The Politics of Global Competitiveness

The Politics of Global Competitiveness

PAUL CAMMACK

OXFORD

UNIVERSITY PRESS

OXFORD
UNIVERSITY PRESS

Great Clarendon Street, Oxford, OX2 6DP,
United Kingdom

Oxford University Press is a department of the University of Oxford.
It furthers the University's objective of excellence in research, scholarship,
and education by publishing worldwide. Oxford is a registered trade mark of
Oxford University Press in the UK and in certain other countries

First Edition published in 2022

Impression: 1

Published in the United States of America by Oxford University Press
198 Madison Avenue, New York, NY 10016, United States of America

British Library Cataloguing in Publication Data
Data available

Library of Congress Control Number: 2021941308

ISBN 978–0–19–284786–7

DOI: 10.1093/oso/9780192847867.001.0001

Printed and bound by
CPI Group (UK) Ltd, Croydon, CR0 4YY

Preface

This project has its origins in a book published over two decades ago, *Capitalism and Democracy in the Third World*, in which I identified a 'doctrine of political development' that aimed to adapt political participation everywhere to the constraints imposed by a global system of competitive capitalism (Cammack 1997). Since then, the dramatic widening and deepening of the capitalist world market, concurrent revolutions in technology and production, and the commodification of everything down to the most basic building blocks of life itself, have meant that our everyday lives are even more shaped by the logic of global capitalist competition. The international organisations I discuss here—the Paris-based Organisation for Economic Cooperation and Development and the Washington DC-based World Bank—did not feature prominently in that book, which was primarily a critique of theories of political development. But they have been the focus of my work since, as it has become increasingly apparent that they consistently seek to push the world market forward, through the promotion of a politics that tutors states in the art of subjecting their populations to the rule of capital, in order to maximise the surplus value extracted from them.

The book builds on work produced at intervals over the last twenty years. In particular, I argued in articles published in the early years of this century that since 1990 the World Bank has been systematically promoting the proletarianisation of the world's poor (their equipping for, incorporation into, and subjection to competitive labour markets), along with the creation of an institutional framework within which global capitalist accumulation could be sustained and legitimated through policies of controlled participation and 'pro-poor' propaganda. I saw its objective as the systematic transformation of social relations and institutions in the developing world, in order to generalise and facilitate proletarianisation and capitalist accumulation on a global scale, and build specifically capitalist hegemony by infusing all areas of life with its logic in an effort to bring all thought and behaviour into line with it; and I described my overall project as a 'new materialist' approach to the governance of global capitalism (Cammack 2001, 2002, 2003, 2004). The term 'new materialist' has been used in different contexts since; in my usage it simply denoted the application of a classical Marxist perspective to the contemporary world, and the new circumstance of completion of the world market, and transformation of the 'production of life itself'.

I pursue the same approach here, broadening the focus in two ways. First, building on a first sketch of the 'politics of global competitiveness' (Cammack 2006), I extend my own research to the OECD as a significant architect of global competitiveness, and to a lesser degree to the European Commission. Second, I develop a new theoretical framework that treats 'production' and 'social reproduction' together, and takes as a starting point the insistence by Marx and Engels in one of their earliest outlines of their historical materialist approach that its focus was on the production of life itself, 'both of one's own in labour and of fresh life in procreation', by social individuals, and that the family must be understood 'in relation to the history of industry and exchange' (Marx and Engels 2010a, 43). Here I owe a debt to Daniela Tepe and Jill Steans (Tepe-Belfrage and Steans 2016), who prompted me in this direction.

A different version of the first chapter was published as 'Marx on Social Reproduction', in *Historical Materialism*, 28, 2, 2020, and I draw also on 'The OECD and the World Market: Antecedents of Deep Marketisation', *Globalizations*, 61, 6, 2019. In addition, I have drawn on a number of my review essays of recent OECD and World Bank texts and secondary sources published at *What's Worth Reading* (https://whatsworthreading.weebly.com), where fuller versions will be found.

For the works of Marx and Engels, I use the widely available Penguin/New Left Review editions of the *Grundrisse* and the first volume of *Capital*. Otherwise, I use the text of the *Collected Works* published in fifty volumes by Lawrence & Wishart between 1975 and 2004. Textual references are to the facsimile electronic edition published as a whole in 2010, and the bibliography includes the original date of completion or first publication of each text as appropriate. Throughout, where gender-neutral terms (e.g. Mensch, Menschheit, Individuum) were used in the original German and the English 'man' or 'men' is used in translation I have amended to men and women, humanity, individual, and so on as appropriate, and included the German in square brackets to signal the change.

During the years in which I have been engaged on this project, I taught successively at the Department of Government (now Politics), University of Manchester, the Department of Politics and Philosophy, Manchester Metropolitan University, and the Department of Asian and International Studies, City University of Hong Kong. It is scarcely an exaggeration to say that I enjoyed every minute, and I am grateful to colleagues in all three institutions for the stimulating work environment they provided. My intellectual debts are far wider, but all the same I would like to thank Toby Carroll, William Case, Greig Charnock, David Pool, Alex Nunn, Sophia Price, Gareth Api Richards, Stuart Shields, Japhy Wilson, and Ralph Young in particular.

Since I retired in 2015, I have been privileged to be an Honorary Professorial Research Fellow at the Global Development Institute, University of Manchester—a position without which it would have been impossible to complete this project. I am very grateful to Professor David Hulme for supporting this appointment.

My life would have been very different if I had not set off in 1971 to teach English Literature at the Universidad Austral in Valdivia, Chile, during the period in office of Salvador Allende. It is now fifty years since Patty and I met, and I cannot imagine my life without her. I dedicate this book first of all to her. In case I never write another one, I dedicate it also to my daughters, Daniela and Ani, and my granddaughter Artemis (Temi). They are under no obligation to read it.

Contents

Introduction		1
Critical Approaches to the Politics of the Global Economy		2
The Politics of Global Competitiveness		12
The Structure of the Book		15

1. Social Production in a Capitalist World Market — 17
   Workers in the World Market — 17
   Social Production under Capitalism — 22
   Social Reproduction and the Politics of Global Competitiveness — 27
   Family, Production, and Exchange, 1867–2020 — 32
   A Crisis of Social Reproduction? — 41

2. The OECD and the World Market — 45
   Antecedents — 45
   1948–1990: The Project Gestated and Developed — 49
   1990–2013: The Project Refined — 58
   The Politics of the OECD—'The Time for Reform Is Now' — 72

3. The World Bank and the Global Rule of Capital — 75
   1979–1989: A Blueprint for Global Development — 76
   1990–2001: Producing a Global Proletariat — 82
   2001–2013: Global Social Production as a Connected Whole — 89
   The Politics of the World Bank—Doing Business — 100

4. The General Law of Social Production — 105
   The Core Project: Combatting Joblessness — 106
   The OECD: Employability Skills for the Twenty-First Century — 116
   The World Bank: Governance of the General Law — 122
   The European Pillar of Social Rights as a Constitution for the
   General Law — 130

5. The Social Politics of Global Competitiveness — 135
   Work — 140
   The World Market — 152
   Proletarianisation and Global Competitiveness — 161

6. Capitalising on COVID-19?   164
   Crisis as Opportunity   165
   A Unified Theory of Adaptability and Resilience   167
   Capitalising on COVID-19?   171
   Conclusion   183

Bibliography   187
Index   199

Introduction

Marx's analysis of the 'bourgeois mode of production' in *Capital* and else-where is a *critique*, intended to identify its laws of operation and its contra-dictions, and to reveal the inequality and exploitation behind the apparently benevolent façade of exchange between equal parties in the market. The Organisation for Economic Cooperation and Development (OECD) and the World Bank (officially the International Bank for Reconstruction and Development, IBRD), in contrast, embrace global capitalism without reserva-tions, and promote it energetically. In doing so, however, they are neither oblivious to its contradictions, nor ignorant of its laws of operation. On the contrary, their understanding of these as reflected in their policy recom-mendations and discourse shows them to be very good students of *Capital*, or at least of the political economy to which Marx directs his critique. They share Marx's insistence that capitalism must develop across the world market as a whole, or not at all; they recognise its need for a propertyless labour force, stripped of access to the means of production and obliged to offer itself for work in order to survive; they attach just as much significance as Marx does to the uninterrupted division of labour, and the continuous application of science and technology to the process of production; they appreciate that as capitalism develops, it increasingly needs workers who are versatile, flexible, and mobile; they grasp precisely the significance of the fact that capital cannot stand still, but must continually seek out new opportunities for investment, and open for itself new sources of exploitable labour and new markets; they know very well that it is competition between capitalists that impels them individually to act in ways that drive forward the process as a whole; they embrace the fact that its expansion will therefore be marked by continual processes of creation and destruction; and they entirely accept that periodic crises, sometimes severe, are an inevitable aspect its development. Above all, they take for granted that capitalism is a *social* phenomenon, grounded in the fundamentally antagon-istic relationship between capital and labour, and that therefore the authority of capital over labour must be continually asserted for capitalist accumulation to continue.

The Politics of Global Competitiveness. Paul Cammack, Oxford University Press. © Paul Cammack 2022.
DOI: 10.1093/oso/9780192847867.003.0001

They have a shared commitment, that is to say, to a politics of global competitiveness; and if that has not been noticed, it is because they have not been considered *together*, as partners in a single universal project, and have too often been assumed to pursue more limited objectives—whether on behalf of the 'rich countries', in the case of the OECD, or of the 'West' and its multilateral corporations, in the case of the World Bank. There are significant insights all the same in the critical literature on these and other organisations that play a major part in managing or governing the world market, and I consider some in this introduction, as a prelude to outlining my own approach and giving an overview of the structure of the book.

Critical Approaches to the Politics of the Global Economy

Critical approaches to the politics of the global economy tend to see institutions such as the OECD and the World Bank as bastions of a world economy run by and for the 'West'. Both have their roots in the Second World War and its aftermath: the World Bank, along with the IMF, directly from the United Nations Monetary and Financial Conference held at the Mount Washington Hotel, Bretton Woods, New Hampshire, in July 1944, and the OECD indirectly in 1961, via the Organisation for European Economic Cooperation (1948), set up explicitly to build an integrated 'world market' under US hegemony. In the 'neo-Gramscian' perspective inaugurated by Robert Cox (which transposed Gramsci's analysis of hegemony from the domestic sphere to international politics and 'world order'), the United States was seen as hegemonic in that other capitalist states saw benefits in its leadership, and consented to it. Whereas the earlier *Pax Britannica* had been based 'both on the ascendancy of manufacturing capitalism in the international exchange economy, of which Britain was the centre, and on the social and ideological power, in Britain and other parts of northwest Europe, of the class which drew its wealth from manufacturing', the *Pax Americana* that succeeded it reflected the ascendancy of a new transnational managerial class with 'its own ideology, strategy and institutions of collective action', whose 'focal points of organisation, the Trilateral Commission, World Bank, IMF and OECD, develop both a framework of thought and guidelines for policies' (Cox 1981, 141, 147). In a subsequent article that expanded on the Gramscian roots of this approach, Cox identified the international organisation as a 'mechanism through which the universal norms of a world hegemony are expressed', and 'the process through which the institutions of hegemony and its ideology are developed':

international organisations embody the rules which facilitate the expansion of hegemonic world orders; are themselves the product of the hegemonic world order; ideologically legitimate the norms of the world order; co-opt the elites from peripheral countries; and absorb counter-hegemonic ideas (Cox 1983, 172). In short, they played a number of important roles, under US leadership, in extending and ensuring the hegemony of a transnational managerial class arising from the internationalisation of production.

A number of subsequent studies built on Cox's approach in different ways. While Cox himself expanded on his analysis in a later monograph (Cox 1987), Stephen Gill took up the analytical framework in *American Hegemony and the Trilateral Commission*, depicting the latter (founded in the early 1970s to bring together politicians, business leaders and academics from North America, Western Europe, and Japan) as the vehicle of a 'developing transnational capitalist class fraction' whose elites were 'at the zenith of an emerging transnational historic bloc' (Gill 1990, 94). Gill's main focus was on private international relations councils, with the Trilateral Commission as the main example; he touched only lightly on the IMF, the World Bank, and the OECD, identifying them as agencies involved with and responsive to the agenda of transnational capital. He would subsequently describe an emergent new world order in which 'disciplinary neo-liberalism' ('the means by which individuals are controlled and disciplined in modern societies') was institutionalised in the 'new constitutionalism' ('the quasi-legal restructuring of state and inter-national forms'), with its discourse of global economic governance 'reflected in the conditionality policies of the Bretton Woods organisations, quasi-constitutional regional arrangements such as NAFTA or Maastricht, and the multilateral framework of the new World Trade Organisation' (Gill 1995, 399, 411–12). A later publication identified the IMF's 1997 *World Economic Outlook* and the World Bank's 1997 *World Development Report: The State in a Changing World* as key statements of an intent to strengthen the power of capital, or 'market society', on a world scale, and contrasted the new consti-tutionalism with the older 'more democratic or progressive constitutionalism' that they exhibited at the time of their creation (Gill 1998, 29–30, 37). Mark Rupert's *Producing Hegemony: The Politics of Mass Production and American Global Power* (1995) took a different approach, addressing 'the *political* rela-tions which underlie the capitalist organisation of production, as well as the interstate system, and which allow us to understand the historical construction of these relations without *a priori* reducing one to the other' (Rupert 1995, 15). The focus here was on the revolution in industrial production in the United States in the early twentieth century, as exemplified by Ford, and the

emergence during and after the Second World War of a 'politics of productivity' that aimed to replace class conflict with compromise (Rupert 1995,
45–53). Rupert showed how the revolutionary 'Fordist' formula of high levels
of investment in assembly line production, relatively high wages, and the
cooperation of workers and employers on constant improvements in
productivity ('speeding up') was exported to Europe in the 1950s, through
the Marshall Plan in particular, enabling the rapid recovery and further
development of European factory production. Bastiaan van Apeldoorn's
Transnational Capitalism and the Struggle over European Integration (2002)
was a seminal case study of the European Round Table of Industrialists,
created in 1983 as 'a private forum for Europe's transnational capitalist class'
(van Apeldoorn 2002, 101); he saw it as moving by the mid-1990s from a 'neo-
mercantilist' project based on producing 'European champions' to a neo-
liberal project focused on global competitiveness. He rejected an instrumental
interpretation of its role, identifying instead a 'higher' form of political agency
oriented towards the articulation of 'a "general capitalist interest" expressing a
longer-term and comprehensive view of how the interests of transnational
capital, and of private enterprise in general, can be best secured in terms of the
general institutional and policy framework in which capital operates' (van
Apeldoorn 2002, 3, 105–6); he rejected a narrow 'economic' perspective on
globalisation, insisting that 'it is also, and above all, about the transformation
of social *practices* as, through economic, social, political and cultural processes,
the lives and activities of people across the globe become connected, and social
practices in one part of the world come to affect those in other parts', so that
globalisation 'must not be seen merely in terms of flows of goods and capital,
but also as a process in which social relations themselves become globalised';
and he argued that the general capitalist class interest has to be *constructed*
through reflection on common interests, and turned into 'a coherent and
comprehensive strategy that can then be represented as serving the general
public interest' (van Apeldoorn 2002, 56, 106): the political agency of the ERT
was primarily oriented towards discourse production around the concept of
competitiveness, then towards agenda setting, and only occasionally and
exceptionally towards lobbying (van Apeldoorn 2002, 112–13). Its principal
concern came to be with the relationship between labour and capital, and
particularly with institutional rigidities, forms of social protection, attitudes,
and behaviour that blunted competitiveness, a relative 'unwillingness to work',
and unrealistic expectations regarding job quality. To address these, it advocated a switch from guaranteeing job security to emphasising individual
responsibility, education, training, flexible skills, and continuous learning

(van Apeldoorn 2002, 146). In short, the 'embedded neo-liberal' project that emerged within the ERT was underpinned by a neo-liberal competitiveness discourse that itself was a focus of struggle over meaning. But while 'the agency of the ERT ... played a significant part in giving an increasingly neo-liberal content to the concept of competitiveness' (van Apeldoorn 2002, 159), it still represented a compromise, echoed in the European Commission, with a rival social democratic project of 'social' Europe, which it contested. Invoking Polanyi and the concept of the 'double movement' (Polanyi 1944), van Apeldoorn concluded that in the continental European context 'a class or class fraction that aspires to hegemony must in the longer run articulate its interests both ideologically and materially with those of the "population" at large: that is, it cannot afford to fully ignore the principle of social protection' (van Apeldoorn 2002, 160).

A related line of analysis, inaugurated by Kees van der Pijl's *Making of an Atlantic Ruling Class*, traced the changing relationship between the different 'fractions' of the hegemonic North Atlantic bourgeoisie—namely, national productive (industrial) capital and international money (finance) capital (van der Pijl 1984, 4–20). He saw the Bretton Woods system centred on the IMF as 'meant to provide American capital (and capitals matching their accumulation conditions) with an integrated circuit of capital internationally', and described the OECD as charged with 'coordinating metropolitan economic policy towards the periphery' (van der Pijl 1984, 144, 187). At the same time, he argued that the Bretton Woods institutions initially had little impact: the liberal universalist moment at which they were founded quickly gave way to a reining back of expansionist ambition to the reduced space of the Atlantic world, and Nixon's breaking of the link between the dollar and gold in 1971 sidelined the IMF in particular. He would go on to publish a valuable theoretical statement, *Transnational Classes and International Relations*, that laid out the classical Marxist foundations of the approach of the 'Amsterdam group' of scholars (van der Pijl 1998). William Robinson's *Theory of Global Capitalism* (2004) pushed the case for the control of international organisations by a transnational capitalist class further, identifying not only a nascent transnational capitalist class (TCC), but also an emerging 'transnational state' (TNS), whose apparatus embraced such economic and political forums as the IMF, the World Bank, the WTO, the regional banks, the G7, the 'larger group of 22 countries', the UN system, the OECD, the EU, and the Conference on Security and Cooperation in Europe (CSCE). 'Economic globalisation', he proposed, 'has its counterpart in transnational class formation and in the emergence of a TNS, which has been brought into existence to function as the collective authority for a global ruling class' (Robinson 2004, 88). More detailed corporate network analysis would question the idea of a single, interlocked transnational capitalist class, finding rather that transnational links tended to co-exist with stronger national and regional foundations (Carroll 2010, 33–5).

Other authors focused more on states than on transnational classes, generally seeing the US government as the principal actor, at the head of an alliance of advanced capitalist states. For Peter Gowan, writing on the Bretton Woods institutions at the end of the twentieth century, the powerful states (the US and the European Union) 'control these multilateral organisations for the purpose of furthering their own power and interests. And the entire IMF/WB system is designed to shift the costs of the power-plays of the Atlantic world on to the bulk of humanity, which lives in the South' (Gowan 1999, 129). David Harvey similarly described a 'new imperialism' in which the United States, as the hegemonic 'super-imperialist' state, has overseen the setting up of an international framework for trade and economic development 'through the Bretton Woods agreement to stabilise the world's financial system, accompanied by a whole battery of institutions such as the World Bank, the International Monetary Fund, the Bank of International Settlements in Basle, and the formation of organizations such as GATT (the General Agreement on Tariffs and Trade) and the OECD (Organization for Economic Cooperation and Development), designed to coordinate economic growth between the advanced capitalist powers and to bring capitalist-style economic development to the rest of the non-Communist world' (Harvey 2003, 54–5). The same perspective carried through to *A Brief History of Neoliberalism*, which argued that from the early 1980s the IMF and World Bank became 'centres for the propagation and enforcement of "free market fundamentalism" and neoliberal orthodoxy' (Harvey 2005, 29).

The argument that the system was built to US design and still operates in US interests has been made most strongly by Leo Panitch and Sam Gindin, whose account of the making of global capitalism centres on the idea of 'American Empire'. It argues that the US *strengthened* its hold in the period from 1987 to 2010, and was 'very much in the driver's seat... less due to the crucial proportion of the votes it controlled (as on the IMF Executive Board) than to its close quotidian relationship with the leadership and staff of [the] international financial institutions' (Panitch and Gindin 2012, 234–5). In similar vein, Judith Clifton and Daniel Díaz-Fuentes, pioneers in the critical analysis of the OECD, argued that it was a 'closed club of Western capitalist economies' well into the present century: its staff had 'historically focused and become expert on producing policies designed by and for its members, predominantly advanced Western capitalist economies, using a limited range of Anglo-Saxon inspired neoliberal solutions, particularly from the 1980s' (Clifton and Díaz-Fuentes 2011, 553–4). Matthias Schmelzer, describing it slightly differently as a 'club of the rich to help the poor', highlights its role from the beginning as a community of donors of development aid, drawing attention to the emergence in the predecessor OEEC of developmental initiatives that the OECD itself would take forward (Schmelzer 2014, 173–6).

The broad picture that emerges from these accounts is as follows. First, the World Bank and the IMF were founded at the high point of a brief moment of liberal universalism coinciding with the Second World War and its immediate aftermath: 'in the heady war years Washington planners talked of an Americanized "One World", including both China and the Soviet Union' (van der Pijl 1984, 107); and in May 1942 business leaders brought together under the auspices of *Fortune* magazine identified as the priority once peace was restored the organisation of the economic resources of the world 'so as to make possible a return to the system of free enterprise in every country' (Panitch and Gindin 2012, 67). Second, the organised and coordinated transfer of US production techniques *and* 'anti-communist' labour and union politics to Western Europe through the Marshall Plan promoted a strategy perfectly summarised in the 'Treaty of Detroit' agreed between General Motors and the Union of Auto Workers (UAW) in 1950, the core of which read as follows: 'The annual improvement factor provided herein . . . recognizes that a continuing improvement in the standard of living of employees depends upon technological progress, better tools, methods, processes, and a cooperative attitude on the part of all parties in such progress. It further recognizes the principle that to produce more with the same amount of human effort is a sound economic and social objective' (Rupert 1995, 170–1). Third, the founding of the OECD in 1961 came at a similar moment, again short-lived and ridden with contradictions, in the context of decolonisation and concerns over the appeal of Soviet-style development. George Ball, Under-Secretary in Kennedy's State Department, 'stressed the value of the newly-formed OECD for coordinating economic policy between the North Atlantic states and for jointly organizing their intervention in the underdeveloped world via aid programmes' (van der Pijl 1984, 205), and Kennedy was subsequently instrumental in the creation of its Development Centre. Fourth, in the two decades from 1987 the commitment of the United States to the 'extension of capitalism to world markets', as Alan Greenspan put it (Panitch and Gindin 2012, 247) was sustained and intense. The concerted effort to shift

Central and Eastern Europe towards 'western-style market economies' after 1989 is an obvious example, and as Gowan describes it, it brought together the G7, the Bretton Woods institutions, the OECD, and the EU, following a US-designed blueprint aimed at fragmenting the Comecon region, replacing it with a hub-and-spoke model, and inducing 'a competitive race by East European states to prepare themselves for direct entry into the West European market' (Gowan 1999, 191). Transnational class forces, business associations, and 'think-tanks' were all involved, along with local allies. In the case of Poland, the neo-liberal Balcerowicz Group entrenched in the Ministry of Finance propagated the view that 'the only prospect for future growth and prosperity lay in rapid reintegration into the global economy', worked closely with the European Union, the IMF, and the World Bank from the start, and with the EBRD (European Bank for Reconstruction and Development) from its founding in 1991, and attached itself to 'a specific class fraction connected to the ideological and policy networks of the transnational proponents of neoliberalism present at the outset of Polish reforms' (Shields 2003, 230–1). Later in the same decade, the US Treasury took a particular interest in Korea as the 'Asia crisis' exploded (not least because it was the most recent country to join the OECD), and 'used the IMF negotiations to "crack open all [the] things that for years have bothered them" (as one of the IMF staff put it)', insisting on raising ceilings on foreign investment in Korean corporations from 26 to 50 per cent and reversing recent legislation that placed a two-year moratorium on layoffs, and requiring all candidates in the presidential election campaign under way to sign up in advance to the programme (Panitch and Gindin 2012, 257). As Panitch and Gindin note, heavily indebted *chaebols* (Korean corporations) *and* dissident candidate Kim Dae Jung, who would win the presidency, were favourable to these changes. In fact, according to Bruce Cumings (Cumings 1999, 25–6), whom they cite, 'it was "Korean officials who pleaded to include anti-labour provisions in the reform package," thereby hoping to pass responsibility to the IMF for reversing the labor victory at the beginning of the year and restoring the legislation allowing companies to undertake immediate mass layoffs'; it was only after Kim Dae Jung confirmed that this would happen that the US Treasury pressed its allies to extend loans, and its banks to join the rescue plan (Panitch and Gindin 2012, 259–60).

In sum, for five decades after the Second World War the United States maintained its position as the hegemonic power among advanced capitalist states, and generally led the process of extension of the world market. But although capitalist recovery and growth were significant in this period, and the revolution in production inaugurated in the United States was successfully extended to Western Europe and turned towards 'flexible production' by Japan, the structure of the global economy was little changed: even at the end of the twentieth century, Panitch and Gindin remind us, 'the advanced capitalist countries accounted for 90 percent of all financial assets, 65 percent of world GDP, and almost 70 percent of global exports of manufactured goods; not only did 85 percent of global FDI emanate from these countries, they were also the recipients of over two-thirds of it' (Panitch and Gindin 2012, 211). In 1973 an internal US Treasury memorandum was able to claim that the IFIs (international financial institutions) were aligned with 'a western market-oriented framework', and present them as playing a strategic role 'as a major instrument for achieving US political, security and economic objectives with particular respect to the developing nations'; and a National Advisory Council working paper that described the World Bank as 'essentially an American-run institution' expressed confidence that 'the US can prevent the IFIs from pursuing policies contrary to US policy objectives' (Panitch and Gindin 2012, 155 and ft. 96, 391). Significantly, though, structural adjustment was pursued as much at home as abroad. The disciplinary firepower of the Treasury was turned on New York City when it was facing bankruptcy in 1975, with Treasury Secretary William Simon insisting that the terms of any bail-out should be 'so punitive, the overall experience so painful, that no city, no political subdivision would ever be tempted to go down the same road' (Harvey 2005, 46); and in 1976 he flew to London to impress upon the British Treasury and Bank of England the imperative need to steer the Callaghan government away from Keynesianism, and ensure the acceptance of IMF conditionality in exchange for a loan. The 'Volcker Shock', the elections of Thatcher and Reagan, and Mitterrand's *volte-face* in France pushed this process of structural adjustment forward in the advanced economies just as it was gathering pace in the developing world. It was only in the 1990s, as van Apeldoorn shows, that European-based transnational capital embraced global competitiveness, and only at the end of the century that the longstanding goal of a single market and single currency was realised (across somewhat different areas) in Western Europe. Coming at each end of this period, the generously funded recovery plan for Western Europe after the war and the concerted effort to integrate Central and Eastern Europe by obliging each country to open itself entirely to 'Western' private capital after 1989 (Gowan 1999, 187–247) offered striking evidence of the manner in which the terms under which the expansion of the world market would proceed had been transformed. At the same time, as Otto Holman pointed out, the European Commission's imposition of neo-liberal discipline on central and eastern

European entrants to the European Union went hand in hand with and reinforced its neo-liberal restructuring of the core of the Union itself through the 1990s (Holman 2001, 183).

It was only at the end of the twentieth century, then, that unity was achieved across the North Atlantic on a 'market civilisation' embracing a single market and currency area covering a large part of Western Europe, and the United States and Canada, themselves partners since 1989 in their own free trade agreement. By this time, the norms on which the hegemonic world order rested were emphatically those of disciplinary neo-liberalism, and the potential for their dissemination beyond the capitalist core was illustrated by the processes of incorporation of central and eastern Europe, described above, and of Mexico, with the creation of the North American Free Trade Association, NAFTA, in 1994. Importantly, disciplinary neo-liberalism was not something the 'North' imposed upon the 'South', but rather a key aspect of a new 'world order' taking shape in the 'North' and the 'South' alike, and actively solicited, as we have seen, in Korea, Mexico, and Poland. And if the United States was still acknowledged as leading the process, the character of its leadership had been transformed in the preceding quarter of a century: it was able to lead as it did because similar transformations had taken place not only across the G7, but also in the former periphery of the Soviet Union, as in Mexico under the Salinas regime after 1988. What is more, there were already suggestions that the ability of the United States to command consent from other states or to dictate to the IFIs was under threat. Gowan, from the vantage point of the late 1990s, suggested that the global economy would eventually escape US domination and control: while he saw the World Bank, along with the IMF, as promoting the interests of the 'Dollar-Wall Street Regime' (Gowan 1999, 19–38), he noted emerging differences between the United States and other states, and the Bretton Woods institutions, arguing not simply that the US sought to use the IMF and the World Bank as auxiliary means of extending its hegemony, but more dialectically that the 'Faustian bargain' that this represented involved a major contradiction: successive US governments could force economies in the developing world to open themselves to US and European investment, but they could not control the consequences. So, while the World Bank could be used to restructure domestic economies to enable them to pay off their debts, thereby 'adapting them to the ... US-centred international system', the emergence of a new growth centre in East and South-East Asia would lead in due course to 'the centre of the entire world economy ... shifting out of the control of the Atlantic region' (Gowan 1999, 42, 51). At the same time, cracks were appearing in the relationship between the US and the

Bretton Woods institutions, as when in the wake of the 1997 'Asian financial crisis' the willingness of then Managing Director Michel Camdessus to endorse a report that absolved US hedge funds from responsibility led to demand from other directors, 'unprecedented in IMF history', that their dissent should be recorded in the 1998 annual report (Gowan 1999, 99). For Gowan, the increasing systemic weight of the Asian growth centre meant that attempts to apply pressure in the region in support of US financial interests would necessarily back-fire. Crucially, too, Gowan identified a major deficiency in US reliance on the Dollar-Wall Street regime, describing it as a 'handy escape route for the American productive sector faced with the competitive challenge of Japan and Western Europe', that 'offered a way out from the hard, domestic task of raising productivity levels and reorganising the linkages between savings and productive investment in the US economy' (Gowan 1999, 118). This was a powerful insight. And while Panitch and Gindin argued strongly for the continued hegemony of the United States, they repeatedly identified the costs and potential contradictions involved in the double role of the US government as responsible for its own 'social formation', and for sustaining global capitalism as a whole (Panitch and Gindin 2012, 302, 330, 333–4). Similarly, while insisting that the OECD has 'remained very much a club of the Western, capitalist countries', Clifton and Díaz-Fuentes noted that from the beginning it did not just represent the interests of its members, but also exercised 'soft governance' over them through peer pressure and review; and they argued that its perspective had changed over time, closely mirroring major phases in the international political economy: as its members' relative share of world GDP and exports declined it expanded its membership in the 1990s, and in the early years of the present century it began to engage with emerging economies (Clifton and Díaz-Fuentes 2011, 553, 558–9). Closely related work highlights its promotion of policies resisted by some of its members, such as the 'neo-liberal' reform of labour markets (Mahon 2011) and the 'entrepreneurial' approach taken by its Committee on Capital Movements and Invisible Transactions towards the liberalisation of capital flows (Howarth and Sadeh 2011), and draws attention to the tensions this creates for the Secretariat, between serving member states and developing its own ideas (Marcussen and Trondal 2011).

As Gill noted at the time, the IMF and the World Bank made seminal contributions towards the end of the century to the discursive framing of the new world order. For its part, the OECD produced not only a fundamental analysis aimed at furthering the structural adjustment of labour markets in the advanced economies, the 1994 *Jobs Study*, but also a sequence of documents that looked further ahead to the establishment of the world market on a much more extended scale. In the same year that the World Bank published *The State in a Changing World*, the OECD produced *The World in 2020—Towards a New Global Age*, in essence a manifesto for a politics of global competitiveness. At a point of maximum 'Western' dominance in the global economy, this supposed 'rich country club' looked forward to the coming *displacement* of its members by new competitors from the non-OECD world. The Czech Republic, Hungary, and Poland had recently been admitted to membership, along with Mexico and Korea. Now the OECD predicted, on the basis of relative growth rates, that by 2020 the non-OECD countries, led by India, China, Brazil, Indonesia, and Russia, would come to represent two-thirds of global GDP, and 'become a driving force in the global economy' (OECD 1997b, 15). It embraced the prospect without reservations and urged the advanced economies to adapt accordingly.

The Politics of Global Competitiveness

Having reached this point, I am able to situate the argument pursued through the rest of the book in relation to this body of literature. The starting point is the evidence that the early 1990s witnessed a virtually unanimous convergence, embracing the G7, in which the US was dominant, the European Commission, the OECD, and the Bretton Woods institutions (the World Bank in particular), on a programme of broadening and deepening the world market, and extending marketising reform across the G7 and beyond their borders. This was the period of Clinton's promise to 'end welfare as we know it', the OECD's and the European Union's effort to reform labour markets in Western Europe, and the insistence that the reconstruction of the central and eastern European economies should proceed through the capacity of individual states to attract foreign investment, or not at all, as well as the World Bank's determination to address poverty in the developing world through structural and social adjustment. The programme, that is to say, was universal, and can only be understood as such: a false picture is given if the policies of the OECD and the World Bank are not analysed together, as the work of actors in a common project. First, looking back, the systematic transfer to Western Europe under the auspices of the Marshall Plan and the OEEC in the 1950s of the revolution in production and associated strategy of class compromise rooted in mass consumption was crucial. Second, it is significant that the programme of marketising reform that arose from the faltering of this strategy from the 1970s on was seen as fragile. Van der Pijl, writing in the early 1980s, closed his account by expressing doubt that the successors to social democratic regimes in Western Europe were capable of 'formulating a new comprehensive concept of control [broadly, a hegemonic programme] adequate to the realities of the post-Atlantic world economy while preserving a minimal degree of imperialist unity' (van der Pijl 1984, 276); Gill argued that 'whilst there has been a growth in the structural power of capital, its contradictory consequences mean that neoliberalism has failed to gain more than temporary dominance over our societies', and suggested that 'the very existence of the neoliberal structural adjustment programmes of the World Bank, and of IMF stabilisation measures, shows that economic liberal-isation has a very long way to go before it can be considered the new development paradigm for the majority of the world's population' (Gill 1995, 401–2, 421); Rupert saw the 'corporatist and neo-conservative' response to the weakening of the Fordist class compromise as US capital moved abroad as inherently unstable, arguing presciently that the resulting 'widening of political possibilities could take the form of a redefinition of "Americanism" in a more cosmopolitan culture of resistance within global capitalism, or it could emerge in a xenophobic or racist reaction to global restructuring which blames workers in other countries, or those perceived as "others" within the USA, for taking "American" jobs' (Rupert 1995, 13); and van Apeldoorn was still of the view, nearly two decades later, that the rule of the neoliberal power bloc was 'far from hegemonic', and that Europe's 'deeply running legitimacy crisis' might only be solved if Europe 'comes to serve a different social purpose than maximizing the freedom of capital' (van Apeldoorn 2013, 194, 199, 201–2). Third, van Apeldoorn's description of the ERT as oriented towards the articulation of a 'general capitalist interest' fits both the World Bank and the OECD *throughout their history,* as does his suggestion that the focus of the ERT was 'above all, about the transformation of social *practices*', so that globalisation 'must not be seen merely in terms of flows of goods and capital, but also as a process in which social relations themselves become globalised'. His comment that the 'general capitalist class interest' has to be *constructed* through reflection on common interests, and turned into 'a coherent and comprehensive strategy that can then be represented as serving the general public interest', too, is entirely applicable to these organisations. Fourth, the description that he gives of the content, for the ERT, of 'maximizing the freedom of capital'—a primary focus on the relationship between labour and capital, and particularly on institutional rigidities, forms of social protection, attitudes, and behaviour that blunted competitiveness, a relative

'unwillingness to work', and unrealistic expectations regarding job quality—
and the remedies it proposed—a switch from guaranteeing job security to
emphasising individual responsibility, education, training, flexible skills, and
continuous learning—captures exactly the content of the OECD's 1994 *Jobs
Study*, the 1995 World Development Report, *Workers in an Integrating World*,
and their policy stance thereafter. Both organisations, that is to say, articulated
a politics of competitiveness *centred on* the freedom of capital to exploit
labour, and had done for decades. Fifth, in doing so, neither organisation
was echoing the position of the ERT, or any advanced capitalist state. Both
were reiterating positions that had always been central to their public discourse, and stemmed from the liberal moments at which they were founded.
The OECD argued consistently from 1961 that the advanced countries should
abandon protectionism and embrace competitiveness in their own interest in
order to boost the efficiency and productivity of their own economies, and the
World Bank's first *World Development Report* (1978) began by urging developed countries not to resort to protectionism to keep out manufactures from
developing countries, as they would be 'delaying some of the difficult structural adjustments that are necessary if there is to be a return to a higher growth
path' (World Bank 1978, 14). Sixth, whether or not the ERT accepted or felt
constrained by the need to compromise with a principle of social protection
that ensured that workers would not be entirely at the mercy of market forces,
the OECD and the World Bank do not. Both promote the maximum level of
competitiveness *across the global economy as a whole*, and they do so consistently, in their respective domains, from a classical liberal perspective that
prioritises the organisation of the population at large in order to maximise
its engagement in productive labour; so rather than compromise with a social
democratic perspective on social protection as a *check* on competitiveness,
they have reworked and redefined it as a mechanism to instil and reinforce the
politics of competitiveness on a global scale, in all populations across the world
economy as a whole. Or so, at least, I shall argue.

From this perspective, the primary objective of the governance of global
capitalism through international organisations is the development and management of the world market as a whole. They promote the subjection of
labour to the disciplines of capital (proletarianisation), and the hegemony of
capital on a global scale. As such, their objectives may coincide with but have
always had a different foundation from the interests of the United States or
any larger grouping of advanced capitalist states, or 'Western' multinationals
or transnational classes. Within this overall mission the IMF and the WTO are
focused fairly narrowly on the stability of the international monetary system

(or better, as van der Pijl put it, the provision of 'an integrated circuit of capital internationally') and the rules of trade between nations—or better, on the same lines, the provision of an integrated circuit of trade internationally. The OECD and the World Bank are rather different. They share the lead role in securing and maintaining the hegemony of capital over labour through the management and transformation of social relations, on a global scale. They have not been mere instruments of the 'West', nor have they sought simply to persuade or compel the countries of the South to undergo 'structural adjustment' and open their economies on behalf of the North. In their influential public discourse and direct engagement with individual countries they have consistently promoted the development of capitalism on a *global* scale, and have jointly sought to persuade *all* countries, in the South and North alike, to adjust their economies and societies to the demands of a genuinely competitive capitalist world order. That is to say, they have always advocated a politics of global competitiveness, and in doing so, they have focused increasingly on the economic and social policies that governments should adopt in order to contain class conflict and maximise the productivity of *their own citizens.*

The Structure of the Book

The OECD and the World Bank, then, express and develop the interest of global capital, the 'general capitalist interest', or 'capital in general'. To explore further what this means, I draw in Chapter 1 on Marx's account of the dynamic but contradictory development of capitalism, on a potentially global scale, his expectations regarding the transformation of processes of production through competition and constant scientific and technological revolution, and its implications both for relations of production (between capital and labour) and social relations more generally. At the same time, I address the implications for the evolution of the division of labour not only within industry, but across society as a whole, and particularly for what is conventionally described as the 'domestic sphere', or the household, and its relationship to the sphere of industry, or waged work. I therefore attach central importance to the issue of social reproduction, understood initially as the reproduction of capitalist society and its constituent social relations over time. The central issue here is that Marx argues that the inherent tendency of capitalist development is to subordinate to itself and take over all other forms of production, whereas some socialist feminists and social reproduction theorists insist that women's unpaid labour in the domestic sphere is an essential element in the reproduction of capitalism. The chapter introduces Marx's *general law of social production*, which suggests that as capitalism develops on a global scale, it increasingly demands workers that are versatile, flexible, and mobile and is central to my argument.

The remaining chapters show that the OECD and the World Bank have consistently promoted it, advocating the revolutionary transformation of social relations across the world, precisely in order to subject all people to the logic of capital. Chapter 2 centres on the efforts of the OECD to build the world market from 1961 onwards; Chapter 3 examines the strategies devised by the World Bank to bring into being a global proletariat, from the publication of its first *World Development Report* in 1978 onwards; Chapter 4 considers their joint efforts, predominantly in the present century, to secure the institutionalisation of Marx's 'general law of social production' and build consent for it; and Chapter 5 addresses the social politics of global competitiveness, with its focus on deeper proletarianisation of the household and the informal economy. The final chapter examines the response of the two organisations to the COVID-19 pandemic, showing that they have maintained their commitment to the politics of global competitiveness through successive crises, and assesses the way in which the pandemic has impacted upon it.

1

Social Production in a Capitalist World Market

Marx's critique of political economy provides the basis for my account of the politics of global competitiveness practised by the OECD and the World Bank. The focus on social production in a capitalist world market identifies two fundamental aspects of Marx's approach—first that at its heart is the relationship between the capitalist and the worker, or capital and labour, and second that its field of study is not the world of states, or of empires and colonies, but the world market. This, with its implications for social relations more generally, is the central theme of this chapter. Although it is over 150 years since *Capital* was published, Marx is the most contemporary of social theorists, for the simple reasons that the capitalist world market has become all-encompassing in its effects, and the 'capital relation'—the relationship between labour and capital—now directly or indirectly bears on all social relationships across the world. In Marx's day these were tendencies, intuitively grasped before they were fully theorised. So I adopt two strategies in order to address the contemporaneity of Marx's critique, to which his general law of social production is central. First, I draw on the idea, found in the *German Ideology*, that the history of humanity must always be studied in relation to the history of industry and exchange to compare some empirical aspects of social and family life in Marx's day and today. Second, I consider the implications for the work of contemporary Marxist feminists and social reproduction theorists of Marx's insistence that capital tends to subjugate and take over all other forms of production. This in turn provides the analytical framework for the investigation in subsequent chapters of the OECD and World Bank as international organisations.

Workers in the World Market

The 22-year-old Friedrich Engels wrote in 1843 in his *Outlines of a Critique of Political Economy* that the cycle in which capital was re-invested in labour,

The Politics of Global Competitiveness. Paul Cammack, Oxford University Press. © Paul Cammack 2022.
DOI: 10.1093/oso/9780192847867.003.0002

increased and invested again, would lead to 'the division of humanity [*der Menschheit*] into capitalists and workers—a division which daily becomes ever more acute, and which ... is *bound* to deepen' (Engels 2010, 430). Marx—just two years older—sought him out, and in the following year developed a similar critique of the regime of private property, which he described in the *Economic and Philosophic Manuscripts* as one in which the worker becomes 'the most wretched of commodities', and the product of labour 'confronts it as *something alien*, as a *power independent* of the producer' (Marx 2010a, 270, 272). When it reached its 'accomplished objective form' as industrial capital, he predicted, it would 'complete its dominion over [humanity] and become, in its most general form, a world-historical power' (Marx 2010a, 293). So when the two began to work together to develop the historical materialist approach, they had already made industrial capitalism—*machine production*—their object of enquiry. They had intuited its potential to establish itself on a global scale, producing a two-class society in which the propertyless majority were confronted and oppressed by the products of their own labour; and they saw this as 'anti-human' (Marx 2010a, 291), a *denial* of humanity.

They never wavered from this dystopian vision. 'It is not individuals who are set free by free competition,' Marx would write in his notebook in February 1858, 'it is, rather, capital that is set free' (Marx 1973, 650). There is still no more precise critique of the promotion of freedom for capital that has dominated recent decades than the way in which he dismissed the view that 'free competition is the ultimate development of human freedom':

> It is nothing more than free development on a limited basis—the basis of the rule of capital. This kind of individual freedom is therefore at the same time the most complete suspension of all individual freedom, and the most complete subjugation of individuality under social conditions which assume the form of objective powers, even of overpowering objects—of things independent of the relations among individuals themselves.
>
> (Marx 1973, 652)

And in *Capital*, Volume 1, he would summarise as follows the social reality of capitalist production:

> Capitalist production ... reproduces and perpetuates the conditions under which the worker is exploited. It incessantly forces him to sell his labour-power in order to live, and enables the capitalist to purchase labour-power in order that he may enrich himself.... The capitalist process of production,

therefore, seen as a total, connected process, i.e. as a process of reproduction, produces not only commodities, not only surplus value, but it also produces and reproduces the capital-relation itself; on the one hand the capitalist, on the other the wage-labourer.   (Marx 1976, 724)

These fundamental tenets of Marx's critique of political economy lay bare the immanent laws of capitalist production, and hence the requisites for its continuation: its grounding in the *capital relation*, the relationship between capital and labour, or the capitalist class and the working class; the need on the part of capital to extract commodities *and* surplus value from labour, and to renew continually its capacity to do so, from day to day and year to year; the incessant need to oblige workers to sell their labour-power in order to live; and the need for free competition, freedom for capital, in order to secure this.

Capitalist production is grounded in class struggle, and fraught with contradictions, so its self-reproduction is never guaranteed. At the same time, its inherent tendency is to expand until its hold over humanity is universal. Because capitalists must compete with each other to survive and prosper, they continually seek to create new needs and products, and find new markets. They seek to drive down through innovation the labour time each process of production requires, and drive up the value it generates. Because their capital is tied up in goods until they reach the market, they seek to reduce the time taken to reach it to the minimum, creating a demand for continually improved means of transport and logistical systems. And because they must lay out capital to produce before they can sell, and must do so without knowing when or if their goods will find a market, they create a market for credit, and at the same time run the risk that a glut of unwanted goods will bring about a crisis. So capital is always seeking new opportunities, striving to bring under its control and extract value from all forms of production and all individuals not subject to it, and to find ways of replacing existing production outside the market with new capitalist processes and techniques. In short, capital is driven, through the activities of individual capitalists in competition with each other, to speed up and refine the process of production, to extend the market and the speed with which products can be brought to it, to take over all non-capitalist forms of production, to extract surplus value however and wherever it can, and to deny to the propertyless majority the capacity to survive outside the market. It tends therefore to establish itself on a global scale, and take over all other forms of production. This is 'the universalising tendency of capital, which distinguishes it from all previous stages of production' (Marx 1973, 540).

Marx and Engels identified the world market, not a world of capitalist states, as the focus of their enquiry in their first extended joint account of historical materialism:

> In history up to the present it is certainly...an empirical fact that separate individuals have, with the broadening of their activity into world-historical activity, become more and more enslaved under a power alien to them...a power which has become more and more enormous and, in the last instance, turns out to be the world market.   (Marx and Engels 2010a, 51)

This was an extraordinarily bold statement to make in the 1840s. Prominent in the *German Ideology* and familiar from the *Communist Manifesto* (Marx and Engels 2010b), the underlying dynamic was most succinctly expressed in a lecture Marx gave in 1847, and revised and published in the *Neue Rheinische Zeitung* under the heading 'Wage Labour and Capital':

> If we now picture to ourselves this feverish simultaneous agitation on the whole world market, it will be comprehensible how the growth, accumulation and concentration of capital results in an uninterrupted division of labour, and in the application of new and the perfecting of old machinery precipitately and on an ever more gigantic scale.... The more productive capital grows, the more the division of labour and the application of machinery expands. The more the division of labour and the application of machinery expands, the more competition among the workers expands and the more their wages contract.   (Marx 2010b, 225, 227)

The idea of the world market would remain central: 'the world market and crises' was envisaged as the culminating part of Marx's project in his plan of work sketched out in the late summer of 1857 (Marx 1973, 108), and in the draft 'Chapter on Money', from autumn of the same year, he remarked that it is in the world market that 'production is posited as a totality together with all its moments, but within which, at the same time, all contradictions come into play' (Marx 1973, 227). 'A precondition of production based on capital', he added in the 'Chapter on Capital' around the turn of the year, 'is...the production of a constantly widening sphere of circulation, whether the sphere itself is directly expanded or whether more points within it are created as points of production'. This 'tendency to create the world market', he added, 'is directly given in the concept of capital itself. Every limit appears as a barrier to be overcome. Initially, to subjugate every moment of production itself to exchange and to suspend the production of direct use values not entering into exchange, i.e. precisely to posit production based on capital in place of earlier modes of production, which appear primitive from its standpoint' (Marx 1973, 407–8). The point recurred a few weeks later, in the same draft chapter, with the striking statement that 'value excludes no use value':

> Capital posits the production of wealth itself and hence the universal devel-
> opment of the productive forces, the constant overthrow of its prevailing
> suppositions, as the presupposition of its reproduction. Value excludes no
> use value; i.e. includes no particular kind of consumption, etc., of intercourse
> etc. as absolute condition; and likewise every degree of the development of
> the social forces of production, of intercourse, of knowledge, etc. appears to it
> only as a barrier which it strives to overpower.   (Marx 1973, 541)

It is as this process unfolds that working individuals are entirely alienated from the product of their own labour, and the result 'is the tendentially and potentially general development of the forces of production—of wealth as such—as the basis; likewise, the universality of intercourse, hence the world market as a basis'—and, in due course, and still ahead of us, when the process reaches its highest point, the possibility of a new basis for the 'real develop-ment' of individuals (Marx 1973, 542). This insight, grasped by Marx in a period of intense creativity in late January 1858, was developed further in the 'Economic Manuscripts of 1861–63', where foreign trade and the constitution of the world market are linked to the development of 'world money' and 'social labour':

> it is only foreign trade, the development of the market to a world market,
> which causes money to develop into world money and *abstract labour* into
> social labour. Abstract wealth, value, money, hence *abstract labour*, develop
> in the measure that concrete labour becomes a totality of different modes of
> labour embracing the world market. Capitalist production rests on the *value*
> or the development of the labour embodied in the product as social labour.
> But this is only [possible] on the basis of foreign trade and of the world
> market. This is at once the pre-condition and the result of capitalist
> production.   (Marx 2010c, 338)

The significance of the transformation of different modes of labour into social labour is that all come under the competitive pressure exerted by 'socially necessary labour time'—the labour time 'required to produce any use-value under the conditions of production normal for a given society and with the average degree of skill and intensity of labour prevalent in that society', a measure that continually falls as the level of development of productive forces continues. As Lucia Pradella puts it, the world market 'is not a static sphere, but consists of the process of universalisation of capital'; it is a 'concrete reality', reflected in 'the imposition of its laws over the multiplicity of states'. As with the world market, so with labour itself; the labour theory of value 'is not abstractly national or international, but expresses the logic of capital universalisation, its becoming world' (Pradella 2015, 130, 133, 165); and as a consequence, as Greig Charnock and Guido Starosta argue, 'national developmental processes across the world have been but *an expression of the underlying essential unity of the production of relative surplus-value on a world scale*' (Charnock and Starosta 2016, 4, emphasis original). The world market comes into being, then, not simply as a 'market' in the narrow sense of a sphere of exchange, but as a social realm in which capital rules and production for use (that is, to sustain life) gives way to production for the purpose of accumulation.

Social Production under Capitalism

In Marx's day the capitalist mode of production was in its infancy, the world market was far from complete, and only a very small proportion of the population, even in England, was directly employed in large-scale industry. In *Capital*, however, Marx addressed both the circumstances of workers in his own day, and the situation that would obtain once the capitalist mode of production became dominant. As reviewed in its closing chapters, the historical genesis of capitalism lay in 'primitive accumulation': 'the expropriation of the great mass of the people from the soil, from the means of subsistence and from the instruments of labour ... by means of the most merciless barbarism'; but 'as soon as workers have been turned into proletarians, and their means of labour into capital, as soon as the capitalist mode of production stands on its own feet, the further socialization of labour and the further transformation of the soil and other means of production into socially exploited and therefore communal means of production takes on a new form' (Marx 1976, 928).

In the early stages of development of large-scale industry capitalists were able to rely upon a steady flow of workers, many of them formerly small proprietors on their own account, forced from the land or unable to compete with large-scale production, along with a mass of labour similarly released.

This ready availability of labour explained the apparent paradox that capital 'asks no questions about the length of life of labour power': 'By extending the working day…capitalist production…not only produces a deterioration of human labour-power by robbing it of its normal moral and physical conditions of development and activity, but also produces the premature exhaustion and death of this labour power itself. It extends the worker's production-time within a given period by shortening his life' (Marx 1976, 376–7). It might have appeared that the interest of capital itself pointed in the direction of a normal working day, but 'experience generally shows to the capitalist…a constant excess of population', with the result that capital 'allows its actual movement to be determined as much and as little by the sight of the coming degradation and final depopulation of the human race, as by the probable fall of the earth into the sun.…*Après moi le déluge!* is the watchword of every capitalist and of every capitalist nation. Capital therefore takes no account of the health and length of life of the labourer, unless society forces it to do so' (Marx 1976, 377, 380–1). Far from there being any perceived threat of a shortage of workers, there was a consensus that there was an endemic threat of *excessive* population growth: Marx noted sardonically in the *Economic and Philosophic Manuscripts* that the theory of population of the political economists (Malthus and John Stuart Mill prominent among them) was that there are 'too *many* people' (Marx 2010a, 311). So when he remarked in *Capital* that the 'maintenance and reproduction of the working class remains a necessary condition for the reproduction of capital', but added that 'the capitalist may safely leave this to the worker's drives for self-preservation and propagation' (Marx 1976, 718), he was doing no more than recognising the logic applied by the capitalist classes of his day, who took no care or responsibility either for the welfare of workers or their future supply. At the same time he derided as 'utterly absurd' the 'dogma of the economists', that higher wages 'stimulate the working population to more rapid multiplication', suggesting instead that generational renewal among industrial workers, who faced a life of poverty and an early death, was prompted 'by early marriages, which are a necessary consequence of the conditions in which workers in large-scale industry live, and by the premium that the exploitation of the workers' children sets on their production' (Marx 1976, 790, 795).

In contrast, the future circumstances that he envisaged once capitalist production 'stood on its own feet' emerged from 'the immanent laws of capitalist production itself': competition between capitalists and the 'centralization of capitals', the conscious technical application of science, and the transformation of production would lead to 'the entanglement of all peoples in the net of the world market, and, with this, the growth of the international character of the capitalist regime'. 'The great beauty of capitalist production consists in this,' he added a few pages later, 'that it not only constantly reproduces the wage-labourer as a wage-labourer, but also always produces a relative surplus population of wage-labourers in proportion to the accumulation of capital' (Marx 1976, 929, 935).

As set out in further detail in his account of the 'general law of capitalist accumulation', this reflected a law of population peculiar to the capitalist mode of production: the working population 'produces both the accumulation of capital, and the means by which it is itself made relatively superfluous; and it does this to an extent which is always increasing' (Marx 1976, 783–4). That is to say, the value produced by workers was expended on their wages, the capitalist's own consumption, and new investment; if wages rose because of a temporary shortage of 'hands' (as for instance in time of war), employers responded by investing in labour-saving machinery, and technological improvements driven by competition generally ensured that fewer and fewer workers were required for a given amount of production as new machines augmented or replaced the old, so that workers were continually thrown out of work. Marx's discussion proceeds in two stages, first setting out the hypothetical case of 'simple reproduction', in which the capitalist is assumed to invest only enough from year to year to maintain production on the same scale as before, and consumes the rest, then considering at greater length the process of 'extended reproduction' (in which increased investment leads to the expansion of the capitalist sector) that lay behind the 'general law of capitalist accumulation'. He concludes from his consideration of 'simple reproduction' that as long as the worker is paid only the cost of his subsistence, while what he produces is entirely appropriated by the capitalist, 'the capitalist produces the worker as a wage-labourer', and comments that: 'This incessant reproduction, this perpetuation of the worker, is the absolutely necessary condition for capitalist production' (Marx 1976, 716). So capitalist production 'reproduces and perpetuates the conditions under which the worker is exploited. It incessantly forces him to sell his labour-power in order to live, and enables the capitalist to purchase labour-power in order that he may enrich himself': the capitalist process of production 'seen as a total, connected process, i.e. as a process of reproduction, produces not only commodities, not only surplus value, but it also produces the capital-relation itself; on the one hand the capitalist, on the other the wage-labourer' (Marx 1976, 723–4). And if simple reproduction 'constantly reproduces the capital-relation itself... so reproduction on an expanded scale, i.e. accumulation, reproduces the capital-relation on an expanded scale': 'Accumulation of capital is therefore multiplication of the proletariat' (Marx 1976, 763–4). In summary: 'Capitalist production can by no means content itself with the quantity of disposable labour-power which the natural increase in the population yields. It requires for its unrestricted activity an industrial reserve army which is independent of these natural limits' (Marx 1976, 788). The implications are profound. As summarised by Martha Gimenez in a brilliant analysis first published in 1977, 'capital accumulation is indifferent to and independent from rates of population growth', as 'population will always be "excessive" in relationship to the demand for labour, whatever its rate of growth may be' (Gimenez 2019, 134). Significantly, this means that access to wage labour has always been intrinsically *precarious*; that while for the most part the level of wages might allow the working class 'not only to maintain itself, but also to increase its numbers' (Marx 1976, 727), there was no guarantee that they would not fall towards zero; and that because the 'production of surplus-value, or the making of profits' was the 'absolute law' of the capitalist mode of production (Marx 1976, 769), there was no guarantee either that any particular society dependent upon capitalist production would be able to reproduce itself over time.

The General Law of Social Production

Large-scale industry requires a new kind of individual, who can be subjected to and will 'willingly' accept the disciplines of capitalist production and competition. Here the starting point is the account in *Capital* of the manner in which large-scale industry continually transforms social production:

> Its principle, which is to view each process of production in and for itself, and to resolve it into its constituent elements without looking first at the ability of the human hand to perform the new processes, brought into existence the whole of the modern science of technology. The varied, apparently unconnected and petrified forms of the social production process were now dissolved into conscious and planned applications of natural science, divided up systematically in accordance with the particular useful effect aimed at in each case. (Marx 1976, 616–17)

This in turn subjects workers to 'variation of labour, fluidity of functions, and mobility... in all directions' and gives rise to a *general law of social production*, according to which 'totally developed individuals' are under pressure to be 'absolutely available for the different kinds of labour required of them' (Marx 1976, 617–18, emphasis mine). So the universalising tendency of capital not only tends to create the world market, but also subjects workers to increasing discipline, dependence, and insecurity. Individuals or households who once made and owned the things that they needed to produce for themselves and exchange with other producers to secure the necessities of life—the means of production—are stripped of them and reduced to nothing but workers—forced to work for owners of capital who in turn compete on a global scale. They are thereby placed permanently in a condition of *precarity*, unable to guarantee themselves the means of survival—precarity being, it is important to note, not merely a recent development, but inherent from the start in the concept of capital itself.

In all of this, the development of science and technology was central. Marx and Engels saw 'specific scientific disciplines as developing in response to problems arising in the sphere of production' (Rosenberg 1974, 715), and drew radical conclusions regarding the implications for social production of the industrial revolution and the subordination of the human hand to the machine. In *manu*facture (*manus* being Latin for hand), the worker became responsible for only one stage in the production process, and repeated it over and over, but still controlled the tool. So long as machines were introduced to carry out each step in production without any change to the existing process, says Marx,

> Handicraft remains the basis, a technically narrow basis which excludes a really scientific division of the production process into its component parts, since every partial process undergone by the product must be capable of being done by hand, and of forming a separate handicraft. It is precisely because the skill of the craftsman thus continues to be the foundation of the production process that every worker becomes exclusively assigned to a partial function and that his labour-power becomes transformed into the life-long organ of this partial function.
>
> (Marx 1976, 458, cited in Rosenberg 1974, 719)

Marx later expands on this crucial difference between manufacture and machino-facture:

> In manufacture, it is the workers who, either singly or in groups, must carry on each particular process with their manual implements. The worker has been appropriated by the process; but the process had previously to be

adapted to the worker. This subjective principle of the division of labour no longer exists in production by machinery. Here the total process is examined objectively, viewed in and for itself, and analysed into its constitutive phases. The problem of how to execute each particular process, and to bind the different partial processes together into a whole, is solved by the aid of machines, chemistry, etc.

(Marx 1976, 501–2, cited in Rosenberg 1974, 719)

So, Rosenberg summarises, in machino-facture, 'for the first time, the design of the productive process is carried out on a basis where the characteristics of the worker and his physical endowment are no longer central to the organization and arrangement of capital. Rather, capital is being designed in accordance with a completely different logic, a logic which explicitly incorporates principles of science and engineering' (Rosenberg 1974, 720–1).

This ties in with Marx's insistence that in all forms of society 'there is one specific kind of production which predominates over the rest, whose relations thus assign rank and influence to the others', and its application to bourgeois society: 'Capital is the all-dominating power of bourgeois society. . . . The point is not the historic position of the economic relations in the succession of different forms of society . . . rather, their order within modern bourgeois society' (Marx 1973, 107). And this brings us full circle: the tendency to create the world market is directly given in the concept of capital itself. In the process of its creation, every limit appears as a barrier to overcome, as capital seeks to suspend the production of direct use values not entering into exchange, and displace earlier modes of production that appear primitive from its standpoint.

Social Reproduction and the Politics of Global Competitiveness

Marx took the view that the 'immanent laws' that compelled capitalists to compete incessantly to boost productivity through scientific and technological innovation would mean first that capitalist development would continually expel workers from failing enterprises, creating its own 'reserve army of labour', and that capital would seek to break down all barriers, and take over all more 'primitive' forms of production, transforming all 'use values' into sources of exchange and profit. An obvious implication of this is that the 'domestic sphere' would tend to shrink, without limits, as the sphere of market-based production increased. Second, though, there was no guarantee that the capitalist mode of production itself, if dominant, would provide for the maintenance and reproduction of people's lives either from day to day or from generation to generation, as its immanent laws contained no mechanism to bring this about. His chapter on 'simple reproduction' opened by raising the issue of 'social reproduction', but dismissing the case for considering it as a *separate* issue:

> Whatever the social form of the production process, it has to be continuous, it must periodically repeat the same phases. A society can no more cease to produce than it can cease to consume. When viewed, therefore, as a connected whole, and in the constant flux of its incessant renewal, every social process of production is at the same time, a process of reproduction. The conditions of production are at the same time the conditions of reproduction.   (Marx 1976, 711)

This is consistent with his insistence that the 'individual freedom' created by free competition is 'at the same time the most complete suspension of all individual freedom, and the most complete subjugation of individuality under social conditions which assume the form of objective powers, even of overpowering objects – of things independent of the relations among individuals themselves', and as such a complete denial of humanity. The conditions of production are at the same time the conditions of reproduction because the reproduction of society under capitalism is *nothing more than* the net outcome of the various connected processes of production in a totality in which the capitalist mode of production is dominant, and therefore assigns rank and influence to other modes of production, which at the same time appear to it as barriers to overcome.

In apparent contrast, Marxist feminists and 'social reproduction' theorists in particular have tended to argue over the last 50 years that the household or domestic sphere *does represent* a limit for capital, on the grounds that it 'produces' the worker through the unpaid labour that goes into daily maintenance and the raising of future generations, and thereby provides capitalists with their workforce and subsidises their production. And Marxist feminists have been prominent too among those who have made the same argument about 'informal' economy workers in the developing world.

The classic points of reference here are Margaret Benston, Mariarosa Dalla Costa, and Maria Mies, though as Susan Ferguson reminds us (Ferguson 2020, 88–90), Mary Inman had advanced similar arguments a generation earlier (Inman 1940). Benston argued, in an essay first published in *Monthly Review* in 1969 and republished on its fiftieth anniversary in 2019, that women as a group 'have a definite relation to the means of production and that this is different from that of men', and defined women as 'that group of people who are responsible for the production of simple use-values in those activities associated with the home and family' (Benston 2019, 2, 3), whether or not they were also engaged in commodity production or wage labour. Dalla Costa expanded on this, in an article first published in 1972, and also republished in 2019, arguing that the role of the working-class housewife was 'indispensable to capitalist production', and '*the* determinant for the position of all other women' (Dalla Costa 2019, 18). And in 1986, in *Patriarchy and Accumulation on a World Scale*, reprinted in 2014, Maria Mies extended the argument, following Rosa Luxemburg and drawing on work with Claudia Werlhof and Veronika Bennholdt-Thomsen, to insist that 'the capitalist mode of production was not identical with the famous capital–wage–labour relation, but that it needed different categories of colonies, particularly women, other peoples and nature, to uphold the model of ever-expanding growth'. For Mies, capitalism was also *inherently* patriarchal: 'capitalism cannot function without patriarchy,…the goal of this system, namely the never-ending process of capital accumulation, cannot be achieved unless patriarchal man-woman relations are maintained or newly created' (Mies 2014, 35, 38). And she argued, directly against Marx, that domestic production by the housewife and non-wage labour in the colonies were intrinsic and perennial features of the capitalist mode of production, stating as her thesis that

> this general production of life, or subsistence production—mainly performed through the non-wage labour of women and other non-wage labourers as slaves, contract workers and peasants in the colonies—constitutes the perennial basis upon which 'capitalist productive labour' can be built up and exploited. Without the ongoing subsistence production of non-wage labourers (mainly women), wage labour would not be 'productive'. In contrast to Marx, I consider the capitalist production process as one which comprises both: the *superexploitation* of non-wage labourers (women, colonies, peasants) upon which wage labour exploitation then is possible.
>
> (Mies 2014, 48)

Although these writers differed among themselves (Benston and Dalla Costa disagreed over whether domestic work was directly productive of surplus value, while Mies accorded greater independent significance to patriarchy), they agreed that capitalism required women's unpaid labour in order to reproduce itself. However, other Marxist feminists were less sure. Maxine Molyneux pointed out that single workers and migrants 'whose labour power is usually reproduced on a daily basis without the benefit of female domestic labour, are invariably paid below average wages', and 'tend to rely on services and food obtained on the market'; and she noted that: 'Strictly speaking it is in the economic interests of capital to proletarianise as many workers as possible in order to reap the dual benefits of an increased mass of surplus value and a fall in the value of labour power that accompanies the mass entry of labour into production' (Molyneux 1979, 11, 26). Michèle Barrett, in *Women's Oppression Today* (1980, republished 2014), also questioned the assumption that the oppression of women was inherently functional for capital, and criticised the tendency to conflate 'women's role in the biological reproduction of the species with the historically specific question of their role in ensuring the reproduction of male labour power and in maintaining the relations of dominance and subordinacy of capitalist production', asserting that 'it has not yet been satisfactorily explained how and why it is that *women* should be assigned any special role in these latter two processes of reproduction', and that it had 'yet to be proved that capitalism could not survive without the present form of domestic labour' (Barrett 2014, 27, 180–1). Lise Vogel, proposing a 'social reproduction perspective' as a basis for a unitary theory in contrast to the 'dual-systems' perspective that treated capitalism and patriarchy separately, asserted in *Marxism and the Oppression of Women* (1983, reprinted 2013) that it was only 'women's capacity to bear children' that made them essential for the reproduction of capitalism (Vogel 2013, 134–5). Families were not 'the only places where workers [renewed] themselves on a daily basis', while from a national perspective 'migration and enslavement of foreign populations' were alternative sources of renewal (Vogel 2013, 147). So although she thought that dependence on women's domestic labour would persist, she recognised only one limit: 'An ultimate barrier to the socialisation of domestic labour is constituted by biology. While domestic labour might conceivably be reduced to a minimum through the socialisation of most of its tasks, the basic physiological process of child-bearing will continue to be the province of women' (Vogel 2013, 163).

Different views emerged, then, in this early stage of debate, about the relationship between domestic and capitalist production. At the same time, there was general agreement that there was a strong trend towards the replacement of domestic production by market or state provision (Benston 2019, 8–9; Gardiner 1975, 52; Beechey 1979, 79; Molyneux 1979, 16; Barrett 2014, 176). Looking ahead, Barrett thought it 'not altogether impossible that capital might wake up to the "wastage of talent" involved in the present educational system and attempt to reduce the channelling of girls away from useful technological subjects. The effects of new technology [might] create a situation where the relationship between the household and wage labour [was] less crucial for social production, and hence create conditions for a more equal distribution of childcare' (Barrett 2014, 255). And Dalla Costa herself cautioned against 'tak[ing] for granted that the family as we know it today in the most technically advanced Western countries is the final form the family can assume under capitalism' (Dalla Costa 2019, 18, 28). She also referenced the phenomenon of 'test-tube babies', while seeing it as adverse to the interests of women: 'today such mechanisms belong completely to capitalist science and control. Their use would be completely against us and against the class. It is not in our interest to abdicate procreation and consign it to the hands of the enemy. It is in our interest to conquer the freedom to procreate, for which we will pay neither the price of the wage nor the price of social exclusion' (Dalla Costa 2019, ft. 9, 44). At the same time, Martha Gimenez developed a strong line of argument in relation to procreation, consistent with the analysis of Marx above. In essays published from 1975 onwards and collected in a single volume in 2019, she argued that 'the functioning of the mode of production determines the mode of reproduction', and insisted that 'capital accumulation is indifferent to and independent from rates of population growth' (Gimenez 2019, 12, 133). On the nuclear family, she argued that capitalist development, 'at the same time it selects this family form as the most "functional" for daily and intergenerational reproduction, constantly undermines it through changes in the productive forces in the realms of production and reproduction' (Gimenez 2019, 196). Under conditions of austerity, she suggested, poor households no longer reproduce labour-power, but rather simply produce people, 'and people, in themselves, without marketable skills, have no value under capitalist conditions': 'capitalists are indifferent to the workers' fate *except when it may impinge on their own safety and ability to accumulate.* Workers are left to their own devices, to survive as best as they can within conditions set by the ebb and flows of capital accumulation and the success or failure of working-class struggles' (Gimenez 2019, 247, 294, emphasis original). And on procreation, she noted in a path-breaking analysis first published in 1991, subsequently revised and updated, that the development of new reproductive technologies fragmented biological processes in the 1970s and opened them to manipulation, 'thus bringing unforeseen changes in the social relations within which children are brought into the world': 'as they split intergenerational social reproduction from procreation, [they] give rise to the capitalist mode of procreation', making it 'possible for individuals or couples to purchase the different elements of the reproductive process to "build", eventually, a baby for themselves' (Gimenez 2019, 188–90). A comparison of the situation of families and households in the context of production and exchange as depicted in *Capital* and as they are today will allow us to assess the current state of evidence on these debates.

Family, Production, and Exchange, 1867–2020

Marx was not blind to issues of gender. Nor was he so narrowly focused on industrial production that he ignored or neglected the family, the household, or what has been termed the private or domestic sphere. Just what Marx and Engels meant by 'production posited as a totality, with all its moments' was clear from their earliest work together. They insisted that what men and women are 'coincides with their production, both with *what* they produce and with *how* they produce'; that this focus on production included 'the production of life, both of one's own in labour and of fresh life in procreation'; and that the history of humanity, and by extension the family within which they propagated their kind, was to be understood 'in relation to the history of industry and exchange' (Marx and Engels 2010a, 31–2, 43). In particular, Marx was acutely attentive to the changing gender division of labour in industry, and its impact upon families and households, especially among the working class. In his own day, though, evidence in support of the transformation of household production was relatively limited, and the advance of science and technology which was transforming the division of labour and the character of production so spectacularly had virtually no impact on the production of fresh life in procreation—human reproduction was quintessentially 'primitive from the point of view of capital' in his lifetime. Scientific advances did lead to improvement in available methods to guard *against* conception: rubber condoms became available in the 1850s, following Goodyear's introduction of vulcanised rubber. But as regarded procreation, only one method of production was known; the division of labour involved was simple; the characteristics of the workers and their physical endowments were central. There was little scope (limited perhaps to knowledge of cycles of fertility) for the application of science; and no scope for breaking down the process of production into its constituent parts (conception, gestation, and birth) susceptible to a division of labour, and out-sourcing was not an option.

Marx had more to say, though, about the relationship between the household, domestic production, and industry. He was thoroughly familiar with the use of female and child labour, despite claims to the contrary (Armstrong and Armstrong 1983, 11; Tepe-Belfrage and Steans 2016, 310), and assiduous in exploring and documenting the extent of its empirical occurrence. In the *Economic and Philosophic Manuscripts* he transcribed lengthy sections on the employment of women and children from Wilhelm Schulz, *Die Bewegung der Produktion*, published only a year earlier in Switzerland, detailing the preponderance of female workers in English and American mills; and he noted, from Eugène Buret's *De la misère des classes laborieuses en Angleterre et en France*, first published in 1840, that the large workshops 'prefer to buy the labour of women and children, because this costs less than that of men' (Marx 2010a, 243, 245). In *Capital*, he drew on the reports of factory inspectors and other official documents up to the 1860s (by which time the scale of mechanisation under steam power in textile factories in particular had advanced considerably) to document at length the extent of female and child labour, suggesting that the entry of women and children into the labour force was 'the first result of the capitalist application of machinery!' (Marx 1976, 517). In one specific example, he noted that the leading Birmingham steel-pen factory employed 1,268 female workers from five years old upwards among its workforce of 1,428 in 1861 (Marx 1976, 590, and ft. 71). He also identified the pressure this development placed on the reproduction of labour-power and the sustenance of new life, and remarked on the commodification of forms of provisioning previously carried out within the household, and what has since been called 'depletion' (Rai et al. 2014). First, citing a report from a Dr Edward Smith, sent by the British government to Lancashire, Cheshire, and other places to investigate the state of health of cotton operatives during the crisis caused by the American Civil War (1861–5), he pointed to the ironic consequences of the widespread female unemployment arising from the recession provoked by the interruption to cotton:

He reported that from a hygienic point of view, and apart from the banishment of the operatives from the factory atmosphere, the crisis had several advantages. The women now had sufficient leisure to give their infants the breast, instead of poisoning them with 'Godfrey's Cordial' (an opiate). They also had the time to learn to cook. Unfortunately, the acquisition of this art occurred at a time when they had nothing to cook. *But from this we see how capital, for the purposes of its self-valorization, has usurped the family labour necessary for consumption.* This crisis was also utilised to teach sewing to the daughters of the workers in sewing schools. An American revolution and a universal crisis were needed in order that working girls, who spin for the whole world, might learn to sew!   (Marx 1976, 518, ft. 38, emphasis mine)

And he went on to reflect that:

> Since certain family functions, such as nursing and suckling children, cannot be entirely suppressed, the mothers who have been confiscated by capital must try substitutes of some sort. Domestic work, such as sewing and mending, must be replaced by the purchase of ready-made articles. Hence the diminished expenditure of labour in the house is accompanied by an increased expenditure of money outside. The cost of production of the working-class family therefore increases, and balances its greater income. In addition to this, economy and judgement in the consumption and preparation of the means of subsistence becomes impossible.
>
> (Marx 1976, 518, ft. 39)

These comments identified the household as a site of production in which a gendered division of labour assigns primarily to women tasks directly associated with the reproduction of labour-power from day to day and generation to generation. Along with such responsibilities as cooking, they addressed handicraft production—sewing and mending—and the nursing of children. They noted the social and economic impact of the introduction of women to factory work: the commending of infants to minders who dosed them with opiates to induce quietness; the process of commodification arising from the purchase of goods formerly produced in the home; and the destabilising cycle arising from periodic crisis. Marx was attentive, then, not only to female employment, but also to the impact of industrial capitalism on the household, in terms of both the gendered division of labour and the reproduction of labour-power from day to day. Throughout, the analysis reflected the precept that where the bourgeois mode of production predominates over the rest, its relations assign rank and influence to others, and it saw moments of *crisis* in particular as prompting change. It was consistent, therefore, with the suggestion that every task carried out in the household—from the production of food to that of future generations—was in principle susceptible to being taken over by capital, whether through commodification or out-sourcing.

Over the intervening period, and especially in recent decades, domestic production and the production of life itself have been shown conclusively to be just as susceptible to being overtaken by capital as any other non-capitalist form of production. Scientific and technological revolutions in industrial production have not only led to the virtual completion of the world market and intensified the precarity of labour, but are also transforming families and households, the gendered division of labour, and the maintenance and renewal of labour power from day to day and from generation to generation. Since Marx's day, scientific and technological revolution has given rise to branches of theory and practice—notably in computing, large data processing, logistics, nanotechnology, robotics, and biotechnology—which were either in their infancy or unheard-of in those times. As is familiar, this has in turn enabled multiple connected revolutions in production, trade, and finance, creating new products and markets, and cutting the time and cost of producing goods and bringing them to market. Urban consumers and once remote and isolated rural producers are linked to markets by mobile technology and speedy systems of delivery, while innovations in robotisation and artificial intelligence have brought about specific developments such as sensor-driven fruit picking machines and self-driving vehicles, confirming the acuity of Marx's insight into the tendency for techniques of machine production to advance without regard for the capacity of the human hand. The most advanced forms of production today literally take no account of the capacity of the human hand, eye, or brain, but instead exploit the capacity of the machine to overcome the limits of human physiology, and perform new processes accurately and tirelessly. And the impact upon the family and household has been precisely as Marx's analytical framework foreshadowed.

First, an intensified division of labour has been enabled by recent technological advances. We are now half a century into the global pattern of fragmentation of production, which opens up the whole world as a site for the extraction of value, with individual products routinely assembled over numerous national jurisdictions. More recently, as the digital revolution has advanced, the capacity of capital to seize upon available labour-power literally anywhere in the world has increased beyond all recognition as out-sourcing, freelancing, 'flexible working', and 'zero hours contracts' have proliferated. Digital platforms such as Comatch, Mechanical Turk, MyLittleJob, PeoplePerHour, Taskrabbit, Upwork, or Worksome match workers to tasks which may be the tiniest constituent elements of larger production or service processes, and do so on a global scale for unskilled and skilled professional work alike. Whatever fragment of the labour-power of an individual is available can be targeted and seized by capital.

Second, along with these changes the flexibility of labour has been developed to a point where the 'standard employment contract', with its attendant rigidity and ancillary costs, is becoming a thing of the past. In a single generation, punitive legislation over labour organisation and contracts is well on the way to doing away with it where it most applied, in the advanced capitalist economies, and converting welfare as a source of protection from the market into 'social protection' as a mechanism for increased exposure to it, while policies of deliberate casualisation replace those aiming at enhancing job security (Breman and van der Linden 2014; Freedland 2016). In the developing world, the widespread introduction of deliberately engineered 'precarious work' suggests that the 'standard employment relationship' will *never* become the norm (Kalleberg and Hewison 2013). The trend is towards open-ended, short-term and part-time contracts, to which minimal employment rights are attached, so that every benefit won through struggle by workers without rights is at the same time another step towards the establishment of a new model contract which cuts back rights won earlier, making 'totally developed individuals' available for whatever work is required of them at any time. At the leading edge of this process, a small but growing minority of workers have no job security at all. In the UK, the Office for National Statistics (ONS) estimated that in the final quarter of 2019, the last datapoint before the COVID-19 epidemic impacted on employment, 974,000 workers (3 per cent of the workforce) were on 'zero hours' contracts, up from 0.7 per cent a decade before. Such workers were heavily concentrated in the 16–24 age bracket, where over 9 per cent of workers were on such contracts, and a clear majority of the total (560,000) were women. The accommodation and food industries accounted for 223,000, with 198,000 in health and social work, 88,000 in wholesale and retail, 52,000 in information, finance and professional services, and 51,000 in administrative and support services. The same survey estimated that 4.1 million workers were on 'flexible working' contracts—among them 2,205,000 on annualised hours contracts, and 776,000 'on call' (ONS 2021a, tabs 2–6, 10), from a total of 32.9 million people in employment (ONS 2020a, p. 4).

Third, it is now over 40 years since Heidi Hartmann suggested that '[t]he "ideal" of the family wage – that a man can earn enough to support an entire family – may be giving way to a new ideal that both men and women contribute through wage earning to the cash income of the family' (Hartmann 1979, 19). So the demise of the 'male breadwinner', always something of an ideological construct as far as working-class families were concerned (McCarthy 2020, 17–96), is nothing new. In the UK and elsewhere, this is part of a larger picture in which the 'reform' (that is, reversal) of welfare, combined with austerity politics, intentionally makes survival outside the labour force difficult for all (Nunn and Tepe-Belfrage 2017). The February 2020 ONS overview of the UK labour market estimated that in the final quarter of 2019 the employment rate (the proportion of people aged from 16 to 64 years who were in work) was 76.5 per cent, the highest since comparable records began in 1971. While the proportion for men was

80.6 per cent (barely changed from three decades earlier), that for women, at 72.4 per cent, was also the highest since records began, partly because the rise in the pensionable age for women from 60 to 65 obliged many women to stay in work after 60, and partly because other policies were pushing the mothers of young children back into the labour market. Of the 15.6 million women in employment, over 9.3 million (59.6 per cent) were in full-time work (ONS 2020a, 3–4). The COVID-19 pandemic has since led to rising unemployment, with consequences that are discussed in the final chapter, but all the same the previous conjuncture of expanding welfare, the 'male breadwinner norm' and relative prosperity, a local, temporary, anomalous and unsustainable aspect of capitalist development at an early stage, is now long gone. Across the wider developed world, 'family policy' is increasingly based on the assumption that mothers will work for a wage (Ferragina and Seeleib-Kaiser 2015), and in the European Union in particular, a policy frame of 'social investment' in which the focus is on 'how to support women to enter and remain in the labour market', and the citizen envisaged is 'first and foremost a paid worker, either in actuality or (when a child) in the making' (Saraceno 2015, 257), promotes this objective. In the UK again, the pensionable age for men and women alike is set to rise in stages to 68 by 2039, and it would be rash to assume that we are not set on course for a 'world without retirement' (Hill 2017). In short, circumstances are more conducive than ever to making every available body a wage labourer for capital.

Fourth, changes have taken place in the composition of families and households and in choices regarding childbearing, under the pressure of welfare reform, and in response to changed opportunities in education and work. In 1996, only 44.6 per cent of UK families (34.8 per cent married or cohabiting couples, 9.8 per cent lone parents) had a dependent child or children; by 2019, the percentage had declined slightly, to 42 per cent of families (32.6 per cent married or cohabiting couples, 9.4 per cent lone parents). Over the same period, the percentage of *households* consisting of two-parent families with a dependent child or children (the 'traditional' nuclear family) fell from 24.3 per cent to 22.4 per cent—less than a quarter of households, compared to the 29.5 per cent of households in 2019 that consisted of a single person—in part because of increased longevity, and in part because of the rising numbers of men aged 45 to 64 living alone (ONS 2021b, tables 1 and 5; ONS 2019, 8). As this reflects, there has been a transformation in procreation: in 1971 (England and Wales only), 'women in the 20 to 24 age category were the largest group giving birth, accounting for 36.5 per cent of all live births. By 2010 this proportion had fallen to 19 per cent, and the 30–34 age category, whose proportion had doubled to 28 per cent between 1971 and 2010, accounted for more live births than any other group'. The share of live births to women of 35 and over rose from 7.4 to 19.8 per cent (ONS 2012, 2, 21). This process has continued, as the tendency to delay childbirth has increased: in 2019, the number of children born to women under 20 (17,720) was well below half what it was in 2010 (40,591); more children were born to women over 40 than to women under 20 for the first time in 2013, and the corresponding total was two thirds higher, at 29,618, by 2019. As in 2010, the 30–34 age category accounted for the largest share of live births, standing at 32.8 per cent, with the share to women 35 and over rising more sharply, to 23.7 per cent (ONS 2020b, table 2): 'Nearly half (49%) of women born in 1989 (the most recent cohort to reach 30 years) remained childless by their 30th birthday, compared with 38% for their mother's generation and just over one-fifth for their grandmothers' generation (1961 and 1934 cohorts respectively' (ONS 2020c, 2).

Fifth, the period since Marx's day has seen the increased application of science and technology to the home, with the appearance of a range of domestic or household appliances powered by gas or electricity, and more recently embracing digital and internet-based technologies. The first electric lights date from around the time of Marx's death, though their use in domestic settings was slow to develop, and initially, as with many other subsequent developments, confined to wealthy households. Over the intervening years, refrigerators, electric ovens and toasters, vacuum cleaners, washing machines, dishwashers and the like have become commonplace, and in the current wave of technological advance the 'smart' home and the 'Internet of Things' exploit the potential of miniaturisation, automatic sensors, and connectivity, while domestic robots loom on the horizon (Schroeder 1986; Chin et al. 2019). Such devices may not reduce the time devoted to housework, as the underlying logic is still that of handicraft in a small unit, with limited division of labour and a process of production that is aided by the machine but not otherwise transformed. The tendency for household appliances not to save labour time is a consequence of the relative inefficiency of household production in a small and isolated unit, but the market for such appliances and devices is huge, and the process of commodification of domestic production continues its headlong advance.

Sixth, as the character of households changes, and more women enter the labour force on a long-term and full time or quasi-full time basis, more labour, goods and services are procured outside the home. Dual-wage families in wealthy countries increasingly outsource care and domestic labour to poor women and particularly legal and illegal migrants (Estevez-Abe 2015; Leerkes 2016; Arat-Koç 2018), and such choices are encouraged by the trend to subordinate family policy in developed economies to the demands of the labour market (Ferragina and Seeleib-Kaiser 2015). At the same time, production in the home of the necessities for the daily renewal of labour-power is increasingly replaced by supply from outside, bringing about significant shifts in domestic work and provisioning. The 'typical' family of four or five with a male breadwinner, full-time female housewife, and two or three children, enjoying home-cooked meals prepared from scratch, may offer a rather approximate guide to past reality, but in any case significant shifts in practice have rendered this stereotype completely invalid. Yates and Warde write of the 'de-structuration of the meal', with an indicative 2012 UK survey suggesting a rise in companionless eating, with around a third of all meals eaten alone, and less than a quarter of them requiring cooking or complex preparation (Yates and Warde 2017, 98–106). A revolution in food processing and hence provisioning has taken place since the 1980s. 'Acceleration in food science techniques', Monteiro and colleagues report, 'has enabled invention of a vast range of palatable [sic] products made from cheap ingredients and additives', with the consequence that 'enterprises whose profits derive from uniformly branded ready-to-consume products, have become colossal global corporations' (Monteiro et al. 2013, 22). The most dynamic growth, driven by competition between Western transnationals and emerging local competitors, is in Asia, and the scale of operation is unequivocally that of the world market (Baker and Friel 2016). At the same time, sandwiches increasingly replace cooked meals, and sandwich-making has been captured by transnational capital. Greencore, founded in Ireland in 1991 upon the privatisation of Irish Sugar, is reported to produce 1.5 billion sandwiches and other related food to go products per year (Financial Times 2016). And a new revolution in prepared meal provision is gathering pace, as mobile and web-based platforms such as Just Eat and Deliveroo link advanced networks and logistics with zero hours workers and industrial kitchens to expand options for the purchase and home delivery of 'restaurant' meals. In turn, the rapidly growing market for commercially prepared food is an artefact of social changes in family and household structure—so much so that mobile phone/take-away and ready meal/microwave combinations are replacing cooked meals prepared from scratch across new and old forms of household alike (Jackson et al. 2018).

Seventh, just as in Marx's day, there are hundreds of millions of individuals around the world who are unemployed, under-employed, or situated in the low investment, low productivity 'informal' sector, and therefore potentially available for recruitment and more efficient exploitation by capital. The ILO currently estimates that there were 172 million people unemployed worldwide in 2018, along with a further 140 million 'who are looking for a job but are not able to take up employment, or who are available but are not looking for a job' (ILO 2019, 2). Beyond that, the organisation identifies some 360 million 'contributing family workers who lack effective access to social protection and income security', an additional 1.1 billion working on their own account, with a large proportion engaged in 'subsistence activities that are pursued because of the absence of job opportunities in the formal sector or the lack of a social protection system', meaning that 'just over half (52 per cent) of global workers are wage and salaried employees', with 40 per cent of such jobs themselves classified as informal: 'Overall', it concludes, 'a staggering 2 billion workers are in informal employment, accounting for three in five (61 per cent) of the world's workforce' (ILO 2019, 6). Even if some self-employed or informal sector workers are successful entrepreneurs or flexible workers making an 'efficient' contribution to capitalist accumulation, it is clear that experience *still* shows to the capitalist 'a constant excess of population'—all the more so, in fact, as the commodification of domestic production has 'freed' more women to enter the paid workforce, and the restructuring of welfare has obliged them to do so.

Eighth and last, a revolution has taken place at the same time in the production of life itself, as the process of procreation has been transformed by 'conscious and planned applications of natural science', and seized by capital, confirming the validity of the expectation that the production of life, in *all* its aspects, has to be approached, in principle, in relation to an emerging bourgeois mode of production, with its incessant division of labour, constant technological revolution, universal competition, and the subordination of natural science to capital. This was foreseen by Shulamith Firestone, and underpinned her radical critique of the 'biological family' (Firestone 1970). Procreation, it turns out, is no more immune to capture by capital—breaking the process of production down into its constituent parts, through conscious and planned applications of natural science, and subjugating every moment of production to exchange—than anything else, as witnessed by a host of scientific and technological advances, and the emergence of global industries— some, like gene-editing and the race to create an artificial womb, highly technological (Pelzman 2013; Bulletti et al. 2011; Devlin 2017; Ahuja et al. 2018), and others, like 'contract pregnancy' or commercial surrogacy, organised on a 'handicraft' or 'workshop' basis (Bailey 2011; Hewitson 2014; Pande 2014). The latter, too, relate to only one aspect of a much broader process of the commodification of the human body, which is just as evident in markets for organs, tissues, blood, and stem-cells (Rainhorn and El Boudamoussi 2015), the willingness of human subjects to volunteer for large-scale drug trials (Sunder Rajan 2017), and the commercialisation of breast milk (Newman and Nahman 2020).

A Crisis of Social Reproduction?

At present, as Meg Luxton comments, the question of 'whether women's subordination is essential to capital accumulation or historical and contingent' is still an open one. On the one hand, very substantial changes have taken place, in advanced and developing countries alike, but on the other, the 'informal economy' is predominant in the developing world and visible in advanced economies, and as Luxton goes on to say, it is still true today that 'women typically are expected to do more of the labours involved in having babies, raising children, providing care and immediate provisioning—labours that are outside the immediate purview of formal production but essential for the continuation of human life on a daily and generational basis' (Luxton 2018, 37). The debate over the theoretical status of domestic work similarly continues, with some insisting, with Dalla Costa, that domestic labour directly produces surplus value just as the wage worker does, and others arguing that while it performs the essential role of producing the labour-power that in turn produces surplus value, a distinction between the two forms of labour still needs to be made (Federici 2019, 55; Mezzadri 2019, 2021; Ferguson 2020, 121–30). Either way, there is agreement among these writers that domestic work is still essential to the production of surplus value, and an increasing insistence that the pressures placed upon households and on women in particular over recent decades have brought them close to collapse. In the strongest version of the argument, Nancy Fraser diagnoses a 'crisis of care', arising from 'the pressures from several directions that are currently squeezing a key set of social capabilities: those available for birthing and raising children, caring for friends and family members, maintaining households and broader communities, and sustaining connections more generally': 'No society that systematically undermines social reproduction can endure for long. Today, a new form of capitalist society is doing just that. The result is a major crisis, not simply of care, but of social reproduction in this broader sense' (Fraser 2016, 99). Silvia Federici, who was a participant in the collective that produced Dalla Costa's essay, identifies a 'profound crisis of social reproduction that entire populations across the world are experiencing because of the impoverishment capitalist development is producing, due to the defunding of social programs, the politics of extractivism, and the now permanent state of warfare' (Federici 2019, 56). Fraser's argument that the crisis is 'a more or less acute expression of the social-reproductive contradictions of financialised capitalism' (Fraser 2016, 99) is representative of a wide spectrum of opinion (Walby 2015; Montgomerie and Tepe-Belfrage 2017; Bakker 2020; Mazzucato 2020).

There is no doubting any of this: the evidence that social reproduction is widely threatened to the point of collapse is overwhelming. Fraser goes on to claim that non-waged social-reproductive activity is 'necessary to the existence of waged work, the accumulation of surplus value and the functioning of capitalism as such...Social reproduction is an indispensable background condition for the possibility of economic production in a capitalist society' (Fraser 2016, 102). But what is a crisis for *society* is not necessarily a crisis for *capital*. If the *sine qua non* for capital is to produce and reproduce the worker *as a worker*, by compromising or eliminating other forms of survival, and if there are still seemingly endless reserves of potential workers, what is identified is a contradiction between capital accumulation and the reproduction of a society, but not in itself a contradiction within capitalism. Examples that Fraser gives as reflective of crisis—reliance on poor migrants for caring responsibilities, and the freezing of eggs and use of hi-tech hands-free breast pumps for women deferring motherhood and mothers combining nurturing with paid work respectively (Fraser 2016, 114–15)—actually reflect two of the central means by which capital pursues the general development of the means of production: primitive accumulation in the first case, and scientific and technological revolution in the other. 'If gendered oppression', as Elena Louisa Lange argues, 'cannot be shown to be necessary to the *logic* of capital, then it cannot be shown to be necessary to *capital*' (Lange 2021, 50, emphasis original).

With the development of the 'world market' to what is now a genuinely global scale, pressures on the great majority of households around the world have mounted to such an extent that their ability to reproduce themselves and survive is itself in doubt. In the 'advanced' economies, these changes have come about as a consequence of the twin pressures of increasingly competitive labour markets and the conversion of 'welfare' into a mechanism for reducing as far as possible the capacity to survive without access to a wage. In the developing world, in the absence of such provision, families have been forced to engage with global production chains, or 'export' labour through migration, as survival outside the world market has become increasingly unviable.

However, the OECD and the World Bank, as flag-bearers for the process of capitalist development on a global scale, continue to press forward regardless. They consistently support the further development of the capitalist world market, and continue to promote a common agenda focused on drawing as many people as possible into competitive labour markets, seeing this not as the cause but as the solution to rising poverty, inequality, and distress. The 'politics of global competitiveness' that they espouse actively seeks to open up to capital areas of activity hitherto shielded from it at least in part, and at the same time to exert pressure on everyone, whatever health issues or domestic or other responsibilities they might have, to make themselves 'absolutely available' for wage labour. As we shall see in the following chapters, in their drive to proletarianise the global population, they promote the incursion of capital into forms of production hitherto carried on within the family or household on a 'handicraft' basis, while also seeking to draw what they describe as 'inactive' household members into the labour market, and to bring workers in the informal sector directly under the control of capital. In terms of Marx's critique, they promote the maximum possible development of the 'capital-relation', and in doing so they *actively promote* the general law of social production discovered by Marx, across the fields of 'production' and 'social reproduction' alike. For the last 70 years they have relentlessly pursued the expansion of the world market through the promotion of the uninterrupted division of labour, and the application of new and the perfecting of old machinery precipitately and on an ever more gigantic scale. In doing so, they have understood perfectly that capitalist development is not a matter of economic or financial policy narrowly conceived, but of the subjection of social production as a whole to the logic of capitalist competition. They have actively promoted the dissolution of the 'varied, apparently unconnected and petrified forms of the social production process' and their transformation through 'conscious and planned applications of natural science', and they have done so with a primary focus on the need to maximise the capacity of capital to access and exploit more productively the labour-power of the world's population. They have pursued active policies of proletarianisation which have become comprehensive in scope, and sought to eliminate any possibility for survival other than dependence upon wage labour. They have striven with increasing energy to equip and oblige women to enter the workforce, and they have recently launched a final offensive against the 'informal' economy. In all this, they have shown unconditional commitment to creating social and institutional conditions that hasten the rule of the 'general law of social production' that obliges workers to practise 'variation of labour, fluidity of functions, and mobility... in all directions' and thereby produces 'totally developed individuals' who are continually under pressure to be 'absolutely available for the different kinds of labour required of them'.

Recently, drawing in their own way on developments in neuroscience and related fields, they have turned their attention to the engineering of the consciousness of the poor, with the aim of inducing compliance and even willing endorsement and internalisation of the logic of competitiveness. In doing so, they are working to bring about that 'most complete suspension of all individual freedom, and the most complete subjugation of individuality under social conditions which assume the form of objective powers, even of over-powering objects – of things independent of the relations among individuals themselves' that Marx associated with free competition in his mid-twenties. It would be incorrect, however, to say that they do so without regard for the *contradictions* of capitalism. If on the one hand they insist that the principal causes of poverty and inequality arise from the *insufficient* development of capitalism, on the other they strive, through the policy advice they offer, to alleviate its contradictions as far as is possible, and to defer their maturation. They are serious about *inclusion*, on the grounds that excluded citizens or populations represent foregone production and potential challenge and instability. They are intensely political in their promotion of reform, advocating sequences and strategies intended to neutralise any capacity for resistance. And as a consequence they have no time at all for the proposition that the 'market' should be freed from intervention and left to do its work. Their ideal, on the contrary, is the active interventionist state, accepting the duty to promote competitiveness in its own area of jurisdiction in a manner that conduces to competitiveness across the world market as a whole (by forswearing protectionism and other forms of state support for industry, for example), and aware, to twist a phrase, that the price of competitiveness is eternal vigilance.

2

The OECD and the World Market

The OECD has been remarkably consistent since its founding in 1961. It has sought constantly to build and extend the world market, by guiding governments towards the principles on which a competitive world economy should work. This has meant not only asserting the logic of competitiveness through competition as a universal principle, but also inculcating market-conforming habits of thought and behaviour on the part of the majority who survive by their labour. In classical Marxist terms, it seeks to develop the *capital relation*, tutoring governments on the need for and the means towards securing and renewing the ascendancy of capital over labour. This is the ultimate objective of its constant focus on competitive markets for goods and labour, and hence its opposition to protectionism and its support for competition and welfare reform. This chapter briefly discusses previous liberal initiatives, then traces its emergence and role in international politics through two periods—from 1948 to 1990, in which it came into being as a successor to the post-war Organisation for European Economic Cooperation (OEEC) and developed its own core project from 1961, and from 1990 to 2012, in which new circumstances allowed it to extend it on a global scale. Over the period it intensified its engagement with developing and emerging economies, reached a position of complete convergence with the World Bank, and put forward a universal prescription for an integrated approach to labour market regulation and social protection intended to create a perfectly exploitable global proletariat. Since then, as detailed in Chapter 4, it has worked closely with the European Commission and the World Bank to take the project forward.

Antecedents

Two unduly neglected sources, Craig Murphy's *International Organization and Industrial Change: Global Governance since 1850* (Murphy 1994), and Patricia Clavin's *Securing the World Economy* (Clavin 2013), identify the liberal institutional foundations on which the OECD would build. Murphy's pioneering study of the role of international organisations in promoting global

The Politics of Global Competitiveness. Paul Cammack, Oxford University Press. © Paul Cammack 2022.
DOI: 10.1093/oso/9780192847867.003.0003

capitalism argues that since their inception in the 1860s, 'the greatest impact of the world organizations themselves has been on industrial change' (Murphy 1994, 2). It shows how international public unions such as the International Telegraph Union (1865), the Universal Postal Union (1867), and the International Bureau of Weights and Measures (1875) sought to create the infrastructure that a world market based on private investment and exchange required, and on which the League of Nations and the UN system would subsequently build. It identifies behind the efforts of liberal internationalists to address the tensions arising from the expansion of the world market 'the deeper issue that capitalist industrialism has always rested on inequalities in power; for the system to work, a few must have the ability to change the processes of production, while most must simply submit to the logic of the machine' (Murphy 1994, 21). So, it argues, international institutions not only promoted the infrastructural and institutional development of the world economy, but also sought to mitigate the social tensions and conflicts its development produced, both internationally and within individual class-divided societies: successive revolutions in production prompted waves of institutional innovation, but the second industrial revolution in particular (based on the petroleum, chemical, and electrical industries) produced social dislocations, both international and domestic, to which the international institutions sought to respond. The more successful designers of successive liberal internationalist world organisations, Murphy suggests, have pressed governments to foster industry by creating and securing international markets for industrial goods, *and* sought to 'manage potential conflicts with organized social forces which might oppose the further extension of the industrial system promoted by the activities undertaken to complete the first task':

> People whose interests are tied to older industries, workers subject to the discipline of new industries, and those in the less industrialized world might be helped to adjust to the new order; agreements maintaining existing privileges might be worked out; or states might agree to use coercion to assure compliance with the new order.   (Murphy 1994, 40)

This indispensable analysis, which sees liberal internationalists and the institutions they created as seeking to persuade capitalists to subordinate their short-run individual interests to the construction of a liberal international order from which all would benefit, and approaches the task from the perspective of the class struggle inherent in the subjection of labour to the needs of capital, fits exactly the contemporary roles of the World Bank and the OECD, and captures the enduring logic that drives them.

It is complemented by Clavin's important monograph on the largely ignored Economic and Financial Organisation of the League of Nations (Clavin 2013). The League was unable to secure disarmament and promote a return to peace and stability after the First World War. But from shortly after its founding in 1919, its largely independent Economic and Financial Organisation sought to define a strategy for rebuilding the global economy along liberal lines. Although the initiative barely got off the ground, it established with remarkable clarity the form that the project would take in the future. While the International Labour Organisation (ILO), set up at the same time to contain the threat of labour radicalisation and anti-capitalist mobilisation through the promotion of coordinated reform, struggled in its aim to establish global labour standards (Murphy 1994, 43–4), the EFO pursued a different set of objectives around the development of the world market, and the reconciliation of individual states to its logic. As Clavin shows, it systematically gathered data on the performance of the global economy and of states within it, and sought to make them consistent and comparable. Second, with this data to hand it took an explicitly global perspective, in which its first priority was to identify policies that would be beneficial for the world economy as a whole, and the whole set of individual states and regions composing it. Third, it sought to build support for its project at an international level. Fourth, while it took account of the specific circumstances of the time, it sought to develop a long-term perspective, arguing that states found this difficult to achieve. Fifth, it did so from an ideological perspective of 'liberal internationalism', a perspective not to be confused with a laissez-faire attitude, as it addressed national and global social relations of production, and how they should be reformed and managed. Significantly, it took a developmentalist view of the world economy, insisting that the needs of emerging and developing states and their largely rural populations must be accommodated, and that the policies of the leading states were not only injurious to them, but also irrational and inefficient as regarded their own long-term interests and those of their citizens. Finally, it saw states as hampered in the pursuit of more 'rational' policies by the hold exerted over them by sectional interests, and sought to encourage them to resist such pressures, and to pursue policies conducive to the 'general good', understood throughout in terms of global liberal development. The resulting outlook, based upon the systematic gathering of data, the adoption of a long-term global liberal perspective, the canvassing of support for it from states, and the identification of the opposition of sectional interests as an impediment to its adoption on their parts, would be central to subsequent projects, and it characterises the work of the OECD today.

So for example, a seminal document published in 1935, *Remarks on the Present Phase of International Economic Relations*, articulated a clear global vision that contrasted sharply with the national protectionism prevalent at the time:

> foreigners are purchasers of *our* products; they are those who have to pay *us* the interest on the capital we have lent them; they are those who, by transporting their goods to our country and our goods to their country would provide work for *our* railways and *our* shipping, who, visiting us as tourists, would spend their money in *our* hotels and *our* shops. In short, those '*foreigners*' are an indispensable link in the chain of our activities, or, to express it more aptly, they are members of our body economic; to impoverish them is to impoverish ourselves.   (Clavin 2013, 144)

With its members unreceptive to this message, the EFO secretariat decided that 'the answer to the crisis was to redouble League efforts to inculcate a broader view of states' duties, as well as rights, to the societies they represented and to the international economy as a whole' (Clavin 2013, 159). In particular, it promoted the view that the policy of agricultural protection pursued by industrial countries was 'a parochial strategy that ignored the well-being of peoples beyond Europe's frontiers, *perpetuated inefficiency within Europe*, kept European living standards low, and made its citizens unhealthy' (emphasis mine). The *Final Report of the Mixed Committee of the League of Nations on the Relation of Nutrition to Health, Agriculture and Economic Policy* (1937) argued that 'industrialized countries should concentrate agricultural production on milk and fruit to meet their domestic markets' need for perishables, but, for the good of their own economic development and the balance of the world economy as a whole, they should produce less wheat, sugar, and cereals – the world's major traded commodities' (Clavin 2013, 170–1). Alexander Loveday, the long-serving Director of the Financial Section, took the view that 'governments absorbed economic ideas into policy in an unsatisfactorily haphazard way that stymied League efforts to coordinate policy developments and facilitate cooperation'. He would put it more bluntly in 1942, suggesting to the League's Secretary-General Sean Lester in relation to the problem of combining economic advancement with social security that the League offered a 'system of collaboration' to help 'baby governments' to grow up (Clavin 2013, 201, 285). This reflected the conviction that the self-centred and short-term perspectives of states were an obstacle to reform, and that an 'altered pattern of production, *coupled with social policies intended to ameliorate the worst effects of free trade*, would enable countries to drop protective barriers and reintegrate their economies into the international economy as a whole' (Clavin 2013, 236, emphasis mine). As Clavin summarises, while the EFO remained committed to liberal economics,

> national and international government had to recognize that not everyone benefited equally from free market economics. Social and health policies were essential to ameliorate their sometimes challenging effects and to underline the responsibilities of the world's richer members to its poorer ones. Development should be at the core of their contribution to global relations.   (Clavin 2013, 250)

In *The Transition from War to Peace Economy* (1943) and its final publication, *Economic Stability in the Post-War World: The Conditions of Prosperity after the Transition from War to Peace* (1945), the League expressed the view, again in Clavin's summary, that no man or woman who wanted work should be unemployed for any time longer than it takes to train for a new form of employment, and that all states 'should share in the markets of the world through the liberalization of trade barriers; and the benefits of modern methods of production should be available to all peoples of the world through trade, and "courageous" international measures of reconstruction and development' (Clavin 2013, 329).

The final report privileged the global over the national, proposing a stronger and more centrally coordinated set of institutions than eventually emerged. It also privileged the needs of competitive capital over the rights of workers. It argued the need for counter-cyclical public spending balanced over time, in view of the inevitability of recurrent recessions, and market-smoothing interventions to stabilise commodity prices to the benefit of both producing and consuming countries, but it rejected direct taxation to redistribute national wealth, as this could act as a disincentive on business and check economic progress. In short, the League order was 'explicitly liberal and capitalist' (Clavin 2013, 339). As such, it focused on the political economy of global production and exchange and the perceived logic and needs of 'capital as a whole'. Its work and its general orientation would be revived, after a hiatus, at the OECD.

1948–1990: The Project Gestated and Developed

Structural adjustment—the 'adjustment' of national economies to the global rule of capital—was not initially a policy imposed on the developing world by the United States, the advanced industrial countries, or the IMF and World Bank. Rather, it was the broad framework within which the rebuilding of the world market took place after the Second World War, and its primary focus was on Western Europe. European currencies were slow to achieve convertibility, and it took until 1958 to remove quantitative restrictions on trade within Western Europe (Barbezat 1997, 38). In this period of heightened US hegemony over Europe, the Organisation for European Economic Cooperation (OEEC), founded in 1948 in the context of the launching of the Marshall Plan (or European Recovery Programme—ERP), was envisaged by the US as a vehicle to promote not only economic recovery, but also economic integration to create a single market in Western Europe, and potentially a West European government. The US administration emphatically promoted the benefits of integration in terms of enhanced productivity and global competitiveness, with Paul Hoffman, the head of the European Cooperation Administration, expressing the conviction in 1949 that if a single market were created, 'the massive change in the economic environment would...set in motion a rapid growth in productivity. This would make it possible for Europe to improve its competitive position in the world and thus more clearly satisfy the expectation and needs of its people.' Alongside this, the ERP launched 'the largest international propaganda operation ever seen in peacetime', aimed in particular at making trade unions partners in the pursuit of greater productivity (Ellwood 1992, 154–5, 159–62). The creation of the European Productivity Agency as a branch of the OEEC in 1953 reflected this emphasis, but as Ellwood argues, the upswing in growth and productivity across Western Europe from the mid-1950s stemmed from 'a new kind of boom' based upon consumer durables, rising female employment, and credit ('hire purchase'), and took international planners by surprise (Ellwood 1992, 216–18).

This was the context in which the OECD emerged when it came into being in 1961 as the successor to the OEEC. From the start it advocated the expansion of world trade and the eventual integration of *all* countries into the capitalist world market. But it still took time to develop a coherent project for a restored world market, and to extend its reach accordingly. Some fundamental underlying reasons for this were set out perceptively in 1976 by Miriam Camps, who was involved at a junior level in the US State Department in the creation of the OEEC, and at a more senior level, after a career break, in the 1960s. She noted in 1976 that 'for many reasons the advanced economies confront a need to make structural changes in their patterns of production', but added first that 'there is a hierarchy of interests which, rightly or wrongly, is generally accepted, i.e. one which puts national interests top, global interests bottom, and the interests of allied countries somewhere in between', and second that relevant issues would not 'readily lend themselves to rule-making, until there is some political reality to the concept of a global economy' (Camps 1975, pp. 23–5 and ft. 23, p. 54). The 20 original members inherited from the OEEC were joined only by Japan, Finland, Australia, and New Zealand between 1964 and 1973, and no further expansion took place until after 1990. Even so, its global project, embracing the newly industrialised countries (NICs) in particular, was clearly articulated from the start. Its founding Convention signed in Paris in December 1960 committed it to promote policies designed 'to achieve the highest sustainable economic growth and employment and a rising standard of living in Member countries, while maintaining financial stability, and thus *to contribute to the development of the world economy*; to contribute to sound economic expansion in Member as well as *non-member countries*', and 'to contribute to the expansion of *world trade* on a multilateral, non-discriminatory basis in accordance with international obligations' (emphasis mine). The inclusion of 'development' in its title represented a conscious step forward from the OEEC, and the OECD's Development Advisory Committee and Development Centre (the latter proposed in 1961 by President Kennedy) would play a significant role in relation to non-members and to global policies from an early stage.

The priority given to developmental assistance to less developed areas, over the objections of the US Treasury (Griffiths 1997, 244), arose from concerns over the appeal of the Soviet model in the developing world. Asserting the centrality of this dimension, Leimgruber and Schmelzer describe the OECD as a 'Cold War economic institution' (Leimgruber and Schmelzer 2017a, 5). As they show, though, it was more than that, and it was never simply a mouthpiece for the advanced economies that were its members. From its early days, its leaders stood somewhat apart, adopting a longer and broader perspective. Overall, Leimgruber and Schmelzer conclude, '[e]ven though the OECD was a Cold War institution structurally driven by member country interests and the underlying power structures, the Secretary-Generals (and other powerful officials) exerted a considerable influence on its running and priorities' (Leimgruber and Schmelzer 2017a, 24). Alexander King, who went on from the position of Deputy Director of the European Productivity Agency at the OEEC to become its Director for Science, Technology and Industry and a co-founder of the Club of Rome in 1968, shared with founding Secretary-General Thorkil Kristensen the view that government ministers and bureaucracies were 'post facto mechanisms': 'They only react after events, and do not foresee them. They are not prepared for them' (Schmelzer 2017, 33); a decade later, drawing on interviews conducted with key staff in 1977, Michael Henderson found that the OECD was not a vehicle for US 'super-imperialism', but was rather oriented towards building consensus among the core capitalist states, who at the time were seeking to hold the line against 'less developed countries' that were becoming 'highly competitive in the world market in such areas as textiles, footwear and electronic appliances'. He noted at the same time that whereas national delegates were 'unabashedly state-centric', the OECD secretariat, concerned with the 'maintenance of the viability and good health of world capitalism', exhibited 'a pronounced systemic or international orientation' (Henderson 1981, 809–10). This view is borne out in materials from the *OECD Observer* examined below.

Core Principles of the OECD

The orientation of the OECD as an institution is manifested in two extended statements published in the *OECD Observer* early in 1963, relating to its method of working and policy orientation respectively (note that in the PDF versions of the *Observer* available online at the OECD *i*library, the articles listed as appearing in No. 1 (November 1962) and No. 3 (March 1963) have been transposed in error. So the articles cited here are found attached to No. 1). The first spelled out the system of 'confrontation of economic policies', an elaborate working method carried over from the OEEC in which the member countries used the OECD as a forum to explain and justify their policies, and comment on those of their peers. This approach was intended to allow each country to 'formulate and apply its policy in full knowledge of the international conditions in which it will be put into effect, and of the plans of other governments and the motives behind them' (OECD 1963, 3). This marks the early adoption of policy coordination, mutual surveillance, and peer review as a key set of OECD practices. Crucially, it was intended as a means to reconcile the substantive policy preferences of the OECD on the one hand, and the interests and preferences of states on the other. The 'method of confrontation', it suggested, would *generate* constructive solutions to acknowledged problems through a learning process that was consistent with full national sovereignty, yet could shift state interests towards OECD preferences by countering sectional pressures. The text was explicit on this point:

A country's economic policy is not the pure expression of unalloyed reason. It reflects the prevailing balance of its social and political forces, and is normally under constant sectional pressures, but discussion in an international forum such as the O.E.C.D. helps to put these forces and pressures into better perspective, and to sort out the good from the bad. Publication by the O.E.C.D. of an international view of what are sometimes thought to be purely domestic questions can materially help the formation of more bilateral opinions in the country concerned.   (OECD 1963, 7)

The faith in reason and deliberation as a means of reaching the best solution by the force of the better argument may not always have been realised. But it is revealing of the OECD's idea of itself at its inception, and, just as important, it shows that its method of working was intended to bring about a process of what contemporary jargon calls socialisation: individual countries would in principle *reassess* their interests and *modify* their policies as a result of the highly structured and iterative interaction described. In the process, the danger of capture by vested interests could be mitigated.

A second article in the same issue, this time under the name of Kristensen himself, addressed the view he took of relations with 'other continents', and entered into the *substance* of policy preferences (Kristensen 1963). It is a document of fundamental and enduring importance. After some striking remarks on the tensions between 'federalist' and 'functionalist' approaches to European unification, it suggested, in the light of the considerable deficit in the overall balance of payments of the United States, that the European countries should embrace liberal rather than protectionist agricultural policies. First, this would address the inflationary tendencies whose consequence was that 'Europe [had] lost some of its competitive power': 'it is a common experience that one of the best ways of countering inflationary tendencies is to allow freer entry of goods from abroad so as to strengthen competition and prevent shortages that may push prices up'. Second, it would allow European countries experiencing a 'persistent shortage of industrial manpower' to transfer workers from agriculture to industry, with benefits for both growth and productivity. Such a strategy, Kristensen admitted, would be 'socially and politically difficult'. But it would still be better to 'pave the way for the progressive abolition of protection in order to encourage the movement towards greater efficiency'. He was not optimistic, expecting rather that reciprocal protectionist measures would have the result of making economic and political cooperation all the harder, and lead to 'less efficient production in the protected sectors, and in consequence some slowing-down of general expansion'. 'What is perhaps even more serious', he went on, 'is that *reciprocal protectionism in the two Western continents would probably have the result of also making them protectionist in their relations with the under-developed countries'* (Kristensen 1963, 17, emphasis mine). Nor was this all. Turning to the 'less developed continents', he stressed the need for development aid, perhaps until 'the end of the century', but insisted that in the long run, 'the main problem of the developing countries will probably be their external trade': 'the problems of markets for the products of the less developed countries will be much more important in future than the problems of trade between developed countries'. And after referencing the 'complicated question of stabilising prices or export earnings in respect of tropical products and primary materials' (on which, in fact, both before and after UNCTAD 1964 Kristensen's views were close to those of Raul Prebisch), he concluded as follows:

> The other major aspect is that in the long run we must expect a spectacular increase in the imports of manufactured products originating in the poorer countries. Almost their only wealth is their plentiful low-wage manpower. They must have modern techniques, but like the Japanese they could adopt them gradually. We might perhaps envisage a large scale re-deployment of industrial activity between the continents over the next few decades, which would mean a re-orientation of European industry. It is not too soon to start preparing for this. Whether we like it or not, Europe will be forced in the imminent future to change, not only her day-to-day policy but also her economic and political structure under the pressure of inexorable forces which entail ever-growing interdependence between all the continents. Europe cannot live in isolation. *There is no protection against the fundamental forces of history.*   (Kristensen 1963, 17, emphasis mine)

This insistence on the need for the developed or advanced countries to assist in the development of others, and in due course to welcome competition from their industrial exports and to adapt their societies to meet it is the *essence* of the OECD's enduring sense of its mission. It would be reiterated time and time again—by Kristensen again *after* UNCTAD 1964 (Kristensen 1966, 6), by his successor Emile van Lennep in response to the rise of the Newly Industrialised Countries (NICs) and global production chains in the following decade, and by a host of publications from the Development Centre in the mid-1990s. Direct engagement with India, China, and others thereafter was simply a continuation of this core original mission. From the start, the goal of the OECD was to develop the *global* economy along capitalist lines, in accordance with liberal principles. Above all, as recognised from the start, this would involve finding ways for the advanced countries to carry out 'difficult' social and economic reforms. The OECD, in other words, was and remains an intensely political organisation.

As this makes clear, the primary focus of discussion and of OECD concern was the need for member countries to adjust *their own* economies to the internal challenges they were facing as a consequence of failing competitiveness. This turn towards the reform of welfare and labour markets in response to structural and technological change was expanded upon in 1979, in a report under the name of Secretary-General Emile van Lennep on the sensitive issue of *The Impact of the Newly Industrialising Countries on Production and Trade in Manufactures* (OECD 1979). Pitched into the context of 'North-South' confrontation over calls for a New International Economic Order, and of crisis and readjustment in the advanced and developing economies alike in the wake of dollar devaluation and the subsequent efforts of OPEC to nationalise production and raise oil prices, it invoked the mutual benefits that would flow from enhanced access to advanced economy markets for industrial production in the 'dynamic new exporters' it termed the 'NICs' (including Greece, Spain, and Portugal!). Van Lennep's message was that 'if appropriate policies are followed on both sides, considerable mutual benefits will continue to be derived from increasing trade in manufactures in both directions with the newly industrialised countries'. The focus was on increasing productivity, in advanced and newly industrialising countries alike:

> For the advanced industrial countries these benefits take the form of cheaper goods for consumers, *a spur to increased productivity* and reduced inflation at home, and new and prosperous markets abroad. For the newly industrialised countries they include higher investment, productivity and real incomes, and the foreign currency needed to help finance accelerated economic development.   (OECD 1979, 5, emphasis mine)

This reflected the embrace of greater competition: the rise of manufacturing capacity in new centres of production would extend the world market, and exports to the advanced economies would keep inflation under control by providing cheap wage goods. It would also expose advanced economy producers to increased competition, and it was this that was welcomed as a 'spur to increased productivity': the producers affected would either reorganise the way they worked or invest in new technologies, thereby becoming more productive, or go out of business, freeing workers to be employed more productively elsewhere. At the same time, producers in newly industrialised countries would compete with each other on the world market, and with new producers from successive waves of emerging economies as integration and structural transformation became universal. In making this argument, the OECD was early to recognise the significance of 'new approaches to the organisation of production and marketing':

> Transnational enterprises (and the expansion of intra-firm trade) have been an important feature in the *decentralisation and fragmentation of production processes and the development of new forms of international division of labour*. Through sub-contracting for off-shore processing and assembly, they have moved capital, technology, managerial and marketing skills to suitable locations, making use of 'potential' comparative advantage deriving from low-cost labour, proximity to major markets and political stability in the host countries. (OECD 1979, 10, emphasis mine)

To further this process, the NICs were urged to provide 'a numerous, disciplined, educated and skilled labour force ... an active and efficient entrepreneurial class and an adequate degree of political stability' (OECD 1979, 11). But the main message was addressed to the OECD's own advanced economy members, who were advised against resorting to protectionism to keep out competitive imports. Workers who used to produce goods that were now imported could be 'employed to produce something else', while 'labour-saving investment and rationalisation to meet competition from low labour-cost countries' would bring about further productivity gains. In the process some jobs would be lost, with women and the unskilled particularly affected, some wages would fall, the intensity of work would be speeded up, so 'serious frictional adjustment problems' were to be expected. The policy conclusions that followed dwelled on the need to manage short-term pain for long-term gain: while the long run was positive, 'over the shorter term ... there is no guarantee that the necessary adjustments will come about smoothly or painlessly' (OECD 1979, 14).

Here, as always, the OECD put the extension of the world market first. Three decades later, incoming Secretary-General Angel Gurría would describe the organisation as 'a partner of decision-makers in the political economy of reform' (OECD 2007a, 5), a phrase that is applicable throughout its history. As problems began to accumulate, it became a strong proponent of reform within the leading capitalist states rather than a passive coordinator of their interests, urging them to accept and embrace competition from the developing world. And it would do the same when the 'global financial crisis' broke—quite characteristically urging the case for more reform, and further steps towards truly global capitalism.

In connection with this, Samuel Beroud provides an illuminating account of the 'positive adjustment policies' recommended by the OECD in the 1970s, and traces their origins back to a 1970 report entitled *Inflation: The Present Problem* that set out a mix of policies ranging from trade liberalisation and the reduction of subsidies for agriculture and industry to price-income policies and state support to modernise industrial facilities, labour force re-training, mobility support, and specific policies for regions severely hit by de-industrialisation. The focus was on 'new structural policies to mitigate public discontent caused by...non-accommodating macroeconomic policies', and, crucially, these were intended 'to "help governments to resist political pressure for too early relaxation of restrictive policies," underscoring that "only the effective introduction of policies for internal adjustment of the structure of industry and employment in advanced countries will permit the acceptance of this international development"' (Beroud 2017, 236).

In a complementary analysis, Leimgruber shows that in the crucial period from the mid-1970s to the mid-1980s the OECD turned its energy decisively towards advocating the reform of welfare regimes in the core capitalist states. A key moment here was the convening in October 1980, following nearly a decade of work on the issue culminating in the 1978 McCracken Report, of a high-level conference on 'the welfare state in crisis'. James Gass, the Head of the Directorate for Social Affairs, Manpower and Education (created in 1974), argued that 'we cannot escape the necessity to remodel our social policies while continuing to ensure a minimum of protection', while van Lennep advocated 'new relationships between public services and private action [and the need] to reinforce every one's personal responsibilities'. Leimgruber cites Gass as insisting that 'as an international secretariat we have a duty to tackle political problems from a professional angle and in the interests of all our member countries', and concludes that 'the OECD was not only in the course of adapting itself, but also contributing to the ongoing change of the ideological climate towards the welfare state' (Leimgruber 2012, 296–7). Its adversary here was the ILO, which had played a major part in promoting universal state-financed welfare from the early 1940s, and was staunch in its defence. Right away at this early stage, the OECD took the view that the world had changed, and urged world-market enhancing reform on developing and advanced countries alike. Complementing this, and building on work carried forward under the auspices of the OEEC, the OECD devoted systematic attention from the start to educational reform focused on producing the 'right kind of people' for the world of tomorrow (Bürgi and Tröhler 2018, 86).

Throughout, the focus was on the development of the world market as a whole through internal reform across all its constituent economies, with the intention of bringing the logic of social production into line with the logic of competitiveness. In 1989, OECD Development Centre President Louis Emmerij advocated 'simultaneous as opposed to sequential world economic growth and development' in a summary of the policy conclusions emerging from a symposium held in February 1989 to celebrate the 25th anniversary of the Centre. The edited volume which he introduced, *One World or Several?*, gave evidence of the further refinement of the OECD's global project. In his opening remarks, Secretary-General Jean-Claud Paye identified a gap between 'a world economy that is increasingly integrated and globalised' and 'an institutional political superstructure that does not mesh very well with the integrated economy' (Emmerij 1989, 12), and proposed that the OECD should fill the gap. From the mid-1990s, in changed circumstances, the organisation would develop further a combined agenda embracing domestic reform in the advanced countries and the expansion of the world economy as a whole, with 'jobs' at home and abroad at its centre.

1990–2013: The Project Refined

Calls from the OECD for the accelerated integration of developing countries into the world market multiplied in the 1990s, in tandem with proposals for productivity-enhancing labour market reform in advanced countries. The most significant of the latter was the 1994 *Jobs Study*, commissioned by ministers in 1992, at a moment of economic recession when 'more people were unemployed in the OECD area than at any time before' (OECD 1994, 1). It concluded that 'it is an inability of OECD economies and societies to adapt rapidly and innovatively to a world of rapid structural change that is the principal cause of high and persistent unemployment', and documented falling rates of growth in productivity and GDP per head decade by decade from the 1960s; it then traced the structural problem back to the late 1960s, and the 'weakened capacity of collective bargaining to keep increases in income in line with economies' capacity to pay' (OECD 1994, vii, 63), com-pounded later by the failure of labour market institutions to respond to the changed circumstances after the first oil shock, except in the US, where real wage growth was contained. Paye wrote in the foreword that

> There is no doubt ... that the only way to achieve long-term success is to embrace change. Trying to slow the pace of change and artificially to protect uncompetitive activities would only make delayed adjustment more painful.

All policies should therefore be harnessed to promote adjustment to change, while taking care to reinforce social cohesion, a condition for the long-term success of the recommended strategy.   (OECD 1994: n.p.)

The diagnosis offered in the report itself led to an agenda that remains in place. It identified a persisting 'structural' element to unemployment, beyond the cyclical component produced by recession, growing from 'the gap between the pressures on economies to adapt to change and their ability to do so'; and made urgent by the challenge of global competition and the incapacity of the OECD economies to meet it:

Adaptation is fundamental to progress in a world of new technologies, globalisation and intense national and international competition. The potential gains may be even greater than those which flowed from the opening up of economies after World War II. But today, OECD economies and societies are inadequately equipped to reap the gains. Policies and systems have made economies rigid, and stalled the ability and even willingness to adapt. To realise the potential gains, societies and economies must respond rapidly to new imperatives and move towards the future opportunities. To many, the change is wrenching.   (OECD 1994, 2)

The task of governments, then, was to steer societies 'through the adjustment to new technologies and new forms of global trade'; their challenge was 'to embrace change rather than succumb to pressure to resist it through protectionism or other measures to restrict competition'; and in facing the task of 'designing and redesigning a range of policies across the economy and society in order to help foster—or in some cases, stop hindering—adaptation to evolving ways of production and trade', they would need to transform their societies. Businesses, trade unions, and workers alike would need to be 'innovative to develop the new products, processes, and ways of working that will create new jobs, and help to shape skills to fit with the jobs of the future'. And explicit policies would need to be developed to secure social cohesion, with particular attention to those who would find it difficult or impossible to adapt:

Some people ... will have particular difficulty in making the needed adaptation. The most successful economies and societies will be those which plough back some of the gains from change into accelerating the process by helping them to adapt. Even so, some in society will find it impossible to adapt to the requirements of advancing economies. Yet they, too, must benefit from the progress. Their exclusion from the mainstream of society risks creating social tensions that could carry high human and economic costs

(OECD 1994, 1–2).

This succinct statement carries forward the advocacy of 'positive adjustment policies' devised in the 1970s, and in doing so spells out an agenda that goes well beyond the litany of liberalisation (of trade), privatisation (of state industry) and deregulation (of business) that is generally held to be the core of 'neoliberal' reform in this period. Notably, the agenda of the OECD matches exactly Marx's account of the 'immanent laws of capitalist production': technological revolution, new forms of production and trade, increased competition, and the resulting need for 'new products, processes, and ways of working that will create new jobs, and help to shape skills to fit with the jobs of the future'. Skip forward two decades, and you find the Chief Economist of the OECD, Catherine Mann, noting that for all countries, 'the challenge is to pursue structural reforms to raise growth and create jobs in a sustainable and inclusive way', and warning members and non-members alike that 'structural reform isn't a finite list of measures with an end-date. It is an on-going process to build more productive, inclusive and sustainable economies for our citizens' (Mann 2014, 13). In short, this was and is a permanent imperative, a programme with no end in sight. In seeking to develop the world economy the OECD is seeking to promote and harness the immanent laws of capitalist production: to bring them to bear on capitalists, workers, and states, and to manage the consequences of doing so. Its task lasts, therefore, for as long as capitalism endures.

For the developed countries, the 1994 *Jobs Study*, periodically reworked at regular intervals since (OECD 2006a, 2018), represents a crucial step in this direction. It challenged the idea that rising unemployment or lower wages were caused by technology, imports from low-wage countries, or the general intensity of competition, with their corollary implications for protective controls of various kinds. Technology and innovation historically boosted growth and living standards, while the increase in trade and competition was mostly between OECD countries, and gave rise to a pattern of 'creative destruction':

It thereby fosters economic growth and development, which involve a turbulent process of birth and death of firms, indeed the rise and fall of whole sectors of activity, and the reallocation of production within, as well as between, regions and countries. With this growth and development comes the wholesale destruction of many jobs—around one in ten each year—together with the creation of a similar number of new ones,

(OECD 1994, §2a, 3)

To slow the pace of change, then, 'would be to seek to cut off economies from the forces that have always been the mainsprings of economic growth and betterment'; the best approach, rather, was 'to strengthen the capacity to adjust to rapid change'. In typically didactic fashion, the message was rammed home in a Box entitled **WHAT THE ANSWER IS *NOT*,** the culprits being work-sharing and protectionism. In recent years, the OECD argued, waves of financial-market liberalisation and product market deregulation had 'greatly enhanced the potential efficiency of OECD economies, and also accelerated the pace of change', in the context of new information technologies and 'the trend towards globalisation': 'Yet, in the midst of this tumultuous period when so many forces were testing the flexibility of economies, policies to achieve social objectives were extended, with the unintended side-effect of making markets, including importantly labour markets, more rigid.' Worse, in Europe in particular the public sector had progressively become more important as an employer, while 'the impediments to private sector hiring increased, as the incentive to accept work – particularly low-paying or precarious work – diminished, and as societies demanded more publicly-provided services' (OECD 1994, §2a, 4). In the different US context of a flexible labour market in which the private sector generated highly productive jobs commanding high wages, precarious, low-skill, low-wage jobs also proliferated (mostly taken by women), whereas in Europe, where such jobs were 'by and large, disallowed by society', the result was increased unemployment. In each case, the core problem was the same: management skills, education and training attainments had failed to keep pace with change, and companies had not sufficiently improved productivity. In the face of this challenge, the OECD concluded, the answer was to meet social objectives 'in new, more carefully-designed ways that do not have the past unintended and undesirable side effects', or in other words to restructure welfare to match the logic of the world market:

Hence the challenge is two-fold: to look across the full range of policies that have been put in place over the last 30 years to see where, and to what extent, each may have contributed to ossifying the capacity of economies and the will of societies to adapt; and then to consider how to remove those disin-centives without harming the degree of social protection that it is each society's wish to provide.... This conclusion leads in turn to a number of broad conclusions: for policies to achieve more jobs; and for policies to equip people for these jobs while supporting those who lose out.

(OECD 1994, §2a, 5)

The conclusion, captured in the title of the study and repeated throughout it, was that the imperative was to create jobs, some of them inevitably low-wage, low-productivity jobs. This called for facilitating the development and use of technology, making working time flexible, encouraging entrepreneurship and removing disincentives to hiring by cutting non-wage labour costs, widening wage differentials, weakening employment protection legislation, and attacking product market barriers through competition policy. The 2006 update, presented at length in the *OECD Employment Outlook* of that year, would reassert the core analysis outlined here, but also identify seven new insights and policy lessons: so-called 'activations/mutual obligations' approaches could co-exist with relatively generous unemployment benefits while providing strong incentives for the unemployed to find work, including 'effective re-employment services to help the unemployed find a new job, as well as adequate monitoring of the job-search efforts of the unemployed to ensure that they are actively looking for work, backed up by the threat of graduated benefit sanctions'; it was vital to remove existing barriers to labour force participation among women, older workers and under-represented groups; the balance between security and flexibility had to be changed by making 'secure' jobs more flexible—'flexicurity'; labour demand had to be expanded by pricing back into employment the lower-skilled 'who are excluded by tax, social contribution or institutional arrangements', and by stimulating product market competition, especially in services; there should be a greater focus on effective lifelong learning; stability-oriented macroeconomic policies should accompany and support 'difficult structural reforms'; and, because 'there is no single golden road to better labour market performance', policies should share 'an emphasis on macroeconomic stability, adequate incentives for all labour market participants and strong product market competition', but tailor the precise policy model to fit specific national circumstances and history (OECD 2006b, 12–13). A briefer brochure summarising the revised strategy identified specific new challenges related to these recommendations: population ageing, the need to take advantage of and adjust quickly to changes brought about by technological advances and globalisation, and the likely intensification of adjustment pressures as 'large labour-rich countries, such as China and India, become better integrated in the world economy' (OECD 2006a, 5).

The *Jobs Study*, then, has become the constant framework within which the OECD continues to promote the enhancement of competitiveness among its members, and the better integration of developing and emerging economies into the world market. At the same time, the latter objective was promoted directly in a significant set of publications from 1995 on.

Towards a New Global Age

Three interventions in particular, *Linkages: OECD and Major Developing Economies* (1995), *Shaping the 21st Century: The Contribution of Development Cooperation* (1996), and *The World in 2020: Towards a New Global Age* (1997) capture the comprehensive project that sought to address on a global scale the implications of embracing the politics of global competitiveness espoused by the OECD. Running through all three was an unswerving commitment to the further development of the world market—and its consistent stance, as it had been since the early 1960s, was to advise *all* states on the changes they should make in order to adjust to what was both an inevitable and a desirable future.

In 1995 an agreed memo on *Development Partnerships in the New Global Context* noted that for three decades 'the highest rates of economic growth in the world have been achieved among developing countries, notably in Asia and Latin America', and welcomed both 'expanded trade, capital and technology flows' and 'far-reaching economic and political reforms' aimed at successful integration into a 'highly competitive, interdependent world'. The 'new global context', of course, was the massive opening up of the world market over the previous decade. The OECD advocated a set of 'strategies and programmes that will work to enable the poorest to expand their opportunities and improve their lives', centred upon 'a sound policy framework encouraging stable, growing economies with full scope for a vigorous private sector and an adequate fiscal base', and 'investment in social development, especially education, primary health care, and population activities' (DAC (OECD) 1996, 19–20). The document in which this memo was published a year later by the Development Assistance Committee, *Shaping the 21st Century*, looked ahead to a time, well before the mid-century, when 'the present developing countries will account for half of global economic output', and linked the goal of 'a higher quality of life for all people' to 'increasing the effectiveness of market economies and the efficiency of government' (DAC (OECD) 1996, 5, 8). The social and economic targets proposed were tied to specific strategies centred on 'reinforcing the transformation of institutions and enabling environments to facilitate the emergence of developing economies and transition economies as growing trade and investment partners in the global economy'. In turn, the developing countries were called upon to 'adhere to appropriate macroeconomic policies; commit to basic objectives of social development and increased participation, including gender equality; foster accountable government and the rule of law; strengthen human and institutional capacity; create a climate favourable to enterprise and the mobilisation of local savings for investment; carry out sound financial management, including efficient tax systems and productive public expenditure; and maintain stable and co-operative relations with neighbours' (DAC (OECD) 1996, 13–14). The study concluded with a firm commitment to universal development, centred on the responsibilities of the advanced economies: 'We should aim for nothing less than to assure that the entire range of relevant industrialised country policies are consistent with and do not undermine development objectives' (DAC (OECD) 1996, 18).

In the same period, a substantial set of studies was produced on the theme of *linkages*, exploring the connections between OECD countries and the economies of China, India, and Indonesia in particular among a larger group of 12 MDEs (Major Developing Economies). The core volume took the same starting point as the 1979 report on the NICs: the need to integrate new actors from the developing world into the mainstream at a time of prolonged and intense recession and far-reaching structural adjustment among OECD countries, which was proving 'particularly demanding and difficult', as '[s]tructural changes and deep-rooted unemployment and under-employment problems in industrialised countries have become linked in some perceptions with the emergence of low-wage competitor countries with less stringent social and environmental standards'. For the OECD, in contrast, the 'emergence of a new tier of competitor countries' was at the same time 'their parallel emergence as important and fast-growing customers and partners'; and above all, 'the challenges posed to OECD countries by these important new partners are the challenges resulting from the successful dissemination of a model of development promoted by the industrialised countries themselves. *Not illogically, the countries aspiring to this model also have a powerful expectation that acceptance of the mainstream international system and its rules will bring with it their full and equitable integration into the system'* (OECD 1995, 12, emphasis mine). Dismissing many of the fears articulated as reflecting 'a mix of misperceptions and unwarranted extrapolations from very incomplete information', the OECD nevertheless agreed that 'the emergence of the MDEs as major players in the world economy and the changes in prospect as a consequence do pose challenges for OECD Members along

with the opportunities to benefit from a more dynamic world economy'
(OECD 1995, 16).

The ensuing analysis of linkages in trade, investment, environmental issues
and migration picked up the 1979 notion of trade as helping 'to maintain the
competitive pressures that spur cost-reducing and quality-enhancing innovation and productivity growth'; advocated further out-sourcing of 'back-office'
operations to developing countries; bemoaned the extent of OECD-Member
non-tariff discrimination against non-Members; and noted the shift around
1990 of portfolio and foreign direct investment towards developing Asia in
particular (OECD 1995, 43, 66–102). On international migration it offered the
view that the only long-run solution to the tensions it generated was economic
development coupled with rapid growth of employment, as the achievement of
sustainable, labour-intensive development in the longer term would hold 'the
best hope of influencing the expectations of potential migrants to take a more
positive view of their own country and its prospects, thus diminishing the
propensity to migrate' (OECD 1995, 158).

A year later, a second extended analysis of linkages in the global economy
(OECD 1997a) provided a wealth of empirical detail and analysis, much of it
drawn upon also in *The World in 2020: Towards a New Global Age*, which set
out a comprehensive and accessible account of the OECD's position:

> We stand on the threshold of a 'New Global Age', where all societies have the
> potential of participating actively in the world economy; where the benefits
> of liberalised world trade and investment could flow to all people; where the
> misery and poverty of much of the developing world could become a closed
> chapter of sad history, no longer a reality of the present.   (OECD 1997b, 7)

The 'new age of global prosperity' envisaged would not materialise automatically: 'it will require bold action by governments within and outside the
OECD area to complete the borderless world through free flows of goods
and services, capital and technology, to ensure high and equitable growth
supported by stable and sustainable macroeconomic conditions and wide-
ranging structural reforms' (OECD 1997b, 7). And in what was by this time a
well-honed narrative, the authors of the report went straight to the nature of
the challenge—the need to make 'globalisation' socially acceptable, and to find
policies that would embed its disciplines across populations. Countries should
continue with reforms 'in the liberalisation of trade, investment, and financial
flows, and in strengthening the rules-based multilateral system, to facilitate a
deeper integration between the world's economies'. However,

in some OECD countries, there are already signs of a backlash against globalisation, which is sometimes blamed for persistent unemployment, widening income inequality and de-industrialisation. To tackle these problems, a wide range of domestic policy reforms is necessary and are [sic] being undertaken to make their economies and societies more adaptable and dynamic, so as to realise more fully the benefits of intensifying linkages with a growing number of non-OECD economies, while enhancing social cohesion.   (OECD 1997b, 11)

The OECD envisaged that demographic and technological change, along with relatively higher growth rates in non-OECD countries, would bring about a 'big shift in global economic weight' in which the non-OECD area could become 'a driving force in the global economy', and it welcomed this prospect unequivocally. Recognising that 'economic integration does involve adjustment costs, especially for low-skill workers and industries', manifested in social strains and protectionist pressures, it urged governments to minimise tensions and facilitate structural changes through flexible labour and product markets, the upgrading of skills and competencies, and reformed social policies that would 'support the adjustment rather than hinder it'. And more generally, it advised that changes in governance would be needed, 'to help populations to form *realisable expectations* for both their economic security and their own responsibilities, if social cohesion and political stability are to be secured' (OECD 1997b, 14–16, emphasis mine).

This was a manifesto for genuinely global capitalism, in the form of a 'competition-oriented agenda' (OECD 1997b, 17) in which the populations and policies of the industrialised and developing economies alike were to be aligned with and subordinated to the needs of a fully integrated global capitalist economy. The implications for the domestic policy of OECD governments were spelled out in the approach taken to connections between labour markets and social policy: the 'New Global Age' held out the prospect of 'a world of much greater prosperity, but a world of greater competitive pressures and more rapid structural change', where greater labour and product market flexibility would be necessary. The scenario laid out assumed that OECD countries would implement the policies of the Jobs Strategy, and in particular would reform social protection so that the degree of security it offered would 'encourage individuals to *take risks and be flexible in responding to changes in their economic circumstances*' (OECD 1997b, 19, emphasis mine). Support for lifelong learning to ensure that workers remained productive, the redesign of social security institutions for 'an era when many employees are likely to change jobs, and possibly careers, several times during their working life', and income support systems geared to emphasise reinsertion into the labour market rather than provide an adequate income for those excluded from work, with cuts elsewhere to fund such programmes in the context of pressures on public finances, were essential features of the desirable policy mix. As ever, the emphasis was on the need to turn all citizens into productive servants of capital, and the action to change attitudes that this entailed:

> The emphasis will need to be on 'active ageing', encouraging individuals to participate fully in society regardless of their age. Social protection systems should be adapted to facilitate a more flexible transition from work to retirement. This would contribute to a reversal of the current trend towards ever earlier retirement, which would in itself be the single most effective step that OECD countries could take to reduce the pressure on their social protection budgets. *At the same time, raising the effective age of retirement will require major changes in the attitudes of workers, employers and society.* But it is necessary and desirable and, with increased flexibility in employment parities, does not imply more of a lifetime spent in work.
>
> (OECD 1997b, 19–20, emphasis mine)

While the OECD could help in the development of this agenda in its role as a 'catalyst and pathfinder in international economic cooperation', through its unique structures and methods of work relying on dialogue and peer pressure, the major responsibility for steering reform fell upon governments:

> Strong political leadership, particularly in OECD countries, will be necessary to convince public opinion of the need to strengthen engagement in the international system. Such leadership will also be necessary to strengthen popular support for policy reform and dealing with adjustment problems. Governments must implement a focused and credible communication strategy to raise public understanding of the issues involved.   (OECD 1997b, 24)

In short, governments were called upon, as the end of the twentieth century approached, to implement the 'general law of social production' identified by Marx when the creation of the world market was in its infancy. The programme that the OECD would carry forward in the twenty-first century was fully in place.

Shifting Wealth and Social Cohesion

In the OECD's programme for universal competitiveness and its vision of a 'new global age', *all* countries are enjoined to create productive jobs by putting in place a structure of incentives that encourages individuals to prepare for work and enter the labour market. Global regimes that promote competition are essential to this, but it is a central part of the project that domestic regimes of social protection should support participation- and productivity-enhancing labour market reform. This logic has been reflected particularly in two series of publications: the annual volumes of *Going for Growth* launched in 2005, and the roughly biennial *Perspectives on Global Development* series launched in 2010 with *Shifting Wealth*; and as the global financial crisis began to bite, it prompted intensified engagement with leading developing and emerging economies on these themes. This approach presumes that the liberalisation of global trade and promotion of competition should continue, and insists on the need for the reform of labour markets, welfare, and social protection everywhere in order to promote competitiveness and productivity. Significantly, because it anticipates that the changes it seeks to promote will be disruptive and contested, it continues to place great emphasis upon ways in which populations must be moulded, and social cohesion maintained.

One element of this was a renewed emphasis, in the first volume of *Going for Growth*, on the process of mutual accountability and peer pressure supported by monitoring and structural surveillance across the areas of work and family life, ageing and employment policies, national education systems, and regulatory reform. OECD Chief Economist Jean-Philippe Cotis explained that surveillance processes at the OECD already included country-specific and sector-specific surveys, but did not yet include 'cross-country surveillance of growth, based on systematic benchmarking and with a view to advising member countries on national priorities. In the context of stalling convergence, benchmarking may help expose more clearly the areas where countries are lagging' (OECD 2005, 7; see also Box 1.1, 12–13, Annex 1.A.2, 31–6, and Fig. 4.1, 125). To remedy this, *Going for Growth* was an attempt at 'deep benchmarking', coupled with the identification of five tailored policy priorities for each country, varying in accordance with their overall profile on structural reform. A subsequent issue would offer an overview of 'a new area for research [sic], the so-called "political economy of structural reforms", a field that the OECD has recently investigated in some depth' (OECD 2007b, 168). It was not so new, as it happens, as it reprised themes addressed by the World Bank in the early 1990s, and referenced the same even longer standing collective action arguments regarding diffuse future winners versus specific and immediate losers. In identifying labour market reforms as the most difficult, and seeking in all circumstances to swell the pool of productive workers, it held fast to its original programme. And characteristically, it did not retreat as the global financial crisis erupted, but rather responded with redoubled efforts, deepening not only its analysis of the labour market, but also of its relations with leading emerging economies.

So while for this and subsequent issues the specific policy areas chosen for general discussion are significant as indicators of the overall project, the main interest of the series is in the enhanced mode of engagement with member countries. The policy agenda advanced harked back directly not only to the beginnings of the OECD itself, but to the classical liberal political economy of Adam Smith, with the emphasis squarely placed on labour utilisation and productivity, and competitive product markets. The OECD urged member countries to maximise the number of people in work, raise their productivity, and boost the competitive environment by reducing state control and removing barriers to entrepreneurship, foreign trade (especially in agriculture) and investment. It highlighted the benefits of 'reducing work disincentives through the limitation of the duration of unemployment benefits and the lowering of benefit levels for those out of jobs for a long time', with the German Agenda 2010 offered as a good example, and described pensions as a 'financial disincentive to work at older ages' (OECD 2005, 21). As the 'global financial crisis' began to make itself felt, the OECD insisted that 'the economic crisis facing OECD countries should not be allowed to slow down structural reforms, and opportunities for reforms should be exploited to strengthen economic dynamism and living standards' (OECD 2009, 5). In the following year, in an editorial entitled 'Shifting gears', new Chief Economist Pier Carlo Padoan urged member countries to step away from briefly necessary exceptional measures, and to strengthen reform efforts by reducing anti-competitive product market regulations, boosting active labour-market policies, and promoting green growth (OECD 2010a, 4).

At the same time, the OECD sought to bring the 'BRIICS' countries into the *Going for Growth* framework, with a chapter urging Brazil, China, India, Indonesia, and South Africa to move towards more competition-friendly product market regulation, strengthen property rights and contract enforcement, deepen financial markets and adopt 'multi-faceted strategies to reduce the size of informal sectors' (OECD 2010a, 5–6 and Ch. 7); from 2012 monitoring and policy advice would be applied to these economies as to OECD members. The focus on the emerging and developing economies was not new.

But the intensity of engagement was now stepped up, at an opportune moment when what growth there was in the world economy was entirely from these states. The first of the *Perspectives on Global Development, Shifting Wealth*, reiterated familiar themes: new poles of growth, the imminent prospect that a substantial majority of the world's GDP would originate from the 'South', and the need for policy making at the international level 'to adjust to a world in which developing countries have a growing economic weight' (OECD 2010c, 3). The perspective of the OECD was what it always had been: the structural transformation that had shifted the world's economic centre of gravity away from the OECD and towards the emerging economies was not a threat, but 'an opportunity for the global economy to shift up a gear'. The report noted the 'huge increase in the global labour force due to the integration of China and India into the world economy' (OECD 2010c, 24–5), and welcomed the competition this would create. Specifically addressing the prevalence of informal labour in both countries (though much more in India), it proposed a three-pronged strategy to address it: unlock poor workers in the informal sector from their low-productivity low-income traps and enable them to be more productive, through active labour market policies such as training and skills development; alter incentives by establishing credible enforcement mechanisms for labour laws and regulations, and making formality pay; and boost job creation through supporting small business compliance with formal requirements, and encouraging larger companies to create formal employment opportunities (OECD 2010c, 146).

In the same year the OECD issued its second full-length economic survey of China (the first appeared in 2005), with a comprehensive battery of recommendations aimed to increase China's productivity and competitiveness: upgrade the monetary policy framework; continue financial market opening; lower product market barriers; unify social safety nets; facilitate labour mobility; consolidate pension regimes; and press ahead with health care reform (OECD 2010b, 10). And in May 2010, with the financial support of the European Union Directorate-General for Employment, Social Affairs and Equal Opportunities, the OECD's Directorate for Employment, Labour and Social Affairs convened a 'high-level conference' on the theme of 'Inequalities in Emerging Economies: What Role for Labour Market and Social Policies?', focused on Brazil, China, India, and South Africa. This brought together policy makers from the four countries, and led to the publication of a detailed policy blueprint. It noted that the four countries shared high if declining proportions of the population in extreme poverty and therefore vulnerable to external shocks, underdeveloped labour markets and social policy institutions, widespread informality, limited administrative capacity, and unstable business climates. It then turned its attention to the need to integrate labour market and social policies by finding a balance between allocating labour to its most productive use and protecting workers, following the same logic that it applied to its own members. It condemned the tendency to 'give priority to job security rather than improving labour force skills and employability', as this form of labour reallocation 'imposes large welfare costs on workers and an inefficient job matching that negatively affects labour productivity', and it called for a focus on income support mechanisms rather than employment protection, and the reform of unemployment compensation schemes that 'rarely impose strict requirements on the claimants of the benefit, such as to be registered in the employment services or to search actively for a job' (OECD 2010d, 268, 276). The aim of labour market policies, it insisted, should be to *reduce labour market duality* rather than offer further protection to those already protected; they should be integrated and complemented with other policies to foster entrepreneurship, and improve human capital accumulation. So the Jobs Strategy was every bit as relevant here as to the advanced economies:

> To boost incomes and jobs, the four pillars of the OECD Reassessed Jobs Strategy, conveniently adapted on a country-specific base, can also be applied to BCIS. This means: i) setting an appropriate and solid macroeconomic policy; ii) removing the impediments to labour market participation for groups with more difficulties as well as facilitating the job search; iii) tackling labour and product market obstacles so as to boost labour demand; and iv) facilitating the development of labour force skills and competencies.
>
> (OECD 2010d, 298)

By this point, then, the OECD had a universal policy framework, explicitly applied across the world market as a whole. It advocated the subordination of socio-economic rights to a prior commitment to productivity and competitiveness in a global capitalist economy, working in close partnership with the World Bank, whose commitment to the same agenda is explored in Chapter 4. As the crisis deepened it continued to press the case, with explicit attention to 'the transformation of the integration of China and India in the world economy', urging them 'to finance social risk-sharing arrangements, so helping to cushion people against shocks and *enabling them to take an active part in new opportunities*' (OECD 2012b, 60–1, emphasis mine). Utopian as the goal may sound given the extent of labour informality, the 'high road' of productive jobs in the formal sector, equally open to female and male workers, was much preferred to the 'low road' of informality and low productivity. The challenge posed by inequality was to be addressed by a focus on equal opportunity, health, education, and training, and increased female labour market participation. Overall, the OECD argued, 'social cohesion will be fostered by holistic social protection systems that avoid reinforcing the dual nature of labour markets', while the 'determination of wages and job conditions is key to the distribution of growth' (OECD 2012b, 155, 157).

For the OECD, then, a 'common concern in designing, and especially scaling up, social protection instruments is that they should not have adverse effects on labour market behaviour and undermine growth projects'—transfers may reduce labour supply, if for example, they are contingent on unemployment and therefore 'lure job-seekers into informality or tempt them to ease up on the job-hunting efforts' (OECD 2012b, 174). Workers should share in the benefits of productivity increases, but overall the imperative was to maximise the supply of productive workers. Hence social and economic 'rights' were placed within strict limits:

> there is scope for labour institutions—minimum wages, collective bargaining, unionisation—to help protect workers with limited or no negative effects on labour market efficiency. However... institutions need to be carefully designed in order to avoid unintended negative consequences. Labour institutions that severely limit turnover and create obstacles for new entrants into the formal sector—whether they come from the informal sector or are young people trying to break into the job market—can accentuate the duality of labour markets.   (OECD 2012b, 177)

The Politics of the OECD—'The Time for Reform Is Now'

Miriam Camps felt in 1976 that the scope of the OECD was limited by the lack of 'political reality' attaching to the idea of the concept of the global economy, and suggested that it did not need either executive or operational power: 'What it does need', she went on, 'is the acceptance by governments of its right, its duty, to goad. This right is one that governments may accept in theory; but they will resist it in fact. No government likes to be pushed' (Camps 1975, 25, 46). She made an excellent point. The OECD designed a global project on behalf of 'capital in general' over its first fifty years of existence, but it was one that would achieve genuine purchase only after 1976, in the wake of material developments that made the global economy a political reality in ways that it had not been before. Its aim, promoted across the world market as a whole once it identified the real prospect for a 'New Global Age', was precisely to develop the social relations of production to their fullest extent, while seeking to embed them in a world-wide social order that could ensure and reproduce the rule of capital. Beginning in unpromising circumstances which Schumpeter had diagnosed in terms of the absence of any commitment to the principle of free enterprise, and the blocking of reform by vested interests hostile to the ethos of capitalism (Schumpeter 1954, 409–14), it pursued the re-establishment of the world market through cooperation and the integration into it of developing and newly independent states, challenged the protectionism of the advanced states, and sought to coordinate and modify their behaviour through methods of transparency, dialogue, and peer review. Within this project, 'structural adjustment' was a permanent necessity, mandated by the 'forces of history', requiring the constant adaptation of *all* states to the exigencies of the world market; and inclusion was interpreted as a social 'right' of access to health and a basic education and an economic 'right' to compete in the labour market, in an environment in which macro-level policies fostered high levels of labour utilisation and productivity. Crucially, the process of building the world market was not limited to the provision of physical or institutional infrastructure, or to the creation of regimes to govern global trade, finance, production, and investment, or even to liberalisation, privatisation, and deregulation. Rather, as Murphy suggested, the strategic programme the international organisations devised was addressed primarily to the social conflicts inherent in the development of the world market. It revolved around strategies aimed at mitigating the contradictions inherent in the process, enhancing the hegemony of capital over labour, neutralising dissent, and inducing the changes in mentality and behaviour that global competitiveness demanded. From the start, the focus was primarily on the management of social and class relations across the world market, rather than on narrowly conceived regimes of the kind generally seen as the preserve of these organisations. This has been a constant theme—and the essence of the politics of global competitiveness.

The OECD has not sought to protect the privileged situation of the advanced economies but rather to promote competitiveness in the world economy as a whole—an approach that it understands to be in the long-term interest of the advanced countries themselves. It expects the consequences to be socially disruptive, and has therefore consistently urged its members to take steps to manage the inevitable disruption. In guiding governments towards the principles on which a competitive world economy would work, it has given pride of place to tutoring them on the creation of a framework, implemented through the reform of social protection, that will promote habits of thought and behaviour on the part of the propertyless majority that enable the world market to work. In doing so, it shows an awareness that the world market it seeks to establish can only be built through the adoption by states of policies that infuse their own product and labour markets with competition, and thereby contribute to the competitiveness of the world economy as a whole. Its focus on policy reforms that channel the behaviour of individual citizens in directions conducive to the rule of capital over them, by changing the set of risks and incentives they face, reflects a deep understanding of capital as a *social relation*, albeit an uncritical one framed by a positive attachment to the idea of competition and free enterprise as the source of human betterment and freedom that Marx so scathingly dismissed.

3

The World Bank and the Global Rule of Capital

The World Bank was founded, as its official title (International Bank for Reconstruction and Development) indicates, with the task of assisting in the 'reconstruction and development of territories of members by facilitating the *investment of capital for productive purposes*, including the restoration of economies destroyed or disrupted by war, the reconversion of *productive facilities* to peacetime needs and the encouragement of the development of *productive facilities and resources* in less developed countries' (World Bank 1944, Article 1, emphasis mine). It was concerned, in other words, with encouraging productive investment on a global scale, and in its own language at a later date, the closer integration of developing countries into the world economy (World Bank 1982, 20). In practice, its sphere of activity was limited at first to the 'free world', and its active involvement with the developing world generally followed events it did not initiate—decolonisation, the emergence of 'global production chains' through multinational investment, the decision taken by China in the late 1970s to pursue market-led development, and the collapse of the Soviet Union and return of Eastern and Central Europe to capitalist markets from the end of the 1980s. Its approach is best appreciated in the *World Development Reports* published annually since 1978, except for the years 1998–2001, in which only three appeared. This chapter reviews them, along with the more recent *Doing Business* series, in order to reveal the composite programme that emerged between 1978 and 2013, and argues that, like the OECD, it aimed consistently at creating a genuine world market based on increasing productivity. Importantly, its primary goal is social: it aims to deliver an exploitable global proletariat fully into the hands of capital.

Until 1990, *World Development Reports* were relatively brief, and included an overview of the state of the global economy as a whole. The first three (1978–81) reviewed the global economy and offered broad policy guidelines. The fourth contained a first systematic description of the world market and subsequent reports through the 1980s featured thematic sections alongside the overview of global development. Throughout, the focus was on increasing the

The Politics of Global Competitiveness. Paul Cammack, Oxford University Press. © Paul Cammack 2022.
DOI: 10.1093/oso/9780192847867.003.0004

integration of developing countries into the world market as competitive producers by making the poor productive. This focus has continued to the present. The seminal 1990 issue, *Poverty*, marked a turning point. The first to specify a theme in its title, it dropped the overview of global development, and focused at length on the 'political economy of reform', or the strategies by which interest groups hostile to liberal capitalist development could be out-manoeuvred. Against a background of a commitment to the expansion of the world market, the Bank focused in the first half of the ensuing period primarily on the policies and institutions that would promote the emergence of an exploitable proletariat in the developing world, leading up to a significant reappraisal at the turn of the century of the role of 'social protection' as the means to maximise the availability of labour to capital, and a composite overview of its approach in the 2004 and 2005 issues, *Making Services Work for Poor People*, and *A Better Investment Climate for Everyone*. From then on, following the same logic and focusing more intensively on the majority of the global population as yet not fully available to capital, it shifted its attention to the political economy of the household. This led it to address themes that have generally been associated with 'social reproduction', but which are better seen as integral to social production as a whole. In short, the period since the late 1970s reflects steady movement towards a programme of increasingly com-prehensive social intervention, based on awareness that the rule of capital requires universal command over the labour-power of the vast majority stripped of access to the means of production. Put differently, the Bank has been concerned throughout with the politics of global competitiveness, to be driven forward by the creation and continual reproduction of productive and exploitable workers in competition across the world market.

1979–1989: A Blueprint for Global Development

The 1978–89 *World Development Reports* consistently condemned the protec-tionism and destabilising economic policies of the industrialised countries; on domestic policy, they consistently urged developing countries to focus on improving the productivity of the poor; and the thematic chapters included from 1983 complemented this central core. The very first report urged devel-oping countries to consult with 'an international forum such as the OECD' on the policies required to facilitate the changes in industrial structure that shifting comparative advantage would require, and underlined in its closing sentence that the current need to adjust is not a transient problem: it reflects a continuing, long-term, structural shift. It is important, therefore, that the implications and benefits of global interdependence be fully recognized. It will be to the advantage of all countries to sustain an international environment that supports the efforts of developing countries to sustain rapid growth and alleviate poverty as rapidly as possible.   (World Bank 1978, 66, 68)

This integrated focus on domestic and international policy throughout the decade was well expressed later in the 1987 report:

The experience of developing countries over the past three decades suggests that when direct controls replace market mechanisms, economies work less efficiently. An economy that imposes few barriers to trade and encourages domestic competition is likely to develop an industrial sector that is more efficient in its use of resources and more competitive in international markets. Domestic policy also interacts with trade policy. The success of trade reforms hinges on the ability of firms to expand export production and meet the challenge of increased import competition. The speed of that adjustment depends on the flexibility of domestic product and factor markets. Government policies can aid flexibility by removing barriers to resource reallocation and by encouraging competition in the domestic economy. Outward-oriented trade strategies and government policies encouraging domestic competition are therefore complementary.

(World Bank 1987, 131)

The Bank's position on developing the world market was identical to that of the OECD: it has argued from the first that developed countries should not resort to protectionism to keep out manufactures from developing countries, as they would be 'delaying some of the difficult structural adjustments that are necessary if there is to be a return to a higher growth path'. Open trade policies, in contrast, would contribute to growth by 'fostering a division of labor that accelerates the upgrading of skills and labor productivity in industry, encouraging technological progress', providing an inflow of manufactured articles at lower prices that would reduce inflation, and 'stimulating growth in the developing countries, causing a further expansion in the markets for the industrialized countries' exports' (World Bank 1978, 14). Subsequent reports elaborated further: the 1980 report argued that although lowering the barriers to imports in such areas as textiles, clothing, leather goods, electronics, steel, and some agricultural commodities would 'increase the localized pains of structural change in the developed countries ... there are internal remedies for these pains, and liberalization of trade will pay off in faster productivity growth and lower inflation' (World Bank 1980, 95); in 1985, the Bank not only added that protectionist policies reduced 'the scope for industrial countries to promote improvements in productivity in their own economies', but also pointed out that they could have 'a profound effect on development strategy. They suggest to governments in developing countries that a strategy based on export growth is highly risky, and thus encourage a return to the inward-looking policies of earlier years' (World Bank 1985, 6). Subsequent reports returned regularly to the same themes (World Bank 1986, 127–8; 1987, 27–8, 168–9; 1988, 15–22; 1989,19–20).

Against this background, it was the need to improve the productivity of the poor that was the dominant theme. 'Progress in the developing countries', the first report stated, 'will require a combination of three elements: maintaining high rates of growth in incomes; modifying the pattern of growth so as to raise the productivity and incomes of the poorer sections of the population; and improving the access of the poor to essential public services.' It drew attention to the need to raise the productivity of 'those who have some access to productive assets such as land, even if only as tenants', and to 'increase employment opportunities in both urban and rural areas, particularly by encouraging more labor-intensive patterns of production'. And it went on to spell out further what would be its constant message: 'the employment problem in developing countries is not long-term joblessness as conventionally understood, but absence of productive earning opportunities, so that long hours of hard work yield only small incomes'. At the same time, the poor 'suffer not only from low incomes but also from inadequate access to public services essential to their health and productivity' (World Bank 1978, 26). As a consequence, it promoted from the start strategic intervention rather than laissez faire:

> Because the poor tend to share less than proportionately in growth, since they have only limited access to productive assets, education, and employment, deliberate action is necessary in areas that affect the distribution of increases in income. These include the structure of economic incentives, the allocation of investments, and the creation of special institutions and programs to increase the productivity of the poor and their opportunities for employment.   (World Bank 1978, 65)

Successive reports elaborated extensively on this theme. The 1979 report identified labour and land as the productive assets owned by the poor, and

argued that the most desirable approach to eliminating poverty was to aug-
ment and encourage their productive use, in part through land reform (World
Bank 1979, 91–3), and in 1980 the Bank expanded on the issue of poverty and
human development, the latter term embracing education and training, better
health and nutrition, and fertility reduction (World Bank 1980, 32, 46–70). Its
starting point evoked Adam Smith and Joseph Schumpeter in equal measure:

> Economic growth comes about in two ways, both of which can be powerfully
> influenced by government policy. One is building up a larger stock of
> productive assets and human skills. The other is increasing the productivity
> of these assets, skills, and the country's natural resources. This involves
> moving capital and labor between sectors, developing new institutions,
> inventing and introducing new techniques of production and new products,
> making better choices among existing techniques, and taking steps to cut
> costs and eliminate waste. Growth thus involves continuous change—it has
> aptly been described as a process of perpetual disequilibrium.
>
> (World Bank 1980, 36)

The focus throughout was on producing productive workers for capital: 'Many
of the noncognitive effects of schooling—receptivity to new ideas, competitiveness, and willingness to accept discipline—are directly relevant to productive economic activity', it suggested, while others, such as tolerance, self-
confidence, and social and civic responsibility, were 'more personal or political
in nature, but may also affect economic performance'. It stressed the importance of primary education, for girls in particular, in part on account of its
impact upon the next generation's health, fertility and education (World Bank
1980, 47, 49–50). The underlying formula was simple: 'human development
increases productivity, reduces fertility, and thus promotes long-term growth
in average incomes' (World Bank 1980, 81); or alternatively, in the 1981
report: 'Human development links the creation of productive work opportunities for the poor with the provision of goods and services to meet their
essential needs' (World Bank 1981, 97). Underpinning this, as a permanent
feature of World Bank thinking, was the focus on reducing population growth
to avoid the creation of 'a growing pool of labor which, in a poor country, is
hard to educate, house, keep healthy and provide with capital to raise productivity and employment' (World Bank 1981, 109): the 1984 report would
estimate that by the end of the century, '[n]umbers in the twenty to forty age
group will increase by 19 million in developed countries, less than one-third of
the increase from 1960 to 1980. In developing countries the increase will be
600 million, one and a half times the 1960–80 increase' (World Bank 1984, 100).

From this position, the Bank addressed the 1980s as a decade of transition and crisis, in which the uneven but dynamic development of the world market was faltering. Overall, it judged at a time of sharp recession in 1982, the developing countries 'have been much more successful than the industrialized countries in adjusting to the new situation' (World Bank 1982, 7), but at the same time it distinguished between the relative success of rapidly industrialising middle-income countries and the low-income countries where growth was slow and absolute poverty seemingly entrenched. Among the former, the 'outward-oriented' East and South East Asian semi-industrial economies were identified as much more successful than their import-substitution oriented Latin American counterparts; and among the latter China and South Asia likewise, as compared to Africa in particular. Recovery in the industrial countries, in the meantime, was poor, as unemployment and inflation were aggravated by 'productive capacities that are high in cost and by rigidities in labor markets'. Worldwide, an expansion of trade in manufactures 'was spearheaded by a small group of industrializing countries which, by vigorously promoting exports and diversifying production into new, more skill-intensive product lines, were able to widen their markets even in the recessionary 1973–75 period and provide a base from which to expand thereafter' (World Bank 1982, 10–11). But the Bank noted that all the same the *relative* share of merchandise exports attributable to the newly industrialised countries slipped from just over to just under a fifth of the total between 1955 and 1980, while low-income exporters saw their share drop by two-thirds, from 5.6 to 1.9 per cent. Its response was one that has remained a constant since. It noted that 'although there were marked shifts in relative positions within groups, few countries have moved from one income group to another over the past three decades', and acknowledged that the 'accumulation of educated and skilled people, of physical infrastructure, of directly productive capital, and of institutions which encourage and reward entrepreneurship and savings is a difficult process at low-income levels' (World Bank 1982, 22–3); yet it still insisted that it was 'increasingly an oversimplification to see [the world economy] as driven exclusively by developments in the advanced countries'. It drew attention to 'multiple growth poles' across the world, called upon the advanced countries to eschew protection and sharply increase their aid to low-income countries, and repeated its commitment to 'a world of growing prosperity, linked by efficient flows of trade, capital and labor' (World Bank 1982, 32, 37). All this was in the depths of the deepest global recession since the 1930s; and in the following year, as the expected recovery failed to appear, the Bank simply renewed its call for developed and developing countries alike to pursue readjustment with greater determination.

Following this extended review of the world economy in 1982, a sequence of new thematic sections rounded out the broader analysis from 1983 to 1989, covering successively the topics of the management of development, population, international capital, agriculture and foreign trade, industrialisation and foreign trade, public finance, and financial systems. These successive interventions added up to a comprehensive programme: governments in developing and industrial countries alike should pursue efficiency in their operations, accepting that 'the most important task of national economic management is to enlist the skills and energies of the population at large in raising the productivity of capital and labour' (World Bank 1983, 6, 64–73); in order to achieve such goals, it was imperative to reduce population growth in Africa and South Asia in particular, as the poor have too many children, and rapid population growth is a 'brake on development' (World Bank 1984, 51, 79); international capital flows could 'promote global economic efficiency', so long as the availability of external funding did not 'delay the policy reforms required for adjustment' (World Bank 1985, 1); a global perspective on agriculture revealed 'the large potential gains to the world economy from more liberal trade and domestic policies in all countries' if policies biased *against* farmers in the developing world, and *in their favour* in the industrial world were reversed (World Bank 1986, 14); it was a 'natural' feature of the global economy that developing countries would industrialise over time, and in doing so they should aim to be outward-oriented and competitive in global markets (World Bank 1987, 38, 78–94); sound public finances were essential, and in turn required prudent fiscal policy, efficient revenue mobilisation (simplify, improve administration, don't tax the poor), clear priorities for public expenditures (primary education, basic health, urban and rural infrastructure), appropriate structures of government, and good administration (World Bank 1988, 52–4, 101–4, 131–53); developing countries should look to rely primarily on domestic sources to finance investment, and aim to build financial systems accordingly, mobilising internal savings, allocating them to productive uses, and integrating informal institutions into the formal financial system; and to achieve this, 'financial markets and institutions have to be guided primarily by market forces rather than government directives' (World Bank 1989, 111). This was where the World Bank stood, then, at the end of the 1980s. It had developed a global perspective that it would promote on a genuinely global scale after 1990. From then on, it could be described *in practice* as seeking to build a global proletariat, and providing the governing framework for its efficient exploitation.

1990–2001: Producing a Global Proletariat

Throughout its history the Bank has systematically promoted the proletarianisation of the world's poor (their equipping for, incorporation into and subjection to competitive labour markets), along with the creation of an institutional framework within which global capitalist accumulation can be sustained, and legitimated through policies of controlled participation and pro-poor propaganda. From 1990 onwards, in the context of developments that made the creation of a genuinely global world market a real possibility, it turned to the systematic transformation of social relations and institutions in the developing world, in order to generalise and facilitate proletarianisation and capitalist accumulation on a global scale, and build specifically capitalist hegemony through the promotion of legitimating schemes of community participation and country ownership. In successive *World Development Reports* it set about the conversion of the world's poor into proletarians, stripped of alternative means of survival, and obliged to offer themselves to capitalists for work. It sought to enlarge the scope for the private production of goods through the extension of markets, and the provision of an institutional matrix in which capitalist exchange could flourish; and it addressed the long-term viability of the project by seeking to ensure the preservation of the environment within which capitalism operates, not least by limiting the tendency for capitalist competition itself to destroy it. It set out the reforms necessary to secure the delivery of appropriate numbers of people with sufficient health and education to be exploitable as workers, and specified means by which the infrastructure necessary for capitalist production but not actually produced by capitalists themselves could be provided. Alongside these macro-structural elements, it recommended institutional frameworks that would ensure that workers behaved in such a way as to strengthen rather than to undermine the capitalist regime; that capitalists were nurtured, but at the same time compelled to compete against each other; and that states acted to support and expand domestic and international capitalism. Towards the end of the century, it sought to promote a general acceptance of the global capitalist regime by manipulating information in order to favour pro-market solutions to the problems of further development, while mounting an ideological offensive to persuade the world's population that there was no alternative. And with all this in place, it claimed that the globalised free-market system offered the only solution to the problem of world poverty (Cammack 2004).

The reports published from 1990 to 2001 are best seen, then, as a cycle that began by recapitulating the starting point enunciated in 1978, and developed it in detail over a decade. So the 1978 agenda of maintaining high rates of growth in incomes, modifying the pattern of growth so as to raise the productivity and incomes of the poorer sections of the population, and improving the access of the poor to essential public services was directly echoed in *World Development Report 1990: Poverty*:

> The evidence in this Report suggests that rapid and politically sustainable progress on poverty has been achieved by pursuing a strategy that has two equally important elements. The first element is to promote the productive use of the poor's most abundant asset—labor. It calls for policies that harness market incentives, social and political institutions, infrastructure, and technology to that end. The second is to provide basic social services to the poor. Primary heaíth care, family planning, nutrition, and primary education are especially important (World Bank 1990, 3).

Following this call for the creation of a global proletariat from which labour could be efficiently extracted, and the sketch of a framework within which proletarianisation could be managed, the Bank's next report, *The Challenge of Development*, advocated the vertical and horizontal expansion of markets, and a 'market-friendly' approach to development which assigned the state an essential supporting role. 'A central issue in development, and the principal theme of this Report', it stated at the outset, 'is the interaction between governments and markets. This is not a question of intervention versus laissez-faire—a popular dichotomy, but a false one':

> Competitive markets are the best way yet found for efficiently organizing the production and distribution of goods and services. Domestic and external competition provides the incentives that unleash entrepreneurship and technological progress. But markets cannot operate in a vacuum—they require a legal and regulatory framework that only governments can provide. And, at many other tasks, markets sometimes prove inadequate or fail altogether. That is why governments must, for example, invest in infrastructure and provide essential services to the poor. It is not a question of state or market: each has a large and irreplaceable role.
>
> (World Bank 1991, 1)

The starting point was not 'laissez faire' but the nurturing of *domestic and external competition*, and the Bank would never deviate from this logic of competitiveness. From this point on, three successive reports addressed key requirements for sustainable global capitalism. The 1992 Report, *Development and the Environment* (World Bank 1992), concerned itself with the need to develop means to preserve the global environment in which capitalist expansion occurs; the 1993 Report, *Investing in Health* (World Bank 1993), proposed market-friendly mechanisms which would deliver a proletariat fit for work; and the 1994 Report, *Infrastructure for Development* (World Bank 1994), sought to extend the scope for profit-making in the provision of infrastructure, and to identify market-friendly ways of meeting any remaining deficiency. The Bank then turned to means by which an emerging global proletariat might be managed. Its 1995 Report, *Workers in an Integrating World*, sought to facilitate the untrammelled exploitation of labour by capital across the global economy, ruling out minimum wage legislation in middle and low income economies with large agricultural and informal sectors, proposing that health and safety legislation should be governed by market principles and set at a level 'at which the costs are commensurate with the value that informed workers place on improved working conditions and reduced risk', and stipulating that trade sanctions were not to be used to enforce even basic rights for workers (World Bank 1995, 74–9). It then described the ideal form to be taken by trade unions, actively promoting models of unionisation that would support capitalist development. Unions were not to act as monopolists, distort labour markets, or oppose programmes of reform and structural adjustment, but '[i]f the union involves workers in activities that improve efficiency, unionism can be associated with a more productive organization' (World Bank 1995, 80). Effective unions, from the World Bank point of view, eliminated the need for large-scale state regulation and intervention and helped firms to extract more surplus value from workers, so long as they were prevented from protecting jobs or distorting markets.

The following Report, *From Plan to Market*, was premised on the transition taking place across Russia and Eastern Europe. It sought to define the institutional framework within which a global politics of competitiveness could develop, moving from a consideration of appropriate strategies of transition to set out the essential institutions of a market or capitalist economy. Complementing the preceding report on the need to subject workers to competitive labour markets, the focus here was upon creating a legal framework that defined and enforced property rights, and *forced capitalists to compete*: 'Transition requires changes that introduce financial discipline and increase entry of new firms, exit of unviable firms, and competition' (World Bank 1996, 44). Workers and capitalists *alike* were to be subjected to competition, and the strategic objective of privatisation should be to reorganise ownership to respond to the needs of the market economy. Accordingly, the report set out a comprehensive institutional framework calling for market-oriented laws enforced by market-oriented institutions, complemented at the micro level by market-oriented incentives. 'Economic laws in market economies', it pronounced, 'have at least four functions: defining and protecting property rights; setting rules for exchanging those rights; establishing rules for entry into and exit out of productive activities; and promoting competition by overseeing market structure and behavior and correcting market failures' (World Bank 1996, 88).

The 1997 Report, *The State in a Changing World*, sometimes assumed to mark a change of direction, in fact did nothing of the sort. Rather, it summarised the implications of previous reports for the orientation required of the state in the new international capitalist regime. With the key features of this 'effective state' already defined, it was principally concerned to secure their adoption and legitimisation. It presented the disciplines of capitalism as paths to freedom and empowerment, but still exposed the fundamentally disciplinary character of strategies of participation and decentralisation, opening itself in so doing to Marx's corrective critique of free competition as the most complete suspension of all individual freedom. In time its ideological ploys would become more subtle, but here it moved in a single page from the transparent assertion that '[g]etting societies to accept a redefinition of the state's responsibilities will be one part of the solution. This will include strategic selection of the collective actions that states will try to promote, coupled with greater efforts to take the burden off the state, by involving citizens and communities in the delivery of collective goods' to a mystified version that presented this as empowerment by 'making the state more responsive to people's needs, bringing government closer to the people through broader participation and decentralization' (World Bank 1997, 3). It produced simultaneously the recipe for the disciplinary state, and the rhetoric for selling it as empowering. It first outlined a policy hierarchy in which macroeconomic discipline was guaranteed by strong central control over policy and spending and locked in place through an independent central bank, and commitment to disciplinary multilateral organisations such as the Bank itself, the IMF and the WTO (World Bank 1997, 50–1, 101). It then explained how discipline was to be spread through the system by building contracts and internal competition into direct public provision, and contracting out to private and non-governmental providers where possible (World Bank 1997, 61–98). Alongside this, it assigned to strategies of decentralisation and participation the triple role of exerting pressure on the state to deliver essential services efficiently, sharing the cost of delivery with the 'beneficiaries' themselves, and inducing people to experience tightly controlled and carefully delimited forms of market-supporting activity as empowerment: 'The message, here as elsewhere, is that bringing government closer to the people will only be effective if it is part of a larger strategy for improving the institutional capability of the state' (World Bank 1997, 111). The goal, in sum, was to bring government closer to the entrepreneur, and to lock the rest of the population into the discipline of the market—decentralisation, participation, and 'empowerment' were key strategic aspects of the implementation of the pervasive rule of capital.

The following reports, leading up to the expanded reprise of the 1990 report on poverty under the title of *Attacking Poverty* in 2001, addressed the definition, dissemination, and legitimisation of the comprehensive project it had now set out. The 1998/99 Report, *Knowledge for Development*, proposed the World Bank itself as the lead global institution for the collection and dissemination of the 'know-how' of successful development. Profiling its 'knowledge management system' launched in 1996 (modelled on the similar systems pioneered by international consultancies such as Arthur Andersen, Ernst & Young, and Price Waterhouse), it offered itself as a rapid-response taskforce capable of producing market solutions on demand, declaring that knowledge management was 'expected to change the way the World Bank operates internally and to transform its relationships with all those it deals with on the outside' (World Bank 1999a, 140). It depicted its strategy of accelerating proletarianisation and capitalist expansion, shared by other international institutions and by leading governments, as the authorless outcome of unexplained supernatural forces, and represented the patterns of behaviour and organisation intended to ensure the embedding of pure capitalist disciplines as empowering forces ensuring local agency in the process of managing inevitable change. The 1999/2000 Report, *Entering the 21st Century*, similarly naturalised the conscious creation of a global proletariat and the fostering of a global world market as the work of a remote and unstoppable force called 'globalisation', and characterised 'localisation' not as a strategy imposed from above on behalf of capital, but as a pressure from below that obliged governments to manage the consequences in accordance with local needs:

Globalization, which reflects the progressive integration of the world's economies, requires national governments to reach out to international partners as the best way to manage changes affecting trade, financial flows, and the global environment. Localization, which reflects the growing desire of people for a greater say in their government, manifests itself in the assertion of regional identities. It pushes national governments to reach down to regions and cities as the best way to manage changes affecting domestic politics and patterns of growth.   (World Bank 1999b, 2)

There was nothing new in this attempt to present a set of policies infused with the disciplines and class logic of capitalism as if they were inspired by disinterested benevolence, or to depict the purposive action of human agents bent upon establishing the hegemony of a particular social form of organisation of production as if it were the natural outcome of abstract forces too powerful for humanity to resist (Marx 1973, 87). Here it served as a platform for a comprehensive statement of the project in the following report, in which an explicit call for the development of the world market through the proletarianisation of the world's poor was presented under the slogan of *Attacking Poverty* (World Bank 2001b; Cammack 2002). This report, attended by controversy and the resignation of its director, Ravi Kanbur (Wade 2001), entirely subordinated the participation of civil society to the goal of supporting the rule of capital, while promoting the Bank's 'mission to fight poverty with passion and professionalism, putting it at the center of all the work we do', and its intention to 'reduce by half the proportion of people living in extreme income poverty' (living on less than $1 a day) (World Bank 2001b, v, 6). As presented for public consumption, this was to be accomplished by means of a three-pronged strategy—promoting opportunity, facilitating empowerment, and enhancing security—with women as its principal beneficiaries. But at its heart in fact was a re-engineering of risk in order to promote competitiveness, under the appealing slogan of 'making markets work for poor people'. First:

Investment and technological innovation are the main drivers of growth in jobs and labor incomes. Fostering private investment requires reducing risk for private investors—through stable fiscal and monetary policy, stable investment regimes, sound financial systems, and a clear and transparent business environment.... Private investment will have to be complemented by public investment to enhance competitiveness and create new market opportunities. Particularly important is complementary public investment in expanding infrastructure and communications and upgrading the skills of the labor force.   (World Bank 2001b, 8)

This approach would increase opportunity by providing a platform for expanding into international markets, with policies sequenced to 'encourage job creation and manage job destruction', building the assets of poor people, primarily in health and education, and especially across gender, ethnic, racial, and social divides, and getting infrastructure and knowledge into poor areas— rural and urban. Empowerment, in turn, would require fundamental challenges to social values and entrenched interests, to build open and transparent institutions, efficient and accountable public administration free from corruption, decentralisation that avoided capture by local elites, and the promotion of gender equity, with its beneficial consequences for the education and health of children, and productive activities, when supported by microfinance and farming inputs. Security would be enhanced by a mix of interventions 'to support the management of risks for communities and households' (World Bank 2001b, 10). Here the Bank highlighted its emerging commitment to 'designing national systems of social risk management that are also pro-growth':

> There is demand across the world for national systems of social risk management. *The challenge is to design them so that they do not undercut competitiveness* and so that poor people benefit. Some examples: systems that both provide insurance for the nonpoor and include social pensions for the poor, as in Chile; health insurance that protects against catastrophic illness that could wipe out a family's assets, as in Costa Rica; and *unemployment insurance and assistance that do not compromise the incentive to work.*
> (World Bank 2001b, 11, emphasis mine)

Among all the interventions over the last thirty years intended to disempower the poor by enlisting them in their own subjection to capital, there is a case to be made for this as the most decisive. Not only did it align perfectly the strategies of the Bank and the OECD, but it placed at the forefront a strategy developed elsewhere within the Bank and beyond it to calibrate risk, through institutional reform and particularly through the transformation of first world welfare into potentially universal 'social protection', to make it both a platform and a springboard for proletarianisation and the building of the world market. The source of these formulations was the 'new conceptual framework' for social risk management set out at the Bank in 2000, and the social protection strategy published in 2001. The emphasis in the conceptual framework on 'the double role of risk management instruments – protecting basic livelihood as well as promoting risk taking' (Holzmann and Jorgensen 2000, 1) was echoed in the sub-title of the sector strategy document—*From Safety Net to Springboard* (World Bank 2001a). The approach envisaged a system that would catch individuals falling out of productive economic activity, and propel them quickly back again. Its starting point was the insistence that 'sound macroeconomic policy, sound financial markets, enforcement of property rights, respect of basic labor rights, and growth-oriented policies are the first and best ingredients for dealing with risk and enhancing welfare'. In this context, they argued, social risk management might encourage economic development 'through the encouragement of risk taking, the choice of more productive technologies and the way in which it deals with gender, but it may also hamper it through the elimination of risk and introduction of incentives to change individual behaviour' (Holzmann and Jorgensen 2000, 20, 23).

This was not the first time the Bank had addressed the issue of influencing behaviour through the institutional management of incentives: the 1990 Report had drawn on academic work on the political economy of reform to set out a six-part strategy that advocated building on discontent with previous forms of economic management to defend market-oriented policies as progressive; moving decisively on reform fundamentals as 'crises can strengthen support for policy change, weaken antireform interest groups, and increase politicians' willingness to rely on technocrats'; seeking external aid and investment to increase the sustainability of reform; building coalitions of those who benefit; sequencing reforms carefully with respect to political and economic objectives; and compensating losers, both among the poor and the politically powerful, such as formal sector workers, in the short term (World Bank 1990, 115; Cammack 2012, 363–8). However, the explicit call here to restructure risk through the replacement of 'welfare' with strategic 'social protection' was a significant step in an all-out effort to subject the global poor to the discipline of capital, and imbue 'welfare spending' with a single logic—the creation of as large and productive as possible a global labour force, motivated to conform to Marx's 'general law of social production'. With it would come a remarkable effort, advanced intermittently over more than a decade, to bring 'production' and 'social reproduction' together into a single frame, addressing global social production as a connected whole.

2001–2013: Global Social Production as a Connected Whole

Over the first two decades of the present century, *World Development Reports* fall into one of three categories. Some restate and refine the broad framework developed since 1990, in conjunction with the *Doing Business* series inaugurated in 2004. Others address one-off ancillary issues, generally applying the same overall logic. A third group directly addresses the completion of the process of creating a global proletariat by targeting specific overlapping groups of workers the Bank regards as insufficiently productive by virtue of their incomplete incorporation into capitalist labour markets— women, and workers in agriculture and the 'informal' economy—and by devising techniques to bring about participation and compliance. This prompts a growing focus on the relationship between households and labour markets around the world, and the need to draw every propertyless individual into productive paid work. In other words, the Bank engages directly with the social process of production 'viewed...as a connected whole, and in the constant flux of its incessant renewal' (Marx 1976, 711), bringing the conditions of production and reproduction together in a single frame. As this process has advanced, and come to focus increasingly on institutional reforms intended to alter the choices individuals might make in relation to entry and continuation in the labour market, it has become clear that it is as much a strategy of 'behavioural adjustment' as of structural adjustment.

The 2002 and 2003 reports, *Building Institutions for Markets* (World Bank 2002a) and *Sustainable Development in a Dynamic World* (World Bank 2003a) returned to and built upon themes broached a decade earlier, while those of 2004 and 2005, *Making Services Work for Poor People* (World Bank 2003b) and *A Better Investment Climate for Everyone* (World Bank 2004a), as the titles suggest, developed in detail the agenda set out in *Attacking Poverty* in 2001. These were important interventions in terms of public communication and the definition of a global agenda, but they did not greatly expand the strategic scale of the project. However, with the arrival of François Bourguignon as Chief Economist, replacing Nicholas Stern, the agenda shifted in successive reports on *Equity and Development* (World Bank 2005) and *Development and the Next Generation* (World Bank 2006a). The first of these noted that differences in life chances across nationality, race, gender, and social groups were 'likely to lead to wasted human potential and thus to missed development opportunities', and associated this situation with the tendency for 'social distinctions that stratify people, communities and nations into groups that dominate and those that are dominated' to be 'reinforced by the overt and covert use of power', thereby stifling mobility (World Bank 2005, 2); the second focused on five youth transitions with 'the biggest long-term impacts on how human capital is kept safe, developed, and deployed: continuing to learn, starting to work, developing a healthful lifestyle, beginning a family, and exercising citizenship' (World Bank, 2006a, 2). In both, the focus was on creating the optimal conditions for a competitive market-based economy to flourish. So the first underlined strongly that 'the policy aim is not equality in outcomes': 'If individual incentives are blunted by income redistribution schemes that tax investment and production too steeply, the result will be less innovation, less investment, and less growth' (World Bank 2005, 2, 3); the second recalled the core message from the 1990 report, that 'labor is the main asset of the poor', and stressed the need for 'policies and institutions that broaden the opportunities for young people to develop their human capital and use it productively in work' (World Bank 2006a, 2, 5). And while the first extended the argument for equity to the international level, calling for 'leveling the playing field in the functioning of global markets and the rules that govern them—and the complementary provision of aid to help poor countries and poor people build greater endowments' (World Bank 2005, 4, 16–17, 206–23), the second focused on young people in their families and local communities, through the triple lens of 'opportunities', 'capabilities', and 'second chances'. Overall, it concluded, '[p]olicies must stimulate young people, their parents, and their communities to invest in themselves' (World Bank 2006a, 11, Fig. 9, 21). In both, the emphasis was on changing institutions and incentives in order to change behaviour.

Against this background, the Bank turned its attention to the area most conspicuously characterised by excess labour and low productivity. The 2008 report, *Agriculture for Development*, was firmly set in the liberal frame of 'incentives and investments', and embraced the incessant process of technological advance and division of labour central to capitalist accumulation, noting that 'rapidly expanding domestic and global markets; institutional innovations in markets, finance, and collective action; and revolutions in biotechnology and information technology all offer exciting opportunities to use agriculture to promote development'. At the same time it argued that 'accelerated growth requires a sharp productivity increase in smallholder farming combined with more effective support to the millions coping as subsistence farmers' (World Bank 2007a, xiii). It sought in particular to release female labour from the rural household by re-working institutions and incentives so that household and individual behaviour would re-orient towards increasing productivity, and entering local markets and global value chains. The Bank envisaged a system in which production would mainly be in the hands of smallholders, with the private sector driving the organisation of value chains that bring the market to smallholders and commercial farms while the state 'corrects market failures, regulates competition, and engages strategically in public–private partnerships to promote competitiveness in the agribusiness sector and support the greater inclusion of smallholders and rural workers' (World Bank 2007a, 8). This led to an agenda expressed in four objectives: improve access to markets and establish efficient value chains; enhance small-holder competitiveness and facilitate market entry; improve livelihoods in subsistence farming and low-skill rural occupations; and increase employment in agriculture and the rural nonfarm economy and enhance skills (World Bank 2007a, 19, and Box 10.1, 228). With three-quarters of the poor in developing countries living in rural areas, the Bank addressed the perverse rationality of the rural household, and the need to transform its dynamics in order to unleash smallholder productivity *and* produce a flow of appropriately skilled workers into non-farm employment and urban labour markets. The promo-tion of entrepreneurship among smallholders, linking them to global value chains, would free labour from the rural household, while the provision of appropriate skills would in turn generate a pool of labour for non-farm rural employment and migration. In other words, this was a recipe for a new wave of 'primitive accumulation' on a massive scale. The livelihood strategies of rural households that opted for low-productivity, low-risk, low-return activities were rational, given their weak asset endowments, and vulnerability to market failures, state failures, and uninsured risks. Furthermore, the resulting syn-drome was reinforced by social norms, particularly around the gendered division of labour: 'Shifts in household strategies that might lead to pathways out of poverty', the report concluded, 'are not gender neutral.' To encourage entrepreneurship, policies were required 'to enhance household's ability to manage risk and to cope when hit by a shock'; otherwise the household was subject to 'asset depletion', with 'differential effects along gender lines, and woman (or girls) in poor households often bear[ing] the largest burden' (World Bank 2007a, 84, 89–90).

'With labor as the main asset of the poor,' the report advised, harking back yet again to the formulation from 1990, 'landless and near-landless households have to sell their labor in farm or nonfarm activities or leave rural areas.' An active policy agenda for the rural labor market therefore required not only 'a better rural investment climate for agriculture and the rural nonfarm econ-omy', but also investments in schooling and training to convert unskilled to skilled labor' (World Bank 2007a, 202). The Bank then turned to female labour:

> The supply of female labor is both a household decision and a determinant of the household's balance of power. Changing the balance of power as women

enter the labor force in turn changes the household's decision. A traditional society in which women do not work outside the farm can remain that way for a long time, even as conditions outside the household, such as female wages, are changing. But once women start working, the change can be very rapid, with lots of women coming out of their homes to be active in the labor market. This suggests that there can be high payoffs to one-time interventions by governments or nongovernmental organizations that assist women's entry into the labor force: once it has started, it will stick as a new self-fulfilling pattern has been established.   (World Bank 2007a, 204)

The upshot of all this, then, was a composite policy package focused on extracting productive labour (and especially female labour) from the rural sector—by promoting entrepreneurship (funded by microcredit), keeping children, and especially girls, in school through conditional cash-transfer systems, and investing in rural education with a primary focus not only on broad-based occupational skills or specific job-related skills, but also, given 'today's rapidly evolving and globally competitive economy,... personal capabilities such as flexibility, resourcefulness and communication' (World Bank 2007a, 222). To underline the point again, this was a programme to break open the rural household, and give a push to Marx's general law of social production throughout the rural world.

Following the 2008 Report the Bank produced the important but self-explanatory two-volume *Reshaping Economic Geography*, a detailed empirical analysis of the envisaged world market, and two successive single-issue reports, *Development and Climate Change* (World Bank 2009a) and *Conflict, Security and Development* (World Bank 2011a). It then brought a gendered perspective on proletarianisation front and centre, in *Gender Equality and Development* (World Bank 2011b). Six years earlier it had launched a gender action plan that presented gender equality as 'smart economics' (World Bank, 2006b), and the opening lines of the 2012 Report echoed it: 'Gender equality is a core development objective in its own right. It is also smart economics. Greater gender equality can enhance productivity, improve development outcomes for the next generation, and make institutions more representative' (World Bank 2011b, xx). It went on to spell out a comprehensive programme for bringing girls in the developing world through childhood and schooling and into the labour force as productive workers, beginning with the recognition of the substantial part that women already played. 'Women now represent 40 percent of the global labor force, 43 percent of the world's agricultural labor force, and more than half the world's university students', it commented.

'Productivity will be raised if their skills and talents are used more fully.' Following the logic of social production as a connected whole, it then addressed household dynamics: 'Greater control over household resources by women can enhance countries' growth prospects by changing spending patterns in ways that benefit children. And improvements in women's education and health have been linked to better outcomes for their children in countries as varied as Brazil, Nepal, Pakistan, and Senegal.' Third, it added, completing the agenda for the report, '[g]ender equality matters for society more broadly. Empowering women as economic, political and social actors can change policy choices and make institutions more representative of a range of voices' (World Bank 2011b, xx). In short, women were to be weaponised in the World Bank's drive to reduce rent-seeking, and to reform the household so that it responded efficiently to the needs of capital. Gender equality was not only smart economics, it was smart social reproduction too.

For the Bank, gender gaps in productivity and earnings were 'driven by deep-seated gender differences in time use (reflecting social norms about house and care work), in rights of ownership and control over land and assets, and in the workings of markets and formal institutions, which work in ways that disadvantage women'. But attitudes and norms could be reshaped:

> In today's globalized world, forces such as trade openness and the spread of cheaper information and communication technologies have the potential to reduce gender disparities by connecting women to markets and economic opportunities, reshaping attitudes and norms among women and men about gender relations, and encouraging countries to promote gender equality.
>
> (World Bank 2011b, xxi)

So along with measures to reduce female mortality and to reduce disparities in earnings and productivity, the Bank argued that 'policies need to address the combined influence of social norms and beliefs, women's access to economic opportunities, the legal framework, and women's education and skills'. And to limit the reproduction of gender inequality across generations, it argued for building human and social capital through cash transfer programmes, facilitating the transition from school to work with job and life skills training programmes, and shifting aspirations with exposure to positive role models (World Bank 2011b, xxii–iii). Strikingly, the Bank shows no concern at all for the impact of a falling birth rate, in part because reductions in infant and childbirth mortality will eliminate the 'missing millions' of females who do not survive beyond infancy or young womanhood. On the contrary, it argues that 'in countries and regions with rapidly aging populations, like China and

Europe and central Asia, encouraging women to enter and remain in the labor force can help dampen the adverse impact of shrinking working-age populations', adding later that women's greater control over marriage and fertility is important not only in itself, but because later marriage and lower fertility make women more available for participation in the labour force, and that it is therefore essential to boost women's ability within the household to voice their preferences regarding number and spacing of children, to educate men, and to increase the quality of family planning services (World Bank 2011b, 5, 11, 32). For girls and boys equally, the focus is on the transition from school to work. In short, the evidence could not be stronger that the objective of the Bank is a productive working class rather than a numerous or even demographically balanced population overall—every child, one might say, a child wanted by capital.

Empowering women within households by increasing both incomes and control over household assets and procreation, the report suggested, will lead to a more productive society, both in the short and the longer term. The message was consistent throughout, building towards a penultimate chapter— 'The political economy of gender reform'—that looked forward to 'a new equilibrium where women have access to more endowments, more economic opportunities, and more ways to exercise their agency—and where *this new arrangement becomes the dominant order*' (World Bank 2011b, 329, emphasis mine). It identified the household as the crucial cog linking growth (markets and formal and informal institutions) on the one hand, and gender equality (endowments, economic opportunities, and agency) on the other. Where incremental reform was blocked by path dependence or institutional rigidities, bold transformative action would be necessary, and 'policy implementation and enforcement must follow through to produce sustainable behavioral change' (World Bank 2011b, Fig. 8.1, 331, 332).

Against this background the 2013 World Development Report, *Jobs*, produced at the deepest point of the greatest global recession since the 1930s, was an unqualified statement of commitment to a liberal capitalist global economy based upon the readiness of the vast majority of the world's population for productive paid work:

> Jobs are the cornerstone of economic and social development. Indeed, development happens through jobs. People work their way out of poverty and hardship through better livelihoods. Economies grow as people get better at what they do, as they move from farms to firms, and as *more productive jobs are created and less productive ones disappear.*
>
> (World Bank 2012a, 2, emphasis mine)

Beyond their value to the individual, though, different jobs have different social impacts. On the positive side,

> Jobs *for women* can change the way households spend money and invest in the education and health of children. Jobs *in cities* support greater specialization and the exchange of ideas, making other jobs more productive. Jobs *connected to global markets* bring home new technological and managerial knowledge. And in turbulent environments, jobs *for young men* can provide alternatives to violence and help restore peace.
>
> (World Bank 2012a, 2–3, emphasis mine)

Conversely, 'some jobs can have negative spillovers. Jobs supported through transfers or privilege represent a burden to others or undermine their opportunities to find remunerative employment. Jobs damaging the environment take a toll on everybody. Thus it is that some jobs do more for development, while others may do little, even if they are appealing to individuals.' What matters, then, is what will produce 'good' jobs—jobs connected to the world market that reallocate labour from low-productivity to high-productivity work, and ideally favour the employment of women (World Bank 2012a, 3; cf. Fig. 2, 160). In terms that added a focus on women to an otherwise classical agenda that Adam Smith would have recognised, four main forces behind increases in national per capita output are identified, in a box entitled 'What drives economic growth?':

> The first is the use of more capital per unit of labour. The second is an increase in the number of people working, relative to the total population. This happens when fertility declines and the share of adults in the total population increases; it also happens when women shift their work from household chores to income-generating activities. The third mechanism through which output can grow is by making people themselves more productive. The acquisition of skills, also known as human capital accumulation, allows a person to do more using the same amount of capital. The fourth mechanism is technological progress, measured as changes in total factor productivity. Technological progress amounts to combining capital, labour, and skills more efficiently, while applying new knowledge.
>
> (World Bank 2012a, Box 3.1, 99)

Everything in the World Bank's current approach to development, perfected over 30 years, pivots around this succinct paragraph, highlighted in this seminal 2013 report. At the centre of its approach, in other words, is not the shallow 'neoliberal' agenda of privatisation, liberalisation, and deregulation, but the much deeper classical concern with maximising the proportion of the population in work, and the productivity of their labour. Its focus is explicitly on global social production as a whole, with households entirely subordinated in their activity to the needs of capital. The Bank typically presents this vision with its accompanying legitimising ideology: 'good' jobs 'build agency, and provide access to voice', in contrast to insecure jobs or 'jobs that people find demoralizing', in which 'lack of status, job security, or voice at work can lead people to feel disempowered and hopeless about the future and to stop participating in social networks' (World Bank 2012a, 126, 132). The strategy is one of embedding the hegemony of capital over labour through encouraging the proletariat around the world to see competitive labour markets and exploitation by capital in its most advanced forms as empowering. To the extent that the human targets of this ideological framing echo the same ideas back, 'social cohesion' is achieved, and social cohesion and the hegemony of capital over labour become synonymous:

> A program in Tunisia uses the process of writing an undergraduate thesis to teach students basic entrepreneurial skills. Students are mentored by professors and private sector coaches to develop business plans. The initial results of the program show that the program motivated students and gave them confidence to take risks. A male participant from Tunis explained, 'I have become more independent. My behaviour has changed. I use my new skills, I am more disciplined.' Students also explained that the program expanded their professional networks by giving them opportunities to interact with mentors. 'I now have a social network. I know whom to consult,' explained a female participant.   (World Bank 2012a, 143–4)

The 2014 World Development Report, *Risk and Opportunity—Managing Risk for Development*, published in late 2013, reaffirmed the Bank's commitment, in the context of the enduring global crisis, to a strategy of behavioural adjustment aimed at altering the attitudes and behaviour of the global population in ways conducive to a general politics of competitiveness. It aimed to do this from the bottom up, starting with the household and its relation to the labour market, and moved a step further in the development of new communicative strategies in order to do so. The foreword, under the name of President Jim Yong Kim, identified as a concern 'the missed development opportunities that arise when necessary risks are not taken': 'Pursuing opportunities requires taking risks, but many people, especially the poor, are often reluctant to do so, because they fear the potential negative consequences'; the report 'calls for individuals and institutions to move from being "crisis fighters" to becoming "proactive and systemic risk managers"', and, he suggests, is 'a valuable guide both for mainstreaming risk management into the development agenda, and for helping countries and communities strengthen their own risk management systems' (World Bank 2013a, xiii). A conspicuous feature of the report was its innovative approach to selling its message. Its initial framing statement, 'Taking on risks is necessary to pursue opportunities for development. The risk of inaction may be the worst option of all' was followed by a 'visual representation' in cartoon form (World Bank 2013a, Box 1.4 and Drawing 1.6), and an inspiring profile of the enterprising Gomez family, who found themselves unable to raise a loan to improve their farm, so sold it, moved to Lima, found precarious jobs, and scraped the money together to allow their daughter to study English and look for work with exporting companies. A discreet note at the foot of this full-page highlighted box identifies this as a 'fictional story'—with a video in nine languages available on the World Bank website (World Bank 2013a, Profile 1, 7). Although a much heavier academic analysis of risk-making under uncertainty followed, the orientation of the report was already clear, and the general framework developed was quickly directed to the implications for households and communities in a world where the great majority must find jobs in competitive labour markets or risk disaster. The model developed placed cognitive and behavioural biases that impair risk management at its centre, and the empirical focus moved directly to the links between households, communities, the enterprise sector and the financial system, backed by an enabling state and a supportive international community (World Bank 2013a, 17, and Diagram 3, 19). In effect, then, this report re-presented the Bank's approach as developed from 1990 onwards from the perspective of individuals and households, thereby conceiving it in a way that it made it possible to ground its strategy not on macro-economic policy but on the re-shaping of incentives, individual attitudes, and behaviour, and social and community norms, and advise states accordingly. It did so by turning the spotlight on gender relations within the family:

> Many households,...particularly poor ones, struggle to help individuals cope with shocks and are unable to support their search for opportunities. As units, they face the challenges both of protecting and insuring their members against common shocks, such as illness and income losses, and

of accumulating sufficient assets and human capital to grow their income. To meet these challenges, households need to have sufficient resources and to be closely connected to their community, to markets, and to good-quality public goods and services. In addition, *family dynamics and social norms sometimes limit the extent to which members can collaborate effectively, increasing the vulnerability of certain individuals within the household— typically women, children, and elderly adults—in the face of shocks.*

(World Bank 2013a, 109–10, emphasis mine)

The ensuing analysis centred on the need for the 'empowerment' of women within the family. In the consistent view of the Bank, the complex dynamics that increase the vulnerability of some members and motivate a low-risk, low-productivity, low-return approach to managing risk are fundamentally gendered. Traditional divisions of labour in agriculture can penalise women and fail to maximise joint income; gender-specific property rights often limit women's ability to acquire, sell, transfer or inherit property; purchase of household appliances that would save women's labour time are spurned by men who control domestic finances; women are the first to cut their food intake in times of shortage; male domestic abuse of women increases in times of economic crisis; a reluctance to invest in the education of girls limits their chances of entering the labour market; and daughters are married off at an early age to suit a family coping strategy with little regard for their security or future prospects. In a context in which poor households are driven to dispose of productive assets or take children out of school to cope with crises, thereby reducing the chances of generating resources in the future, the ability of a household to increase its labour supply either temporarily or permanently 'depends critically on the ability of women to participate in the labour force' (World Bank 2013a, 120), but a large share of the female population still remains outside it. Correspondingly, the policy proposals made have a strongly gender-specific quality. Public policies can 'redress the balance of power and reduce inequities within the household': 'In many cases, a combination of regulatory reforms, targeting of public programs, and social norms that empower women to take greater control over decisions regarding family planning, work, and financial management can increase their bargaining power in the household, while reducing the vulnerability and improving opportunities for children'; women's empowerment 'can be achieved not only by enhancing access to the labour market but also by making women the beneficiaries of cash transfer and other social programmes' (World Bank 2013a, 123–4), and by giving them property rights; and information campaigns and recruitment services can increase the chance that young women will enter the labour market, and postpone marriage. In sum, the Bank itself characterises the policy recommendations of the 2014 Report as falling into 'two complementary groupings: policies to *empower households*, and policies to *empower individuals within households* to better manage their risks' (World Bank 2013a, 130, emphasis original).

The Politics of the World Bank—Doing Business

While the *World Development Reports* were addressing a range of issues, and focusing increasingly on the ways in which individual behaviour could be manipulated, the Bank, in conjunction with its private finance arm, the International Finance Corporation, launched a new annual series, *Doing Business*, aimed at promoting the reform of business regulation. First appearing in 2004, a year before the OECD launched *Going for Growth*, it followed on from the 2002 *Private Sector Development Strategy—Directions for the World Bank Group*, which also informed the 2005 World Development Report, *A Better Investment Climate for Everyone* (2004), and was introduced as follows:

> Private initiative, unleashed in competitive markets, is key to promoting growth and poverty reduction, in parallel with public sector efforts.... PSD is about a good balance between the complementary functions of the state and the private sector. It is about judicious refocusing of the role of the state, not about indiscriminate privatization. Sound government policies that provide room for private initiative and that set a regulatory framework, which channels private initiative in ways that benefit society as a whole, are critical. This in turn requires institution- and capacity-building.
>
> (World Bank 2002b, i)

Doing Business was a comprehensive programme of surveillance of business-related regulatory policies, initially covering the five areas of starting a business, hiring and firing workers, enforcing contracts, getting credit, and closing a business—all of which it wished to make simpler and easier, within a regulatory framework supportive of entrepreneurship and competitiveness. The first, *Understanding Regulation*, opened with a clear statement of the Bank's philosophy: 'A vibrant private sector—with firms making investments, creating jobs, and improving productivity—promotes growth and expands opportunities for poor people' (World Bank 2004b, viii). It went on from there to argue that while macro policies—stabilisation, price liberalisation, privatisation, and trade barrier reductions—were important, the quality of business regulation and the institutions that enforced it were equally significant. Its primary intended target was local firms in developing countries, and its analysis reflected close cooperation with academic specialists and professional associations in such areas as private law, credit market institutions, and insolvency practice. Succinctly expressed, the aims of the project were to motivate reforms through country benchmarking, inform the design of reforms, enrich international initiatives on development effectiveness, and inform theory (World Bank 2004b, ix–x). Setting out its longer term programme, the Bank announced that the 2005 and 2006 issues would cover registering property, dealing with government licenses and inspections, and protecting investors, and paying taxes, trading across borders, and improving law and order respectively; and while currently 'the *Doing Business* project does not focus on the political economy of reform, as more data become available, the project will include exploration of political economy issues and measurement of reform impact' (World Bank 2004b, x). In addition, case studies and explorations of the size of informal business sector, and the determinants of entrepreneurship were promised.

Notably, *Doing Business in 2004* gave a clear and early indication of the argument central to *World Development Report 2013: Jobs*. Citing 'an 18-year-old Ecuadorian' from the World Bank survey *Voices of the Poor* ('First, I would like to have work of any kind')—incidentally, repeated at the start of *Doing Business 2011*—the Bank went on: 'Not any job will lead out of poverty. If it were simply a matter of creating jobs, having the state employ everyone would do the trick. This has been tried in some parts of the world, notably in communist regimes. What is needed is to create productive jobs and new businesses that create wealth' (World Bank 2004b, xii). *Doing Business*, then, was central to the Bank's strategy for global competitiveness, and this first issue concluded with a critique of 'heavier regulation', endorsing the need for public regulation while suggesting that governments should only regulate where they had the capacity to enforce, and accepting that in some situations (where monopolies cannot be restrained through regulation, quality cannot be assured without state control, or public safety is jeopardised), 'nothing short of government ownership can foster a good business environment'; it ended with a summary of principles of good regulation which again confirmed that competitiveness was the mainspring, in a permanent programme of reform: 'simplify and deregulate in competitive markets; focus on enhancing property rights; expand the use of technology; reduce court involvement in business matters; and make reform a continuous process' (World Bank 2004b, 92).

In the event, *Doing Business in 2005: Removing Obstacles to Growth* introduced new indicators on registering property and protecting investors, and *Doing Business in 2006: Creating Jobs* brought in dealing with licences, paying taxes, and trading across borders. The exercise continued with the accumulated set of ten indicators in *Doing Business 2007: How to Reform* and thereafter. The creation of 'good jobs' in the formal sector was the principal goal—not only in the 2006 issue, where it was flagged as the theme, but in 2007, where the volume opened by noting the paucity of formal jobs in the private sector in Bolivia, India, Malawi, and Mozambique, and urged that '[r]eform can change this, by making it easier for formal business to create more jobs. Women and young workers benefit the most' (World Bank 2007b, 1). Here the promised 'political economy of reform' began to emerge, along familiar lines, with the recommendation that reforms were best initiated in the early months of a new government, and with a listing of the four steps to successful reform: start simple and consider administrative reforms that don't need legislative changes; cut unnecessary procedures, reducing the number of bureaucrats entrepreneurs interact with; introduce standard application forms and publish as much regulatory information as possible; and remember: many of the frustrations for businesses come from how regulations are administered (World Bank 2007b, 5).

With some modifications (for example, the introduction of 'getting electricity' from 2009, the shifting of 'employing workers' to a separate annex in 2011, and the introduction of contracting with the government as an indicator in 2020), the annual has continued along similar lines ever since, extending its coverage from an initial 133 to an eventual 190 countries. Throughout, the focus has been on creating good jobs in the formal sector, with an emphasis on women and young workers as the major beneficiaries. And as the global financial crisis developed, the Bank echoed the OECD's call for flexibility in the firing and hiring of workers, and highlighted the 'challenge of finding the right balance between worker protection and labor market flexibility' (World Bank 2009b, 19–20). Its 2010 issue, subtitled *Reforming through Difficult Times*, offering a summary statement that captured the essence of its approach:

With the global financial and economic crisis, unemployment has risen sharply around the world. This makes the need for governments to adopt policies that stimulate job creation ever more pressing. At the same time, adequate safety nets have to be in place to protect workers from sudden job loss, help them transition between jobs and prevent more people from slipping into poverty. Both are critical for an economy's competitiveness.

(World Bank 2010, 22–3)

Comparing the OECD's parallel exercise, *Going for Growth*, the complementary and overlapping agenda of the two series is apparent. Both focus directly on boosting the productivity of labour and the competitiveness of markets for products and services across the world. So as the *World Development Reports* from the early 2000s onwards moved onto a distinctive social agenda that allowed the Bank to promote itself as a sponsor of opportunity and inclusion, the *Doing Business* reports became the primary vehicle alongside them for promoting regulatory reform and seeking to generalise competition-based capitalist development. In doing so, they gave evidence of the coherence of the Bank's initiatives and publications across the board, and its close coordination with the work of the OECD.

The very first *World Development Report* had declared that the Bank was 'in a unique position to analyse the interrelationships between the principal components of the development process', and carried the following advisory statement: 'The judgments expressed ... do not necessarily reflect the views of our Board of Directors or the governments they represent' (World Bank 1978, iii). Repeated in every subsequent report, this was not an empty formula. At no point has the World Bank adopted, in these reports, a perspective that reflects the practice of either the United States or any combination of developed states. On the contrary, it has been consistently critical of them whenever they have failed to promote the development of the world economy through the practice and pursuit of a politics of competitiveness, particularly when this failure has stemmed from the protection of specific interest groups.

From the start, then, the focus of the *World Development Reports* was on producing an ever more productive global proletariat available to capital, and doing so without limits. When the 'global financial crisis' hit, the Bank committed itself even more strongly to this strategy, seeking to reinforce it rather than back away—a process that culminated, five years into the crisis, with the 2013 and 2014 Reports, on 'good' formal sector jobs in the world market and the necessary recalibration of risk. As the discussion of *Doing Business* shows, the 2013 focus on good jobs, linked to productivity and exports, drew not only on policy positions that dated back to 1978 and had been reinforced ever since, but also on a decade of close work with the great majority of economies around the world, with a focus not only on macro-economic policy, but also on the detail of capacity-building and institutional and behavioural reform that would equip states to promote competitiveness in their own economies, and thereby contribute to cementing its logic across the world economy as a whole.

4

The General Law of Social Production

In the alienated world of capitalist accumulation driven forward by class struggle, Marx argued, a key element of competition-driven scientific and technological revolutions was the effort on the part of capital to break each process of production down into its constituent elements 'without looking first at the ability of the human hand to perform the new processes'. As this tendency gathered momentum across an expanding world market, he predicted, workers would increasingly be obliged to practise 'variation of labour, fluidity of functions, and mobility . . . in all directions', giving rise to a 'general law of social production', according to which 'totally developed individuals' were under pressure to be 'absolutely available for the different kinds of labour required of them' (Marx 1976, 616–18). Incessant scientific and technological revolution, that is to say, would give rise to incessant struggles over the versatility, mobility, and flexibility of labour. Over 150 years after the publication of *Capital*, this vision has not yet been fully realised. But in the second decade of the twenty-first century, at the height of the global crisis, it emerged as the central objective of the international organisations charged with the governance of the global economy.

This chapter first invokes the theme of 'making work pay', then profiles a joint project between the OECD, the World Bank, and the European Union, whose executive Commission has been equally committed over the last three decades to the politics of global competitiveness. It documents a sustained collaborative exercise derived from the *Europe 2020* competitiveness agenda and inaugurated by the annual series launched by the Commission in 2011, *Employment and Social Developments in Europe*. The issue on which the three organisations worked was joblessness and 'under-employment': the joint project they pursued aimed at increasing both participation and productivity in labour markets around the world. At its heart was a commitment to 'make work pay', by refining labour activation programmes and reforming benefit or 'social protection' regimes so that both would incentivise waged work. The joint project took this forward through detailed and innovative case studies of labour markets in 12 member states of the European Union. At the same time, the architects of the joblessness project understood that the creation of the

The Politics of Global Competitiveness. Paul Cammack, Oxford University Press. © Paul Cammack 2022.
DOI: 10.1093/oso/9780192847867.003.0005

kind of labour force it envisaged also required a regulatory framework that compelled capitalists to compete, and impelled the continuous revolution in the means of production of which the uninterrupted division of labour was a part. It was explicit, therefore, in insisting that the assault on joblessness had to be accompanied by continuing efforts to maintain and extend a competitive and dynamic environment for business, on a global scale. To this end, it argued for a comprehensive politics of global competitiveness, with the versatility, mobility, and flexibility of labour at its heart. Related work by the OECD and the World Bank outside the project itself also addressed these themes in the same period: the OECD's *Skills Outlook* series inaugurated in 2013, and particularly *Skills Outlook 2017: Skills and Global Value Chains*, directly addressed the uninterrupted division of labour in the context of an increasingly integrated world market, with labour activation and skills training as key links back to the joblessness project; the 'trilogy' of World Development Reports issued by the World Bank between 2015 and 2017, *Mind, Society and Behavior*, *Digital Dividends*, and *Governance and the Law*, set out a comprehensive framework for the governance of the general law of social production on a global scale; and the 2018 Report, *Learning to Realize Education's Promise*, offered a blueprint for a comprehensive regime attuned to the needs of global capital. Taken together, they show that in the aftermath of the 'global financial crisis' the international organisations charged with the management of the global economy renewed their efforts to establish the rule of capital, justifying these efforts on the grounds that irreversible changes had taken place in the world economy, that the fragmentation of labour on a global scale was an established fact, and that if societies around the world were insufficiently productive it was because they were not yet fully responsive to the logic of global competitiveness. So the period saw a decisive step forward in the implementation of a politics of competitiveness on a global scale, and one that can be characterised precisely as seeking to implement the 'general law of social production'.

The Core Project: Combatting Joblessness

The OECD and the World Bank have been set for decades on building a global economy ruled by capitalist competition, and on developing as a means to this end systems of labour regulation and social protection that reinforce the dependence of citizens in the rich and poor worlds alike on waged labour. Efforts to reform the relationship between wages, taxes, and welfare that date back to the 1970s took major steps forward with the OECD's *Jobs Study* of 1994 and the subsequent efforts at the World Bank around the turn of the century to transform welfare into 'social protection' as a springboard into the labour market. These themes came together around the notion of 'making work pay'—described in the lead article in a special issue of the OECD's *Economic Studies* on the topic in 2000 as 'implemented either through employment-conditional benefits and tax credits or through employment subsidies and payroll tax rebates given to employers' (Pearson and Scarpetta 2000, 12). It is emblematic of the OECD's response to the post-2008 recession that it sought to impose the disciplines of competitive labour markets and press ahead more urgently with the reshaping of social protection and taxation policies to that end—an approach succinctly captured in the suggestion from Mark Pearson and Herwig Immervoll that this was '*a good time* to make work pay' (Immervoll and Pearson 2009). The same thought informed the *Europe 2020* strategy and the joint project on joblessness and underemployment carried out between the OECD, the World Bank, and the European Commission in response to the crisis.

The European Commission's first annual review of *Employment and Social Developments in Europe*, produced under the auspices of the Directorate-General for Employment, Social Affairs and Inclusion, was 'a comprehensive analysis of challenges facing the EU in the areas of both employment and social policy', with a triple focus on 'the number of people considered at risk of poverty; the number of severely materially deprived persons; and the number of people below 60 years of age who are living in households with very low work intensity' (European Commission 2011, 3, 99). It was a central contribution to the Europe 2020 strategy launched in 2010, and another step in the EU's dogged 'continuous adjustment' to the challenge of competitiveness in the wake of the failure of the 2000–2010 *Lisbon Strategy* (Nunn and Beeckmans 2015). The *Europe 2020* strategy itself presented inclusive growth ('fostering a high-employment economy delivering social and territorial cohesion') as the third of three 'mutually reinforcing priorities', the other two being smart growth ('developing an economy based on knowledge and innovation'), and sustainable growth ('promoting a more resource efficient, greener and more competitive economy') (European Commission 2010, 3). An 'agenda for new skills and jobs' was one of seven 'flagship' initiatives, along with research and innovation, enhanced education systems that would facilitate the entry of young people into the labour market, high speed Internet as part of a digital single market, resource efficiency, an 'industrial policy for the globalisation era to improve the business environment, notably for SMEs, and to support the development of a strong and sustainable industrial base able to compete globally', and a 'platform against poverty' that would enable people experiencing poverty and social exclusion 'to live in dignity and take an active part in society' (European Commission 2010, 4). Judging that the Lisbon process had failed to transform productivity, and that the crisis had exposed 'structural weaknesses' that needed to be addressed, the Commission redoubled its efforts to promote a politics of global competitiveness, rather than thinking of changing course:

> Europe is left with clear yet challenging choices. Either we face up collectively to the immediate challenge of the recovery and to long-term challenges – globalisation, pressure on resources, ageing, – so as to make up for the recent losses, regain competitiveness, boost productivity and put the EU on an upward path of prosperity ('sustainable recovery'). Or we continue at a slow and largely uncoordinated pace of reforms, and we risk ending up with a permanent loss in wealth, a sluggish growth rate ('sluggish recovery') possibly leading to high levels of unemployment and social distress, and a relative decline on the world scene ('lost decade').
> (European Commission 2010, 6–7)

The aim was to raise the employment rate of the population aged 20–64 from its then 69 per cent to at least 75 per cent, 'including through the greater involvement of women, older workers and the better integration of migrants in the workforce' (European Commission 2010, 8). On the 'jobs' side of the agenda for new skills and jobs, member countries were enjoined to implement national pathways for flexicurity, 'to review and regularly monitor the efficiency of tax and benefit systems so to [sic] make work pay with a particular focus on the low skilled, whilst removing measures that discourage self-employment', and to 'promote new forms of work-life balance and active ageing policies and . . . increase gender equality' (European Commission 2010, 17).

Taking as its starting point the increasing prevalence of wage polarisation and non-standard work, and the understanding of 'taking an active part in society' in the *Europe 2020* definition of poverty as inclusion in the job market, on the grounds that 'having a job remains the best safeguard against poverty and exclusion' (European Commission 2011, 53, 104), the review of *Employment and Social Developments in Europe* noted that poverty was almost as prevalent in households with only one member in work as in jobless households, and conducted a detailed examination of joblessness, under-employment and in-work poverty. It found that among the population at risk of poverty or social exclusion, 'four adults in ten of those aged 18–59 are inactive but not retired, compared to one in five within the whole population', and identified students, the disabled and 'persons not employed and fulfilling domestic tasks, such as care for children or other dependants' as significant sub-groups (European Commission 2011, 121). Its key contribution was its focus on the labour intensity of households, measured as 'the ratio between the number of months that all working age household members have worked during the income reference year, and the total number of months that could theoretically have been worked by the same household members' (with 0–0.2 'very low', 0.2–0.4 'low', 0.4–0.6 'medium', 0.6–0.8 'high', and 0.8–1 'very high' (European Commission 2011, 105–6). In-work poverty, it suggested, was linked with *individual* low pay, low skills, precarious employment and involuntary part-time work, but also with *household* circumstances, 'such as size and composition of households and low work intensity':

> The latter reflect situations where there are too few adults in the household who are working or, if they are, not working enough to achieve an adequate income (working too few hours or only working for part of the year). In this respect, single and lone parent households, as well as one-earner families, are seen to face the highest risks of poverty.   (European Commission 2011, 141)

Higher household work intensity was to be achieved by means of 'policies that support wages and incomes; policies supporting the labour market participation of groups at risk of poverty; and policies to provide access to enabling services'. While a full-time, permanent job was the best protection against poverty, the crisis had provoked a general shift from permanent to part-time work and temporary contracts, each associated with lower hourly rates of pay (European Commission 2011, 141, 146). Assuming that this shift was permanent, and explicitly rejecting the 'one breadwinner family model' ('The empirical evidence shows that in most countries the one breadwinner family model does not really protect from poverty'), the Commission concluded that 'it is paramount to monitor the situation of the in-work poor in the near future, and to assess the effectiveness of policies in supporting labour market participation of all adults in the household, in providing a living wage, and in facilitating upward transitions for those trapped in low-paid or precarious jobs' (European Commission 2011, 179–80). Subsequent issues would develop these themes further, highlighting for example the prevalence of long-term employment among those under 35, and the negative implications for competitiveness (European Commission 2012, 14, and Chs 1 and 6; European

Commission 2014, 21). By 2018, anticipating 'some degree of replacement of low-skilled labour by automation as well as a decrease in standard (full-time, open-ended) employment', it was arguing that 'better education and the upgrading of the skills of the European labour force are key to reaping the benefits and minimizing the risks of transformations in production', and calling for the rethinking of social protection 'to make the European labour market even more inclusive, particularly for youth, women, older workers and people with disabilities' (European Commission 2018, 3).

In the same period the Commission financed a World Bank study on joblessness, whose results were presented at a workshop in Brussels in May 2014 with OECD experts also present, and published as *Portraits of Labour Market Exclusion* (Sundaram et al. 2014). It built on and complemented another World Bank study published in the same year, *Back to Work: Growing with Jobs in Europe and Central Asia*, which drew on case studies of Poland, Romania, Tajikistan, and Turkey, and followed the 2013 World Development report, *Jobs*, in arguing that

> to get more people back to work by growing with jobs, countries need to regain the momentum for economic and institutional reforms that existed before the crisis in order to: (a) lay the fundamentals to create jobs for all workers, by pushing reforms to create the enabling environment for existing firms to grow, become more productive, or exit the market, and tap into entrepreneurship potential for new firms to emerge and succeed or fail fast and cheap; and (b) implement *policies to support workers so they are prepared to take on the new jobs being created, by having the right skills and incentives, unhindered access to work, and being ready to move to places with the highest job creation potential.*   (Arias and Sánchez-Páramo 2014, 2, emphasis mine)

Portraits of Labour Market Exclusion took related themes forward in a genu-inely collaborative project. Identified as a 'joint product', it involved two policy officers from the Commission's Directorate General of Employment, Social Affairs and Inclusion, the first concerned with the inclusion of disadvantaged groups and the second with social services and active inclusion, alongside World Bank specialists in labour economics and social protection (Sundaram et al. 2014, 11). Taking the sharp 4.5 per cent contraction of European economies from 2008 and the accompanying increase in youth and long-term unemployment as its cue, the report highlighted the dangers of 'deteri-oration of skills and detachment from the labour market': 'With government budgets under stress and an environment marked by demographic changes, using the labor force at its full potential is key. Knowing what the out-of-work population looks like is fundamental to a holistic approach to policymaking with respect to the inactive and the unemployed' (Sundaram et al. 2014, 17). This was explicitly an exercise in profiling in order to identify mechanisms that would facilitate labour market activation, with the more attractive term 'portrait' preferred for purely presentational reasons:

> To this end, this report presents 'profiles' or 'portraits' of individuals who have no or limited labor-market attachment....The portraits...identify distinct groups of individuals who are the potential clients of income – and employment – support policies by examining detailed labor market, demographic and social circumstances....In this sense, the portraits help move the dialogue on activation from a labor market-centric view to a broader dialogue that includes social policy as a whole.   (Sundaram et al. 2014, 17–18)

In short, the report explored the relationship between social protection programmes such as family and maternity benefits and social policy issues such as retirement ages, in order to advance 'more successful labor market inclusion of citizens'. Three key supply-side variables were identified: 'labor supply conditions (household-level incentives to work and physical ability to work), prior work experience, and human capital' (Sundaram et al. 2014, 21). The objective was to look *behind* aggregate data for six countries (Bulgaria, Estonia, Greece, Hungary, Lithuania, and Romania) to establish whether the inactive population fell into distinctive groups or 'clusters', and how if at all each could be drawn more successfully into the labour market. It found six such groups in all six countries: middle aged job losers; youth not in employment, education, and training; early retirees (accounting for around half of the out-of-work population in Romania and 30 per cent in Hungary), including the disabled; inactive women and stay-at-home mothers; long-term unemployed; and rural unemployed. Groups identified were classified in terms of activation need (risk of poverty) and potential (closeness to labour market), and barriers to labour market activation were mapped for different prioritised groups in order to identify appropriate activation strategies. The newly unemployed, young educated rural unemployed, and middle-aged heads of household were identified as relatively easy to incorporate through such strategies as help with job search and matching, while the 'harder-to-serve', facing high labour market and social barriers (low education, skills, and experience, combined with disability or high childcare and related responsibilities) would require much more extensive activation (Sundaram et al. 2014, 41–6). The report underlined that while some women (such as low-educated rural inactive mothers without work experience in Romania) were highly disadvantaged and others (such as younger, more educated stay-at-home mothers in Greece, Hungary, and Bulgaria with some work experience) less so:

> In general, women face important disincentives and barriers to work, which are reflected in the appearance of female out-of-work clusters in all the countries analysed. Labor taxes and social protection systems create strong deterrents for second earners (generally women) to seek formal jobs. Along with these disincentives, women also face labor market barriers such as lack of services (child or elder care), limited flexibility in work schedules, and imperfect access to productive inputs, networks and information. Adverse attitudes and social norms may also limit women's access to jobs and in many cases reinforce each other.   (Sundaram et al. 2014, 46)

There are no great surprises here, any more than there are in the policy advice that follows: greater access to social and public services near home, professional training, 'windows' for mothers in public works programmes that include child care and training opportunities, short periods of 'second chance' schooling with a focus on professional skills, community-based social work and entrepreneurship education, training in job hunting and basic functional skills, temporary mobility support for transportation and housing, and improved access to child care and after-school care. The point is that these issues are raised specifically with a view to drawing women, including those described as 'hard to reach', into the labour market: the list concluded by emphasising that 'improving flexibility in work schedules – including part-time and home-based work – in order to facilitate combining work with other responsibilities would make it easier for women to hold jobs' (Sundaram et al. 2014, 46).

The stage was set, then, for a systematic effort to squeeze more labour out of the citizens of the European Union, by accessing the labour-power of women with household responsibilities in particular through reforms to regulatory frameworks that would make non-standard part-time and home-based work pay. The overall aim was not to cut the social protection budget, but to use it to maximise employment. Hence the report recommended 'reducing or eliminating the abrupt withdrawal of social benefits when a person starts formal work, and eliminating filters that make a household ineligible for a benefit if one of its members is employed', and underlined that the challenge lay in 'expanding social protection systems without creating disincentives to work'

(Sundaram et al. 2014, 47). This was the background to individual country case study chapters that identified the specific mix of clusters in each, reviewed existing policies, and recommended tailored improvements in a final section, 'From Profiling to Activation'. They were preceded by two reflections that placed the study in a broader framework that echoed the general law of social production. The first was a succinct five-point summary of *Back to Work* that noted that its findings 'intersect with those of this report' (Sundaram et al. 2014, 48). The second was a short section on 'broader policy issues' that concluded by reminding readers that

> while active labor market policies, activation and job-matching support can help smooth frictions in the labor market, they will not lead to stable, sustainable employment. Demand for jobs comes from the economic activity of firms and the social sector; therefore the integration of labor market policy with regional economic development policy is especially important. Broad economic reforms to the business climate that strengthen job creation and entrepreneurship will likely be effective in fostering the attachment to the labor market of the out-of-work population.   (Sundaram et al. 2014, 51)

At this point the OECD emerged as a full partner in the joblessness project. Its Head of Employment-Oriented Social Policies, Herwig Immervoll, had been involved in the 2014 study, and he now took charge of a new six-country project (Estonia, Ireland, Italy, Lithuania, Portugal, and Spain—to which Australia was later added), reported in OECD *Social, Employment and Migration Working Papers* from 2016 on (Nos 192, 205–10, 226). The lead paper of the project acknowledged the financial assistance of the European Union Programme for Employment and Social Innovation 'EaSI' (2014–2020, EC-OECD grant agreement VS/2016/0005, DI150038), described it as 'part of a joint project between the European Commission (EC), the OECD and the World Bank', and noted 'multiple rounds of discussions with the World Bank', involving among others two of the authors of the 2014 volume, Natalia Millan and Michele Zini; the series was launched at a 'project kick-off seminar, held at OECD in Paris on 3 March 2016 with the participation of the EC, World Bank, and representatives from twelve countries, and during a seminar held at the European Commission, DG EMPL, on 17 February 2016' (Fernandez et al. 2016, 3). The OECD study was concerned not only with joblessness, but also with underemployment, and weak labour-market attachment. Fernandez and his colleagues aimed 'to provide individual and household perspectives on employment problems, which may be missed when relying on common labour-force statistics or on administrative data, but which are relevant for targeting and tailoring support programmes and related policy interventions' (Fernandez et al. 2016, 4). These are not headline-grabbing documents. They reflect systematic backroom work conducted over recent years among leading bureaucracies with an international focus, aimed consistently at fine-tuning the politics of global competitiveness in its most crucial area—the labour market. They aimed for 'an improved understanding of the characteristics and labour-market barriers of out-of-work and "low-work-intensity" individuals': sharing the approach reviewed above, the overview document noted that standard labour-market statistics provided information about correlates of employment barriers such as the age or number of children, but not about limited work experience or care responsibilities as such, or about the incidence of multiple simultaneous barriers. In addition, their use of identical categories across countries made them ill-suited to documenting labour-market challenges in different national contexts, while 'available comparative statistics typically adopt[ed] an individual perspective and lack[ed] data on the socio-economic *household context* which shapes individual employment opportunities and incentives' (Fernandez et al. 2016, 7, emphasis mine).

From this point, the paper outlined barriers to employment arising from a lack of work-related capabilities, work incentives or employment opportunities, and found, in line with the World Bank study, that such broad groupings contain very different subgroups, with individuals with labour market difficulties facing multiple, overlapping barriers. The approach was strictly instrumental, aiming to identify the obstacles to getting as many people into as much productive work as possible by addressing individuals *within* households, and recognising that those in which it was interested tended to move between non-employment and different types of precarious work. It included 'individuals with unstable jobs working only sporadically, those working persistently with restricted working hours, and those with very low earnings (due to, for example, being partially unpaid, or working informally)', but it made no attempt to distinguish between 'voluntary and involuntary joblessness or reduced work intensity', on the grounds that 'those saying they do not want employment, or prefer to work part-time or part-year, may do so as a result of employment barriers they face, such as care obligations or weak financial incentives, and which policy could address' (Fernandez et al. 2016, 9). Focusing on the working age population in its target countries and noting that 8 per cent were full-time students who were not available for work, it found that only 41 per cent were full-time employees (in a range from 36 to 58 per cent). Among the rest, 15 per cent were unemployed, and 10 per cent self-employed; a further 10 per cent had 'care duties', 7 per cent were part-time workers, 5 per cent were retired, and 3 per cent 'unfit to work'. In principle, more than half of the working-age population, in the admittedly difficult year of 2013, were potential targets for the extraction of *further* waged labour, if the right combination of activation and labour support policies could be found.

The subsequent country case studies explored the claim that there was 'enormous scope for activation and employment support policies to address potential employment barriers and strengthen labour-market attachment' (Fernandez et al. 2016, 45). Each examined the 'faces of joblessness', analysed current policies for activation and employment support, and addressed policy challenges and priorities for selected groups. In large part, they followed similar lines to the World Bank studies, making detailed analysis superfluous. In summary, the groups identified for closer attention were older labour-market inactive individuals with limited work experience and low skills or health limitations in Lithuania (Pacifico et al. 2018b, 45–55) and Estonia (Browne et al. 2018a, 39–50); prime-age long-term unemployed with limited work experience and scarce job opportunities in Lithuania (Pacifico et al. 2018b, 55–64); the 'working poor' in Estonia (Browne et al. 2018a, 50–4); unemployed young and prime-age adults with low work experience in Spain (Fernandez et al. 2018, 57–66); 'discouraged younger adults with limited work experience' in Italy (Pacifico et al. 2018a, 38–40); prime-age long-term unemployed with low education and scarce job opportunities, long-term unemployed youth without any past work experience and with scarce job opportunities, and youth with unstable employment, some recent work experience and often low skills in Portugal (Düll et al. 2018, 45–65); unskilled mothers with care responsibilities and limited work experience in Estonia (Browne et al. 2018a, 54–62); low-skilled women in unstable jobs in Spain (Fernandez et al. 2018, 57–66); labour-market inactive mothers with care responsibilities and limited work experience or without any past experience in Italy (Pacifico et al. 2018a, 40–1); and mothers with limited work experience and with care responsibilities, parents with higher-income partners and care responsibilities, and economically vulnerable parents without any past work experience and with care responsibilities in Ireland (Browne et al. 2018b, 46–68). As is evident, no attempt was made to match categories exactly from country to country; the emphasis was spread across the board, but fell most heavily on youth, and mothers or parents.

Overall, the joblessness project, developed in successive waves by the World Bank and the OECD, in partnership with the European Commission, profiled the populations in a group of 12 EU countries from former Central and Eastern Europe or from the relatively under-developed periphery of Western Europe, engaging closely with the governments of the countries concerned with a view to identifying specific 'clusters' from which more paid work could feasibly be extracted, and seeking to specify mechanisms through which this could be achieved. It was a crucial aspect, therefore, of a broader process of activation of the 'general law of social production', complemented by the continuing independent work of the OECD and the World Bank in this area. The following sections address this complementary work.

The OECD: Employability Skills for the Twenty-First Century

The core focus of the OECD on reforms conducive to 'higher productivity and labour utilisation' (OECD 2012a, 18) reflects a classical liberal agenda that can be traced back to Adam Smith (Smith 1999, 104–6). In 2013, it published the first of what would be a biennial series that took up exactly this theme, the *OECD Skills Outlook*, reporting in the inaugural issue the results of a survey of adult skills produced by the Programme for the International Assessment of Adult Competencies (PIAAC). The focus was on 'the skills needed for the 21st century': proficiency in key information-processing skills, their socio-demographic distribution, and their use in the workplace (OECD 2013, 45–186). It found, uncontroversially, that proficiency in literacy, numeracy, and problem-solving in technology-rich environments was 'positively and independently associated with the probability of participating in the labour market and of being employed and earning higher wages', and also with other aspects of well-being such as good health, a reported sense of political efficacy, and a propensity to engage in volunteering activities (OECD 2013, 224). The 2015 edition, *Youth, Skills and Employability*, noted that seven years on from the global economic crisis, 'more than 35 million 16-29 year-olds across OECD countries are neither employed nor in education or training', with young people twice as likely as prime-age workers to be unemployed, and its proposed remedy was forthright:

Young people are best integrated into the world of work when education systems are flexible and responsive to the needs of the labour market, when employers are engaged in both designing and providing education pro-grammes, when young people have access to high-quality career guidance and further education that can help them to match their skills to prospective jobs, and when institutionalised obstacles to enter the labour market, even for those with the right skills, are removed.   (OECD 2015b, 3)

It called for a 'whole-of-government' approach: solid labour market institutions and skills-friendly tax policies to foster employment of low-skilled youth; encouragement for end-of-studies internships within a framework combining flexibility and obligations to firms; programmes targeting students at risk of difficulties in school to work transitions; systems of mutual obligations between youth and institutions ('Receiving social benefits should be backed with requirements to register with the public employment services, take actions and receive help in order to prepare for the labour market, including through further education'); adoption of a 'work-first strategy that encourages employment through efficient job-search assistance and training, monitoring and financial incentives'; comprehensive, high-quality guidance and counselling systems; and, most significantly, a lowering of the gap in employment protection legislation between temporary and permanent contracts (OECD 2015b, 114).

Behind this activity lay the OECD's conviction that the multi-faceted technological revolutions taking place would revolutionise the world of work. In 2015 it inaugurated a project that led to the publication in 2017 of *The Next Production Revolution*, which celebrated a 'confluence of technologies', ranging from 3D printing and advanced robotics to artificial intelligence, bio-production, nanotechnology and the creation of new materials. It noted that this would 'inevitably disrupt today's industries, and incumbent firms [would] be challenged as new technologies redefine the terms of competitive success', and signalled the need for 'forward-looking policies on skills, labour mobility and regional development' (OECD 2017c, 15): 'Aligning framework policies that promote product market competition, reduce rigidities in labour markets, remove disincentives for firm exit and facilitate growth for successful firms is critical'; and

Effective systems for life-long learning and workplace training are essential, so that skills upgrading matches the pace of technological change and retraining can be accessed when needed. Digital skills, and skills which complement machines, are vital. Also important is to ensure strong generic skills – such as literacy, numeracy and problem-solving – throughout the population, in part because generic skills are a basis for learning fast-changing specific skills.   (OECD 2017c, 16)

Against this background, the *OECD Skills Outlook 2017: Skills and Global Value Chains* broadened the agenda, organising its analysis around a theme central to the activation of the general law of social production across the global economy as a whole. It used the fragmentation of production across the world market and its manifestation in global value chains to reiterate the need for a 'whole-of-government' approach to productivity, covering trade, innovation, investment, and industry as well as skills. As in 1979, the focus was on fragmented production as a 'spur to productivity' in the advanced economies through competition (OECD 1979, 5). Now, though, the OECD premised its analysis upon a (somewhat premature) vision of an *entirely* homogenous global labour market:

> Economies used to be split into a sector exposed to international competition and a sheltered sector. Workers could enjoy higher wages in the exposed sector in return for accepting higher risks (e.g. unemployment risks), while government could design specific policies for this sector. This distinction has now disappeared. Any job in any sector can be the next to benefit or suffer from globalisation: in many OECD countries, up to one-third of jobs in the business sector depend on foreign demand.   (OECD 2017c, 19)

In effect, the OECD argued that the world market is now complete, and fully integrated. At the same time, it saw increasing digitalisation on the one hand and the continued development of global value chains on the other as complementary strategies: while digitalisation might 'enable further fragmentation of production', technological innovations such as automation 'could stimulate renewed localisation of production in advanced countries, especially if policies enable this' (OECD 2017c, 19). Either development was grist to the OECD's mill, and it concluded that the only way forward, in all parts of the global economy, was further investment in skills, whether to realise the productivity gains offered by participation in GVCs and to transfer them to smaller firms to the benefit of the whole economy, to protect workers against potential harm in terms of job losses and lower job quality, or to enable specialisation in the most technologically advanced manufacturing industries and complex business services that are expected to lead to innovation, higher productivity and job creation. To the extent that the proliferation of GVCs had prompted a backlash against globalisation, then, the answer was not protection, but the habituation of workers to a genuinely global labour market on the basis of confidence in their own ability to compete. So 'the challenge for countries is not only to seize the economic and social benefits of GVCs but also to explain their consequences better *so that citizens can have informed views on the issue and vote accordingly*', and it is 'investing in skills' that 'can ensure that all individuals understand the challenges and opportunities of globalisation, feel more confident in the future, shape their own careers, and *cast informed votes*' (OECD 2017c, 19, 20, emphases mine). Stepping beyond its habitual concern with policy, the OECD projected its analysis into the electoral arena: the general law of social production—the obligation placed upon workers to be versatile, flexible, and mobile in all directions—would not simply be enforced by forms of labour market discipline and complementary social protection regimes alone, but *reinforced* through the democratic political process, in the hope that it would be internalised and lived by those under the strongest obligation to sell their labour-power on the market, who would be led to define themselves and their aspirations in terms of the logic of competitiveness. In other words, the aim was to perfect, through political messaging emanating from the state, the alienation that Marx saw as intrinsic to 'free competition'.

It is this focus on leading workers to conform to the requirements of a globally competitive labour market rather than the identification of global value chains as a unique one-size-fits-all first choice strategy that shapes the OECD's approach. Global value chains have a crucial role, just as they did when the OECD first addressed the issue of the global fragmentation of production half a century before (OECD 1979; OECD 2017c, 24). But in the new circumstances arising from the completion of the world market, 'countries increasingly compete through their skills': 'Industries involve the performance of several types of tasks, but all require social and emotional skills as well as cognitive skills.' And 'policies are needed that prepare workers for a world in which skills requirements are evolving fast, by facilitating the development of skills at various phases of life' (OECD 2017c, 27–8, 32). This calls for a high level of coordination across government, as 'the risks of misalignment between policies and international competitiveness objectives are large'. In short, the 'whole-of-government' approach that the OECD advocates for developed and developing countries alike is intended to orient the 'whole of government' to imposing the disciplines of global competitiveness: ensuring that trade, tax, and competition policies and skills policies are aligned, and supported by liberal migration policies, and that strict employment protection legislation and non-compete clauses do not 'hinder the needed structural changes' (OECD 2017c, 34). The emphasis is on strategies for developing skills and innovation across the population as a whole rather than on GVCs *per se*, as countries seek 'to specialise in activities that create as much value as possible and to offshore other activities' (OECD 2017c, 39). Integration into global value chains is one means among others of achieving higher levels of productivity, and the idea that raising participation in GVCs should be an objective in itself is misguided. Rather, migration, global value chains, and the digital revolution are complementary strategies. An appropriate mix varied over time as circumstances change enables the flexible exploitation of a skilled and motivated labour force, both in entering global value chains advantageously and in offsetting the tendency towards the outsourcing of high value-added operations. Skills are needed in order to benefit from GVCs, and in turn participation in higher value-added tasks in value chains introduces new skills that can disseminate across the economy as a whole, and small and medium enterprises (SMEs) in particular. 'Overall, if the concept of economic upgrading is to be used at a country level – for instance as a policy objective – it could be understood more generally as achieving productivity gains from participation in GVCs through the development of skills or innovation' (OECD 2017c, 58). GVCs are a crucial feature of a highly integrated and advanced world market that exhibits an uninterrupted division of labour and constant technological revolution, but there is no *particular* merit in having production spread over a number of competing territorial jurisdictions (states). Rather, GVCs fit into a broader picture in which continuous advances in skills and productivity at national level, with competition in labour, goods, and services markets across the world, produces a world market characterised by competitiveness at every level.

At this point the OECD's analysis moves directly onto the terrain mapped by Marx's general law of social production 150 years earlier. While educational attainment as conventionally measured is tending to equal out between developed and developing economies, the emphasis is shifting from level of education to 'the quality of skills, their effective use and efficient allocation of skills to industries' (OECD 2017c, 74). And while cognitive skills are important, 'skills linked more closely to social and emotional aspects of jobs... are particularly valued by employers'. The OECD highlights two requirements: the *skills mix* at the individual level, and the need for a *pool of workers*. So first, each individual 'needs to have high levels of several types of skills, rather than specialising only in one skill', and second, most technologically advanced countries 'require pools of workers with reliable skills'. As to specific characteristics, the OECD recognises cognitive skills, and social and emotional skills, or 'personality traits', and converts a list of skills derived from recent literature into indicators for its own Survey of Adult Skills. The skills are reading and writing, numerical skills, and computer use; interacting and communicating, creative problem solving, self-organisational ability and flexibility on the job, and managerial and organisational competencies; and conscientiousness and job engagement, openness to experience and cultural diversity, and trust. The resulting indicators are literacy, numeracy, problem-solving in technology-rich environments, ICT skills and STEM skills; self-organisation, managing, and communicating, and marketing and accounting skills; and readiness to learn (OECD 2017c, Fig. 3.1, 77). This leads into a complex and detailed static analysis based on the varying mix of skills from country to country as revealed in the survey of adult skills, but in the final chapter a more dynamic perspective is adopted as the OECD turns to the question of how countries can develop skills and anticipate changing needs. The platform here is a strong mix of skills across the spectrum, including entrepreneurship, close links with the private sector in curriculum development, and exposure to work experience. The goal is not to provide industry specific skills, but general employability: one of the benefits of work experience is that it can signal 'the demand for different types and combinations of skills', while work-based learning experience in a supplier network not only provides exposure to up-to-date equipment and expertise, but also enhances 'social and emotional skills necessary to succeed on the job' (OECD 2017c, 136). So while there is a place for firm-specific skills, 'employment protection legislation must balance workers' needs for income, skills development and job security with employers' need to adjust the workforce in an increasingly changing world of work'. This can be achieved by 'attaching employment protection and social insurance to workers rather than to jobs, and by delinking these entitlements from job tenure, either by linking them to work experience or making them independent from these criteria' (OECD 2017c, 140–1). Restrictions on worker mobility should be minimised by eliminating 'non-compete' clauses, under which employees agree not to use information learned during employment in subsequent jobs for a set period of time. Governments should carry out skills forecasting or anticipation exercises, 'to facilitate the rapid development of standards in new occupations or in occupations with changing skills requirements' (OECD 2017c, 143), and provide organised learning opportunities for adults beyond formal education: 'Workers in high-technology-sectors need to keep pace with rapidly changing techniques. Workers in low-technology industries and those performing low-skilled tasks must learn to be adaptable.' Tax breaks can support investment in skills, but if they are only available for training connected to current employment they may be 'ineffective in assisting workers who need or want to change careers, and may therefore reduce labour market flexibility and exacerbate skills mismatches' (OECD 2017c, 152, 155).

In short, the volume as a whole develops Marx's succinct and elegant formulation recalled at the beginning of this chapter—under the general law of social production, workers are under pressure to be 'absolutely available for the different kinds of labour required of them', and need to be 'totally developed individuals' capable of 'variation of labour, fluidity of functions, and mobility... in all directions'. The OECD's *Skills Outlook* series makes the realisation of this law in practice its central task.

The World Bank: Governance of the General Law

From 2015 on the Bank issued what it described as a 'trilogy' of reports— *Mind, Society, and Behavior*, 2015, *Digital Dividends*, 2016, and *Governance and the Law*, 2017—which together 'examine how policy makers can make fuller use of behavioral, technological, and institutional instruments to improve state effectiveness for development' (World Bank 2017, 29). Taken together, they constituted a regime for the governance of the general law of social production. The 2018 report that followed, *Learning to Realize Education's Promise*, rounded off the regime by making the case for a primary focus on learning and acquiring skills, or accumulating 'human capital'. *Mind, Society, and Behavior* addressed developments in behavioural economics, neuroscience, cognitive science, and psychology, suggesting that 'paying attention to how humans think (the processes of mind) and how history and context shape thinking (the influence of society) can improve the design and implementation of development policies and interventions that target human choices and action (behavior)' (World Bank 2014, 2). As Bank President Jim Yong Kim put it in his foreword, its main message was that 'when it comes to understanding and *changing* human behavior, we can do better' (World Bank 2014, xi, emphasis mine). In short, the report represented an attempt, in the tradition of *Nudge* (Thaler and Sunstein 2008), to go beyond the effort to change behaviour through incentives (conditional cash transfers, social protection, and labour market reforms) to work directly on mental processes (World Bank 2014, 25–34). Alongside techniques such as default options and 'commitment devices', the emphasis was placed on social relations in the family and community. 'Sociality,' the Bank declared, 'can serve as a starting point for new kinds of development interventions': as social preferences, networks, norms, and learning all affect decision-making, 'interventions may be able to target social identities as a means of changing behavior' and 'achieve their objectives by harnessing some social pressures and diminishing others' (World Bank 2014, 43, 46, 50). The perspective was that social norms could be activated, worked around, or changed through legislation or persuasion, in accordance with their utility, and that 'norm change may be a necessary component of social change' (World Bank 2014, 51–5).

The Bank claimed the right to work surreptitiously on states of mind inconsistent with behaviour conducive to capitalist accumulation and competitiveness, deploying its machinery of mind management and behavioural correction across six substantive issue areas: poverty, early childhood development, household finance, productivity, health, and climate change. In what amounted to a medicalisation of development, it offered both scientifically informed diagnoses and appropriate interventions (tested through randomised controlled trials before being marketed as a certified cure). Described as *remedies* (World Bank 2014, 80), policies were removed from the context of purposive political action on behalf of a particular set of interests, with policy making presented and experienced as an objective scientific process bringing unquestionably good things to the poor.

At the core of the report, and most prominent in the chapters on poverty and productivity, was a focus on the problematic character of the mental processes of the poor and the social norms that regulated their behaviour, and their resulting failure to exhibit the future-oriented and individualistic risk-taking mentality that capitalist development required. Poor people, the Bank argued, were prone to 'engage in behaviors that ostensibly perpetuate poverty', not because of 'deviant values' or 'a culture of poverty particular to poor people', but because 'the context of poverty ... modifies decision making in important ways': 'The constant, day-to-day hard choices associated with poverty in effect tax an individual's *bandwidth*, or mental resources' (World Bank 2014, 80, emphasis original). So first, 'poverty generates an intense focus on the present to the detriment of the future'; second, 'poverty can also create poor frames through which people see opportunities', blunting the capacity to aspire and to take advantage of the opportunities that do present themselves; and third, the environments of people living in poverty—such as the absence of physical and social infrastructure—make additional cognitive demands.

The Bank noted that 'poor households often benefit from forms of social insurance, tapping resources from friends, neighbours, family, and social groups such as burial societies, or rotating pools of credit', and argued that while such practices 'may very well be welfare enhancing', they carried their own set of costs as 'the diversion of assets to cover social obligations like these may come at the expense of investment in private opportunities' (World Bank 2014, 85–6). One field experiment, first published as a Bank Policy Research Working Paper in 2012, found that in Kenya budding female entrepreneurs in particular were willing in a laboratory experiment to 'pay a price to keep their earnings from a game hidden', and proposed a 'rotten kin theorem' to describe the social pressure to share income with relatives and neighbours facing hardship (Jakiela and Ozier 2016). Another, also from Kenya, targeted 'norms that may require investments in social capital to the detriment of private opportunities' and suggested that 'using a simple metal box with a padlock and designating savings for a particular purpose can help increase savings for people who must assist others in their social network' (World Bank 2014, 86). Hostility to such norms was not new. The 1989 report had argued that 'informal short-term credit may entail hidden costs', as 'traditional obligations of mutual support can be a problem for those who wish to accumulate capital. The desire to protect personal savings from family and friends creates a strong demand for less accessible savings instruments when these become available' (World Bank 1989, 113). But neither there nor here did the Bank formally acknowledge the other side of the coin—that the erosion of such mutual help networks not only frees resources for entrepreneurial activities, but also increases pressures on households and individuals to secure their livelihoods in the market, and thereby intensifies pressure towards proletarianisation. It was seeking to address a situation in which the majority of the propertyless poor were not yet obliged to sell their labour-power in the market in order to survive, or to act in other ways that allow capitalist production 'to stand on its own feet' (Marx 1976, 874). Hence its resort to 'nudges'—sometimes as elaborate as the exploitation of a South African TV soap, *Scandal!*, in which World Bank input led to the main character 'depict[ing] poor financial behavior before changing her habits', putting a part of her salary into a special bank account from which she could not draw and which would give her good interest on her savings (Berg and Zia 2013, 5, 49, cited in World Bank 2014, 4, 76, 122).

This orientation towards creating present and future citizens inclined to conform to the logic of the general law of social production was most prominent in the chapter on productivity, which paralleled precisely the contemporaneous work of the Bank on inefficient labour markets but turned the focus onto the developing world, where too few of the poor were oriented towards investing or working to maximise their income. In Ghana, small-scale entrepreneurs who were given cash loans used them in part to finance household needs or help relatives. In Kenya, bicycle taxi drivers did just enough work to meet their daily needs, then went home, while shopkeepers wasted time wandering about in search of small change and socialising instead of coming to work with a float. In India, fishermen fished less as the value of their catches increased, opting for days off instead of going to sea. The Bank points out that such workers are insufficiently disciplined by a contractual employer-employee relationship: 'divides between intentions and actions and the neglect of potential opportunities may loom even larger [for the self-employed] ... because they do not have contracts with an employer inter-ested in their level of effort or explicit work arrangements that dictate what is expected of them' (World Bank 2014, 135). On its own terms, this is correct—these individuals can make the choices they do because they are outside the compulsion of the capital relation, and hence able to *resist* the logic of competi-tiveness. This is the situation that the Bank seeks to change.

The second of the trilogy of reports on behavioural, technological, and institutional instruments to improve state effectiveness for development turned its attention to the potential of the digital revolution to knit the world market together, and the need both to overcome the digital divide and to develop 'analogue complements' that would ensure 'a favourable business climate, strong human capital, and good governance' (World Bank 2016, 2). The Bank had no difficulty in slotting the digital revolution into its perennial narrative: 'The stakes are high, because the digital revolution leaves behind countries that do not make the necessary reforms' (World Bank 2016, 38). And while it argued strongly for the inclusion of the 60 per cent of the world's population without access to the Internet, the lessons it drew were squarely focused on the world economy as a whole, and the need, and opportunity, to increase the level of competitiveness. It welcomed unreservedly the capacity of the digital revolution to reduce costs, raise efficiency, and boost the product-ivity of labour, most conspicuously by improving the availability of informa-tion and the efficiency of supply (logistics and inventory control) and markets, enabling firms to access fragments of flexible labour-power and monitor permanent and casual workers in real time, and individuals to commodify resources primarily devoted to 'self-reproduction'—houses (Airbnb), cars (Uber and similar services, delivery), and even moments of leisure time. It then addressed the potential for perfecting the governance of the relationship between labour and capital—the 'capital relation'—and its mediation by the state. First, it reminded its readers that as technology progresses, some skills become obsolete: 'Workers must acquire new skills that help them become more productive with the help of that technology. Adjustment takes time and will be painful for many, but this is how economies progress' (World Bank 2016, 18–19). It acknowledged that while skilled workers may gain, those without skills 'will need to seek work in lower-skilled, nonroutine occupations, such as janitorial services, hospitality, or personal care', and that rising demand for such services will perhaps not be enough 'to prevent downward wage pressure as the available workforce in these sectors grows' (World Bank 2016, 22). Despite this, 'the benefits will come to those who embrace the changes the internet brings, not to those who resist them.... Not making the necessary reforms means falling farther behind those who do, while investing in both technology and its complements is the key to the digital transform-ation' (World Bank 2016, 29). One major lesson drawn, the need for reforms to education and training, would receive detailed treatment in the 2018 Report. A second, the need and opportunity to reform systems of taxation and social protection to bring workers from the informal economy into formal employment (suitably redefined to fall short of the standard employment contract), would be central to the 2019 Report, *The Changing Nature of Work*. But it was outlined here, in terms that led the Bank to focus squarely on the shift identified in Marx's general law, from the 'monstrosity' of a 'disposable population held in reserve, in misery, for the changing require-ments of capitalist exploitation' to one in which 'partially developed' individ-uals were replaced by 'totally developed' individuals, absolutely available for the different kinds of labour required of them (Marx 1976, 618):

> The on-demand economy leads to more informal employment, transferring insurance and occupational obligations to freelance workers. Strict labor regulations, common in developing countries, and overreliance on labor taxation encourage faster automation by making hiring more expensive. It would be better to strengthen workers' protection independently from work contracts by delinking social insurance from employment, offering inde-pendent social assistance, and helping workers retrain and find new employ-ment quickly. In many countries this requires major reforms. And countries just starting to develop social protection systems and deepening labor laws should design them for the 21st-century workplace, rather than copy what industrialized countries created for a very different world of work.
>
> (World Bank 2016, 36)

Underpinning all this was an unconditional embrace of constant technological and scientific revolution driven by entrepreneurship, innovation and compe-tition between capitalists. *Digital Dividends* set out at length, in a section headed 'More trade, higher productivity, and greater competition' (World Bank 2016, 55–70), the manner in which the digital revolution could trans-form the capitalist system through the three channels of trade, capital utilisa-tion, and competition: making markets more efficient and inclusive, facilitating the unbundling of tasks, raising firms' productive utilisation of capital and labour, intensifying competition, and creating new business models: 'These new business models dissolve the boundaries between the online and offline economies and can help break existing regulatory barriers to entry in sectors that are often protected from competition' (World Bank 2016, 67). The Bank embraced this prospect without reservations, citing a range of examples that have become familiar, from the creation of money (Kenya's M-Pesa) to Internet-based banking (China's Yu'e Bao and WeBank), online retail and wholesale (from Amazon and eBay in the US to Alibaba, Flipkart, and Snapdeal in China and India), and global developments in ride and room sharing and food and courier services.

As elaborated later in the report, with the fast pace of technological change, and its implications for job creation, destruction, and reallocation, 'labor regulations, taxation, and social protection systems [would] have to support labor mobility and adapt to the changing nature of work' (World Bank 2016, 101). So the Bank embraced '[i]ndependent contracting, casual work, freelancing, and other new forms of work in online labor markets and the sharing economy' not by calling for the abolition of social protection and celebrating the emergence of an entirely rightless proletariat, but by outlining new forms of social protection appropriate to the 'new world of work', centred as foreshadowed above on delinking social insurance from the labour contract. First, 'all individuals should be registered in the same social insurance system, regardless of where they work, with subsidies for the poor or low-wage earners, and with finance coming from general revenues'; second, the labour market disruptions that accompany technology change should be met by intermediation and retraining services, and social assistance where transition brings difficulties, potentially in the form of a guaranteed basic income; third, workers should be given 'a stake in digital capital', whether through pension funds, mutual funds, or even more directly in firms active in the digital economy; and fourth, if the solution is to protect workers rather than jobs, a first step would be to 'do away with regulations that almost prohibit flexible work arrangements' (World Bank 2016, 280). The ideal workers, in this vision, would be members of an essentially homogenous *global* proletariat, linked by competition across global production and value chains, and reproduced as workers by a social protection regime that impelled them to seek paid work up to the limit arising from their domestic circumstances or physical impairment, provided a minimum safety net in periods of unemployment without impairing the incentive to seek work, *and* equipped them to renew their skills and remain competitive in the labour market when out of work.

The third part of the 'trilogy', WDR 2017, *Governance and the Law*, addressed the role of the state in terms similar to those applied to the poor in the 2015 report, identifying a situation in which the institutions conventionally seen as central to development fail, with the result that ineffective policies persist, and effective policies are not chosen. But in doing so it drew on themes it had developed over three decades. The Bank's standard strategy of looking for ways of neutralising opposition and building winning coalitions for reform was now addressed in terms of establishing '*commitment, coordination,* and *cooperation*' as 'the three core functions of institutions that are needed to ensure that rules and resources yield the desired outcomes', with the first of these to be secured by 'commitment devices' that provide incentives to work within the rules, with 'credible commitment' to pro-growth policies and property rights paramount, or 'an environment in which firms and individuals feel secure in investing their resources in productive activities'. Coordination was essential, to address market failures and thereby ensure that firms and individuals wanting to invest and innovate believe that others will also do so; and cooperation involved 'citizens' willingness to contribute to public goods and not free-ride on others' (World Bank 2017, 5–6 and Table 0.1, 7). Appropriate policies (such as those to strengthen labour markets, overcome gender barriers, or prepare countries against shocks) were 'often difficult to introduce and implement because certain groups in society who gain from the status quo may be powerful enough to resist the reforms needed to break the political equilibrium'; so successful reforms 'require adopting and adjusting institutional forms in ways that solve the specific commitment and collective action problems that stand in the way of pursuing further development'; and states should strengthen the capacity of law to enhance contestability, change incentives and reshape preferences (World Bank 2017, 29). The rule of law, in this conceptualisation, is not a neutral framework, but a means of structuring risk in such a way as to promote competitiveness at every level of society; and vested interests are dangerous because states must secure the 'continual reallocation of resources across sectors and firms': 'In a dynamic setting in which new companies enter the market while uncompetitive firms exit, inputs reallocate between firms, giving way to innovation, competition, and productivity' (World Bank 2017, 45).

The focus of the report, then, was the perennial issue for elite perspectives on democracy: how to bring about 'coalitions between reforming elites and organized citizens that support reform initiatives and overcome the opposition of other elites', now addressed with an explicit analysis of electoral politics. While citizen agency 'can help translate favorable conditions into effective reforms that drive positive change', elections may also 'legitimize socially undesirable policies; political and social organizations can lead to violence and rent-seeking; and deliberation can be captured by private interests and opportunistic elites'; and voters, the Bank says, 'not only lack information, but also have systematic biases in favor of economic policies that have been proven wrong empirically' (World Bank 2017, 225–6, 229). After extensive review, it concludes that 'chances to promote institutional change and policy reforms are maximized when the incentives of reformers from above (elites) and mobilization from below (citizens) converge and mutually reinforce each other against defenders of the status quo' (World Bank 2017, 241). Throwing caution to the winds, the Bank now proposed that these issues must be addressed at a global level, suggesting in the final chapter that 'dynamics of governance do not play out solely within the boundaries of nation-states', and responding to the ever-present danger of 'populist' opposition to 'globalisation' by noting that international actors (such as itself) can affect the domestic policy arena by changing the dynamics of contestation, shifting actor incentives, or shaping actor norms, by entering the policy arena, providing alternative sites for contestation, empowering or shaping incentives by providing resources, and shifting the preferences of citizens and elites (World Bank 2017, 257 and Figure 9.1, 258). In analytical terms, nothing here was new. The novelty was that the fundamentally political role the Bank now envisaged for itself amounted to and was recognisable as a proposal for a global constitution derived from the general law of social production.

The 2018 report that followed the 2015–2017 trilogy, *Learning to Realize Education's Promise*, followed lines already familiar from the work of the OECD, as the two converged on the issue of the skills required for the future world of work: all that is required here is to note the terms of convergence and their absolute fidelity to the trinity of versatility, flexibility and mobility. It opened with the statement from Bank President Jim Yong Kim that 'providing education is not enough. What is important, and what generates a real return on investment, is learning and acquiring skills' (World Bank 2018a, xi). The main body of the report then made the case at length, tracing weak skills in the workforce to learning shortfalls during school years: 'The problem isn't just a lack of trained workers; it is a lack of readily trainable workers...Lack of skills reduces job quality, earnings, and labour mobility.' And the skills needed in the labour market are multidimensional: foundational skills must be supplemented by higher-order cognitive skills such as problem-solving, and socio-emotional skills such as conscientiousness, while specific jobs require specific technical skills (World Bank 2018a, 9). The report was primarily concerned with the multiple compound causes of failure, and their much heavier incidence on the poor and disadvantaged; it gave equal priority to making skills central and to making their acquisition universal; and it concluded that the future of work would place a premium on learning: 'rapid change will increase the returns to learning how to learn, which requires foundational skills that allow individuals to size up new situations, adapt their thinking, and know where to go for information and how to make use of it' (World Bank 2018a, 27).

The European Pillar of Social Rights as a Constitution for the General Law

The response of the European Commission, the OECD and the World Bank to a decade of global economic and financial crisis, then, was to devise, severally and together, a battery of strategies—behavioural, institutional, political, and social—aimed at perfecting the rule of capital over the citizens of developed and developing countries alike. As the outlines of the global constitution they proposed emerged, it became clear that the logic at its heart was that of the general law of social production identified by Marx as the necessary outcome if the revolutionary tendencies inherent in the capitalist production process continued unabated. Central to Marx's conception was the suggestion that the *catastrophes* of large-scale industry would make '*recognition* of variation of labour and hence of the fitness of the worker for the maximum number of different kinds of labour into a question of life and death'—putting an end to a situation, familiar in his day, in which 'variation of labour imposes itself after the manner of an overpowering natural law' (Marx 1976, 618, emphasis mine). This analysis is directly applicable to the response depicted in this chapter to the 'global economic and financial crisis'—the first such major crisis to follow the drawing of all nations 'on pain of extinction' into engagement with the bourgeois mode of production. The project developed by the European Commission, the OECD and the World Bank in the second decade of the twenty-first century aimed explicitly at increasing participation in and dependence on the labour market across the world, by modifying social protection regimes to make 'inactivity' cost, and work pay. Precisely, it recognised that for the global capitalist system, the fitness of the worker for the maximum number of different kinds of labour was a question of life and death. In their different ways, the OECD's *The Next Production Revolution* and *Skills Outlook* series and the World Bank's trilogy that concluded with *Governance and the Law* took a 'whole-of-government' approach that started from a perception of the completion of the world market, and brought revolutions in technology, production, and the division of labour together as the basis for a radically transformed prescription for the relationship between governments and citizens, to which the notion of education as concerned exclusively with the universal inculcation of skills and attitudes aligned with the politics of global competitiveness was central. Capping all this off, the promise of *Learning to Realize Education's Promise* was precisely that everyone could be mobilised in the service of global capital.

The process under way in this period, then, was the constitutionalisation of the general law of social production. It rested on a shared vision of 'an uninterrupted division of labour, and...the application of new and the perfecting of old machinery precipitately and on an ever more gigantic scale' (Marx 2010b, 225). The World Bank's report on *Governance and the Law* represented a first attempt to sketch such a constitution with a potential global reach (and to advance its own claims to govern), but the World Bank had no *juridical* authority, so could do no more than offer a blueprint. The situation of the third partner in the enterprise of combatting underemployment and joblessness, and maximising the number of workers who were versatile, flexible, and mobile in all directions, the European Union, was different, and it was the *European Pillar of Social Rights* approved at the November 2017 Social Summit for Fair Jobs and Growth in Gothenburg that came closest to defining the framing conditions for such a constitution. In 20 propositions on employment and social protection, this historic document first defined the ideal worker under capitalism, then set out a regime of social protection with expansive aspirational content that was crucially conditional on and constrained by the logic of global competitiveness. The preamble located the initiative in the new opportunities and new challenges arising from globalisation, the digital revolution, changing work patterns and societal and demographic developments, and made social rights conditional upon success in that environment, with specific reference to *employment* and *productivity*:

> To a large extent, the employment and social challenges facing Europe are a result of relatively modest growth, which is rooted in untapped potential in terms of participation in employment and productivity. Economic and social progress are intertwined, and the establishment of a European Pillar of Social Rights should be part of wider efforts to build a more inclusive and sustainable growth model by improving Europe's competitiveness and making it a better place to invest, create jobs and foster social cohesion.
>
> (European Commission 2017, paragraph 11, 7)

The 20-point content of the pillar was then set out in three 'chapters'— on equal opportunities and access to the labour market (principles 1–4), fair working conditions (principles 5–9), and social protection and inclusion (principles 11–20)—infused with the logic of the general law of social production.

The first chapter stipulates that all EU citizens, regardless of gender, racial or ethnic origin, religion or belief, disability, age or sexual orientation, have a right to be *equipped to compete* in the labour market: 'Everyone has the right to quality and inclusive education, training and life-long learning in order to maintain and acquire skills that enable them to participate fully in society and manage successfully transitions in the labour market' (Principle 1); to equal pay for work of equal value (Principle 2); and to 'equal treatment and opportunities regarding employment, social protection, education, and access to goods and services available to the public' (Principle 3). Principle 4 crucially construes these rights in terms of 'active support to employment' in a mobile labour market: 'the right to timely and tailor-made assistance to improve employment or self-employment prospects', including the right to receive support for job search, training, and requalification, along with 'the right to transfer social protection and training entitlements during professional transitions'. Young people have 'the right to continued education, apprenticeship, traineeship or a job offer of good standing within four months of becoming unemployed or leaving education'; the unemployed have the right to 'personalised, continuous and consistent support', and the long-term unemployed have the right to 'an in-depth individual assessment at the latest at eighteen months of unemployment' (European Commission 2017, 12).

The definition of fair working conditions in Chapter 2 refers to 'secure and adaptable employment', but declares in Principle 5 that while workers have the same rights to fair and equal treatment regarding working conditions, access to social protection and training regardless of the type and duration of the employment relationship, the 'transition towards open-ended forms of employment shall be fostered'; 'the necessary flexibility for employers to adapt swiftly to changes in the economic context shall be ensured'; '[i]nnovative forms of work that ensure quality working conditions shall be fostered. Entrepreneurship and self-employment shall be encouraged. Occupational mobility shall be facilitated'; and '[e]mployment relationships that lead to precarious working conditions shall be prevented, including by prohibiting abuse of atypical contracts' (European Commission 2017, 14). It is thereby made explicit that open-ended forms of employment, the right of employers to respond flexibly to changes in the economic context, and occupational mobility as the norm are not in themselves markers of precarious work. Work is precarious only when *atypical contracts* (which are perfectly permissible) are *abused*.

According to Principle 6, adequate minimum wages are to be ensured 'in a way that provide [sic] for the satisfaction of the needs of the workers and his/her family in the light of national economic and social conditions, *whilst safeguarding access to employment and incentives to seek work*' (European Commission 2017, 15, emphasis mine). Hiring and firing are subject to minimal constraints: workers have the right to a written statement at the start of their employment of their rights and obligations, and, prior to dismissal, to be told the reasons and granted a reasonable period of notice (Principle 7). Social partners have the right to be *consulted*, and workers have the right to be informed and consulted 'in particular on the transfer, restructuring and merger of undertakings and on collective redundancies' (Principle 8). Principle 9 recognises diversity and promotes maximum flexibility in relation to responsibility for care: 'Parents and people with caring responsibilities have the right to suitable leave, flexible working arrangements and access to care services. Women and men shall have equal access to special leaves of absence in order to fulfil their caring responsibilities and be encouraged to use them in a balanced way' (European Commission 2017, 16), and Principle 10 insists on the need for a high level of protection of health and safety, working environments adapted to professional needs, and the right to protection of personal data in the employment context.

Against this background, the new regime of social protection and inclusion is set out in the third chapter in ten principles that envisage a maximally inclusive labour market characterised by varied forms of flexible and mobile labour. Future workers (children) have the right to affordable early childhood education and care of good quality and protection from poverty, while those from disadvantaged backgrounds 'have the right to specific measures to enhance equal opportunities' (European Commission 2017, Principle 11a, 19). However, permanent full-time work is no longer a point of reference. Rather: 'Regardless of the type and duration of their employment relationship, workers, and, under comparable conditions, the self-employed, have the right to adequate social protection' (European Commission 2017, Principle 12, 19). Unemployment benefits are conceived as a means to ensure a speedy return to work: 'The unemployed have the right to adequate activation support from public employment services to (re)integrate in the labour market and adequate unemployment benefits of reasonable duration, in line with their contributions and national eligibility rules. Such benefits shall not constitute a disincentive for a quick return to employment' (European Commission 2017, Principle 13, 19). According to principle 14, 'Everyone lacking sufficient resources has the right to adequate minimum income benefits ensuring a life in dignity at all stages of life, and effective access to enabling goods and services.' But the same principle adds that for those who can work, 'minimum income benefits should be combined with incentives to (re)integrate into the labour market' (European Commission 2017, 20). The following principle states that everyone in old age has the right to resources that ensure living in dignity, but precedes this statement with the caveat that workers and the self-employed in retirement 'shall have the right to a pension *commensurate to their contributions* and ensuring an adequate income' (European Commission 2017, 20, emphasis mine). The remaining principles address health care (Principle 16), people with disabilities (Principle 17), long-term-care, 'in particular home-care and community-based services' (Principle 18), housing and assistance for the homeless (Principle 19), and access to essential services (Principle 20). Only in relation to the disabled is there further reference to employment: 'People with disabilities have the right to income support that ensures living in dignity, services that enable them to participate in the labour market and in society, and a work environment adapted to their needs' (European Commission 2017, 21). At present, then, it is the European Pillar of Social Rights that best represents the constitutionalisation of Marx's general law of social production.

5

The Social Politics of Global Competitiveness

In his preface to *The World in 2020*, OECD Secretary-General Donald Johnson looked forward to a new global age of universal prosperity, but cautioned that it would not materialise automatically. It would require 'bold action by governments within and outside the OECD area to complete the borderless world through free flows of goods and services, capital and technology, to ensure high and equitable growth supported by stable and sustainable macro-economic conditions and wide-ranging structural reforms' (OECD 1997b, 7). The summary overview that followed identified the dynamic performance of a number of non-OECD countries, rapid advances in information and communications technologies, and unprecedented increases in worldwide trade and investment as key factors driving accelerated change. But it noted at the same time that signs of a backlash were already present in some OECD economies, in part because of structural changes in production techniques and in the labour market: 'Knowledge-intensive industries and firms have had above-average employment growth, but there has been a decline in the demand for low-skilled workers relative to skilled labour.' Two conclusions followed. First, further structural reform in order to hasten the process of economic integration would benefit the OECD countries themselves: consumers would benefit from the lower price of goods imported from developing countries, while resources would be 'freed for higher productive uses, such as skill-intensive services and capital equipment, some of which is exported to non-OECD countries, stimulating in turn their development' (OECD 1997b, 12–13). Second, and equally important:

> Such economic integration does involve adjustment costs, especially for low-skilled workers and industries. This can lead to tensions, especially when they coincide with high and persistent unemployment in many OECD countries, which can manifest themselves in social strains and protectionist pressures. In order to minimise these tensions and facilitate these structural changes, governments must ensure flexible labour and product markets,

The Politics of Global Competitiveness. Paul Cammack, Oxford University Press. © Paul Cammack 2022.
DOI: 10.1093/oso/9780192847867.003.0006

foster the upgrading of skills and competencies, and reform social policies in ways that support the adjustment, rather than hinder it, so as to maximise the benefits of closer linkages with non-OECD economies.

(OECD 1997b, 14)

This is the social politics of global competitiveness, and it is at the core of the thinking of the OECD and the World Bank, both of whom aspire to establish the rule of capital on a universal scale.

The World in 2020 assumed that non-OECD country GDP would inevitably surpass that of the then OECD countries well before 2020, and welcomed the prospect. It expected that the 'big five' leading non-OECD economies—China, India, Indonesia, Russia, and Brazil—would by then account for between 30 and 35 per cent of global GDP, with the eventual outcome depending on the mix of policies followed by themselves and their advanced economy counterparts. The IMF's October 2019 *World Economic Outlook* (IMF 2019, Table A, 126) attributes 40.8 per cent of world GDP (PPP) and 63 per cent of world exports of goods and services to the advanced economies (which now include Singapore, Korea, Hong Kong, and Taiwan, as well as the Czech Republic, Estonia, Latvia, Lithuania, the Slovak Republic, and Slovenia, all of the latter now OECD members) and 59.2 per cent and 37 per cent respectively to emerging market and developing economies. The combined GDP of China, India, Russia, and Brazil accounts for 32 per cent of world GDP, and the inclusion of Indonesia (not recorded here separately) would bring it to 34.5 per cent, at the upper end of the 1997 estimate. In comparison, the G7 account for a combined total of 30.1 per cent. China heads the US not only in GDP, but also in its share of world exports of goods and services, at 18.7 and 10.7 per cent versus 15.2 and 10.1 per cent. Overall, the advanced economies still dominate in world exports, commanding a 63 per cent share, while World Bank data shows US corporations still holding dominant positions, although the banking, oil, and mining companies that used to lead have been displaced by the likes of Apple, Microsoft, Amazon, Alphabet, and Facebook, and China's Alibaba and Tencent have forced their way into the top ten (World Bank 2020b, Table 6.1, 141).

At the level of the structure of the world economy, then, things have turned out much as the OECD expected. But its insistence on the rising significance of the non-OECD economies was only the background to its principal message— the sharp contrast between prospective living standards by 2020 under the contrasting scenarios of 'business as usual' and accelerated liberalising reforms. Real GDP per capita might rise by 50 per cent in the OECD area under the first, it estimated, compared to 80 per cent under the second, while in the non-OECD area, where it was much lower, it would double under the first, but could rise by as much as 270 per cent under the second. The key to this was not simply the adoption of policies that promoted the expansion and deepening of the world market, but the reform of governance: 'Changes in governance will be needed to help populations to form *realisable expectations* for both their economic security and their own responsibilities, if social cohesion and political stability are to be secured' (OECD 1997b, 15–16, emphasis mine). The wide-ranging reform agenda that followed made clear why this was so. It was grounded in stable macroeconomic policy geared towards low inflation and 'sustainable' fiscal positions; a free, open and competition-oriented multilateral system of trade and investment entailing a progressive removal of protectionist barriers and obstacles to international migration; closer global financial integration with the objective of the full integration of non-OECD countries into the global financial system; and a single global tax regime (OECD 1997b, 16–19). Beyond this was the need to create labour markets fit for 'a world of greater competitive pressures and more rapid structural change', and able to secure flexibility, higher employment, and social cohesion. These would have to be underpinned by social protection of a kind that would 'encourage individuals to take risks and be flexible in responding to changes in their economic circumstances':

> OECD institutions for social security will need to be re-designed for an era when many employees are likely to change jobs, and possibly even careers, several times during their working life. Restructuring of national labour markets could include a continuing decline in relative demand for unskilled labour. Social and educational policy must focus on these unskilled workers. They are at risk of long-term dependency and social exclusion.
>
> (OECD 1997b, 19)

Hence income support systems should 'emphasise reinsertion in the labour market, rather than just provide an adequate existence for those excluded from work'; the focus should be on lifelong learning, and 'active ageing' to reverse the trend to earlier retirement; and 'raising the effective age of retirement [would] require major changes in the attitudes of workers, employers and society. But it is necessary and desirable and, with increased flexibility in employment parities, does not imply more of a lifetime spent in work.' The primary focus was on OECD members, but the approach was explicitly universal in scope, and it briefly noted the need for institutional reforms in the majority of non-OECD countries, to 'promote "supply-side" capacities, notably private sector development and enterprise competitiveness' (OECD 1997b, 19–21).

This agenda has remained in place at the OECD and the World Bank, and is reflected in the constitutionalisation of Marx's general law of social production. Where OECD Chief Economist Catherine Mann declared in 2014 that 'structural reform isn't a finite list of measures with an end-date. It is an on-going process to build more productive, inclusive and sustainable economies for our citizens' (Mann 2014, 13), the current incumbent of that role, Laurence Boone, proclaims in prefacing the 2019 issue of *Going for Growth*, that 'the time for reform is now' (OECD 2019b, 3). It always has been, whether in times of boom or crisis. The report itself highlights declining labour productivity and sluggish growth in labour utilisation in emerging market and advanced economies alike, and laments that the 'take-up of structural reforms has moderated'; its own summary of priorities for advanced and emerging-market economies, derived from a comprehensive analysis of country by country performance in relation to social and institutional factors shaping labour productivity and utilisation, is as clear and succinct a summary of the social politics of global competitiveness as you could desire. It revolves around providing equal access to education, training, and jobs, regardless of background; enhancing incentives for women to fully participate in the labour market; providing a level playing field for firms in order to foster competition, innovation, and productivity; addressing infrastructure bottlenecks and improving access to public services; and supporting radical innovation and the diffusion and adoption of new technologies (OECD 2019b, 15–18).

Against this general background, recommendations to individual countries (including non-members of the OECD) echo familiar themes. So, for the 'big five', Brazil should increase the effectiveness of social benefits, enhance outcomes and equity in education, reduce barriers to trade, reduce distortions in the tax system, and increase public and private investment in infrastructure; China should ensure a better match between skills available and those demanded on the market, strike a better balance between liberalisation and regulation in financial markets, reduce barriers to labour mobility, and strengthen social security and public service provision, enhance the rule of law and address pollution; India should simplify and modernise labour laws to create more and better jobs for all, reduce administrative and regulatory burdens on business, enhance access to and quality of social infrastructure, pursue financial sector reforms, and improve physical infrastructure and promote an efficient use of energy and water resources; Indonesia should enhance outcomes in education, improve the regulatory environment for infrastructure, reform labour regulations to reduce informality, continue to make energy prices more cost-effective, ease barriers to entrepreneurship and investment, and strengthen institutions to fight corruption; and the Russian Federation should reduce state control over economic activity and other barriers to competition, raise the quality of public administration, lower barriers to foreign direct investment and to trade in services, raise the effectiveness of innovation policy, and improve the quality of the public finances; and to take a single example from OECD members, the European Union should enhance support for innovation, increase competition in service and network sectors, reduce producer support to agriculture, remove barriers to labour mobility within the European Union, and strengthen the drive to fight climate change (OECD 2019b, Ch. 4). This is not quite 'one size fits all'. Rather, it is 'one design suits all', with a different mix of tweaks required, on the part of the *client*, to achieve a fit.

The OECD, like the World Bank, is a fundamentally political organisation. The actions of both represent political interventions, aimed to secure the hegemony in the states with whom they interact of forms of politics that favour the growth and accumulation of capital, and the ascendancy of capital over labour. They take as axiomatic that the process of capitalist development is both contradictory and conflict-ridden, and they weigh in consistently on the side of capital. Their political action is a form of class struggle at a global level, clearly articulated as such, and manifested in strategic programmes that address the social conflicts inherent in the development of the world market by guiding governments towards regimes of governance that will instil competition, induce competition-enhancing attitudes and behaviour on the part of capitalists and workers alike, and neutralise dissent. Their field of action, that is to say, is not a narrow one focused on technical and apolitical policy advice. Rather, it is the management and development on behalf of global capital of social and class relations across the world market that internalise the logic of capital.

As the second decade of the twenty-first century drew to a close, both issued major statements addressing the 'new opportunities and new challenges arising from globalisation, the digital revolution, changing work patterns and societal and demographic developments' that had impelled the EU to produce a new definition of social rights (European Commission 2017, 7). The World Bank's *World Development Report 2019: The Changing Nature of Work* and the OECD's *Employment Outlook 2019: The Future of Work* explored in detail the kind of worker that global capital requires, and the implications for society as a whole. Then, in its 2020 World Development Report, *Trading for Development in the Age of Global Value Chains*, the World Bank turned directly to the development of the world market itself. Viewed as a connected whole, these documents advanced a framework for pushing 'under-employed' workers in the developed world into a higher level of employment, and pulling informal sector workers in the developing world into the formal sector. Informed throughout as they were by strategies for perfecting the means and extent to which labour could be squeezed out of diverse households across their life cycle, targeting women in particular, and shaping social protection to the needs of capital and the labour market, they reflected a comprehensive programme aimed at maximising the extraction of productive labour from the global population as a whole. The complementary strategies for globally competitive labour markets that they present are entirely supportive of a politics of global competitiveness in which workers are subject to Marx's 'general law of social production'—'variation of labour, fluidity of functions, and mobility . . . in all directions'. In other words, they have advanced from the definition of the constitution of the general law of social production to mapping the institutional and legislative reforms required for its implementation. The first section below addresses the account of the worker that global capital requires in *World Development Report 2019: The Changing Nature of Work* and the OECD's *Employment Outlook 2019: The Future of Work*. The second addresses the approach taken in *World Development Report 2020: Trading for Development in the Age of Global Value Chains* to the development of the world market, and the third addresses the social implications through a focus on the family and household.

Work

The *World Development Report 2019: The Changing Nature of Work* calls for investment in 'human capital' to enhance productivity, with a complementary regime of 'social protection' in the specific context of the latest phase of the application of science, technology, and machinery to production in the forms of automation and robotisation. In terms that refer back directly to the 1990 formula—the productive use of the poor's most abundant asset, labour, and the provision of basic services to the poor—it declares the politics of global competitiveness to be inescapable, and calls for a universal model of social protection to support it:

Innovation will continue to accelerate, but developing countries will need to take rapid action to ensure they can compete in the economy of the future. They will have to invest in their people with a fierce sense of urgency—especially in health and education, which are the building blocks of human capital—to harness the benefits of technology and to blunt its worst disruptions. . . . In countries with the lowest human capital investments today, our analysis suggests that the workforce of the future will only be one-third to one-half as productive as it could be if people enjoyed full health and received a high-quality education. *Adjusting to the changing nature of work also requires rethinking the social contract.* We need new ways to invest in people and to protect them, regardless of their employment status. Yet four out of five people in developing countries have never known what it means to live with social protection. With 2 billion people already working in the informal sector—unprotected by stable wage employment, social safety nets, or the benefits of education—new working patterns are adding to a dilemma that predates the latest innovations. This Report challenges governments to take better care of their citizens and calls for a universal, guaranteed minimum level of social protection. It can be done with the right reforms, such as ending unhelpful subsidies; improving labour market regulations; and, globally, overhauling taxation policies.

(World Bank 2018b, vii–viii, emphasis mine)

It is a half-truth to say that the nature of work is *changing*: the present wave of scientific and technological innovation reflects the fact that capital never treats the existing form of the production process as the definitive one, but rather continually transforms not only the technical basis of production, but also the functions of the worker and the social combinations of the labour process. Hence, the rapid development of automation and robotisation, as the latest revolution in the application of science and the division of labour, threatens as always to throw masses of capital and labour from one branch of production to another, and 'by its very nature, necessitates variation of labour, fluidity of functions, and mobility of the worker in all directions' (Marx 1976, 617).

The World Bank understands this perfectly well. It has consistently preached the need for governments to facilitate rather than impede the 'throwing of masses of capital and labour from one branch of production to another', counselled them on forms of 'welfare' conducive to the creation of mobile and flexible labour markets, and devised political strategies to isolate and neutralise opposition. Following the same line here, it argues that if the new technology threatens to produce unequal opportunities and divisive outcomes, it is because not all workers are equally available to be exploited productively by capital—the obvious solution being that they should be. This confirms the direction of travel of World Bank policy advocacy over forty years, and its consistent adherence to a politics of global competitiveness focused primarily on making people around the world available for productive exploitation by capital. It identifies the persistence of informality as 'the greatest challenge for emerging economies', assessing its incidence at more than 70 per cent in sub-Saharan Africa and 60 per cent in South Asia, more than 50 per cent in Latin America, and stuck at around 90 per cent in India, then makes the familiar argument that 'the demand for routine job-specific skills is declining', while the changing nature of work 'demands skill sets that improve the adaptability of workers, allowing them to transfer easily from one job to another' (World Bank 2018b, 19, 23–4).

At the same time, the Bank identifies an unexpected 'convergence in the nature of work between advanced and emerging economies':

Labor markets are becoming more fluid in advanced economies, while informality is persisting in emerging economies. Most of the challenges faced by short-term or temporary workers, even in advanced economies, are the same as those faced by workers in the informal sector. Self-employment, informal wage work with no written contracts or protections, and low-productivity jobs more generally are the norm in most of the developing world. These workers operate in a regulatory gray area, with most labor laws unclear on the roles and responsibilities of the employer versus the employee. This group of workers often lacks access to benefits. There are no pensions, no health or unemployment insurance schemes, and none of the protections provided to formal workers.

(World Bank 2018b, 27)

It responds by calling for common social protection systems and labour regulations on a global scale, through investment in human capital that avoids placing greater regulatory or financial burdens on firms, which must be left free to compete. Governments should not oblige firms to finance pensions and other forms of insurance through payroll taxes, as this does little good if these workers represent only a small share of the workforce, while further demands for employer-provided support (such as a minimum wage, employer-provided health care, or protection against dismissal) deter hiring and the formalisation of labour even further. Social inclusion should be extended to all workers, but governments 'should move away from regulation-based distribution to direct social welfare support'. This is a prescription for making all the propertyless class available for work while perfecting competitive labour markets: the role of the state, just as it was according to the 1990 World Development Report, *Poverty*, is still to make available to capital a working age population, healthy, educated, and ready and willing to work. So 'given the considerable uncertainty about the future of employment, governments should rethink policies that deter job creation, and emphasize policies that protect the vulnerable while still encouraging employment' (World Bank 2018b, 31). This approach has been long in the making, and the means by which it is to be achieved are mostly familiar: an easing of barriers for start-ups and for the exit of unproductive firms, globally coordinated tax regimes, and streamlined business regulation; early years to lifelong learning, as 'a large share of children entering primary school in 2018 will work in occupations that do not yet exist'; an emphasis on adult literacy, skills training for wage employment, and entrepreneurship programmes; and a primary focus on raising the productivity of workers, in ways foreshadowed six years earlier in the 2013 Report, *Jobs*, and extensively canvassed by the OECD (World Bank 2018b, 70–92). Significantly, the Bank has no time for the non-capitalist sector. Informal sector workers, women, and workers in agriculture are alarmingly unproductive, while informal sector firms are 'run by uneducated owners, serve low-income consumers, use little capital, and rarely move to the formal sector' (World Bank 2018b, 94).

In short:

> Work is the next venue for human capital accumulation after school. Poorer economies have much to do because they lag behind advanced economies in the returns to work. Governments can raise those returns by increasing formal jobs for the poor, enabling women's economic participation, and expanding agricultural productivity in rural areas. Formal jobs create more learning opportunities. Empowering women will raise the stock of human capital in the economy. And expanding agricultural productivity in rural areas will provide better work opportunities for the poor. Jobs that generate and build skills will prepare workers for the future.
>
> (World Bank 2018b, 102)

The policy goal of creating stable formal private sector jobs for the poor requires in turn a radical departure from the now obsolete 'Bismarckian social insurance model of earnings-based contributions ... premised on steady wage employment, clear definitions of employers and employees, and a fixed point of retirement', which 'is not a good fit for developing countries, where formal and stable employment are [sic] not common', and 'is also increasingly unsuitable for the changing nature of work in which traditional employer-employee relationships are no longer the norm' (World Bank 2018b, 113). As far as possible, the very poor should receive sufficient 'assistance' to make them available for productive work; beyond that, while a minimum level of support should be provided by the state, individuals should contribute themselves as far as they can, through insurance, to covering the risks inherent in exposure to globally competitive labour markets; and the burden of payroll taxes should be reduced as far as possible, in order to remove inequity across informal and formal sectors, and reduce disincentives to hiring. So the Bank proposes a four-tier system that is structured in terms of risks and incentives, and looks towards universal provision as a springboard to productive work as an ideal end goal. The first level is 'social assistance' through conditional cash transfers and targeting: 'social assistance, especially income support plus interventions, has often raised productivity and resilience among informal workers' (World Bank 2018b, 108). The enhanced role proposed would require 'broader and more permanent coverage than most social assistance programmes currently provide', so it should be expanded only at the same pace as the mobilisation of required resources, taking into account the adverse incentive effects of excessive redistribution. The Bank discusses at length but does not endorse Universal Basic Income schemes, suggesting that these are ideal but not yet feasible: the time is not yet right, it says, for a social minimum provided by a single scheme (World Bank 2018b, 112). At a second level, social assistance 'should be complemented with insurance that does not fully depend on formal wage employment. An arrangement of this nature would provide basic universal coverage, subsidizing premiums for the poor and topping up social assistance. Mandatory earnings-based contributions would also be necessary' (World Bank 2018b, 106). Again, the key concept is effective *individual* management of risk:

A reformed system must ensure that low-income workers have access to effective risk management tools. The right combination of instruments, subsidized for the poorest, is required to cover losses from livelihood disruptions, sickness, disability, and untimely death. Instruments that support stable consumption patterns, or are consumption smoothing, are also important. A comprehensive package of protection in pursuit of these goals would contain, first, a guaranteed minimum insurance with subsidized coverage against impoverishing losses. This instrument would complement social assistance by providing coverage against losses that would be too large to cover through transfers. Second, a mandated savings and insurance plan would allow for consumption smoothing. Finally, market-based 'nudged' or purely voluntary savings would allow people to contribute more, if desired.

(World Bank 2018b, 114)

In keeping with the goal of reducing payroll tax rates, the final level is an employers' contribution modified by reformed labour market regulations. This should take account of the fact that more than half of the global work force is informal, end the practice of expecting labour regulations to substitute for social protection, and make it easier for firms to 'adjust the composition of their workforces', so that they can more readily adopt new technologies and increase productivity. 'Hiring and firing' should be made easier, by shifting from severance pay to unemployment benefit funded by individual savings ('Savings could be drawn on for unemployment or for retraining') or to state transfers set low enough to avoid undermining the incentive to work, combined with active reemployment support measures to 'assist' the unemployed back into work (World Bank 2018b, 116–17).

In its final chapter the report turns to the need for a new social contract ('a policy package that aims to contribute to a fairer society') focused on social inclusion, 'defined as improving the ability, opportunity, and dignity of those most disadvantaged in society'. It asks three questions: 'First, how can society frame a new social contract in the context of high informality and the changing nature of work? Second, if a government is given a mandate to prepare a social contract aimed at improving fairness in society, what would be its basic ingredients? And, third, how can the state finance any proposed reforms?' (World Bank 2018b, 124–5). There are no surprises in the answers. The Bank gives Danish 'flexicurity' as a recent example, and ominously adds 'the economic reforms introducing market principles that began in 1978 in China, the Balcerowicz Plan in Poland in 1989, and the Hartz reforms in Germany in 2003' as examples of 'substantially new social contracts'. It is emphatic that it does not have a revived 'New Deal' in mind: equality of opportunity means investing in early childhood development, and 'boosting social protections, including social assistance and insurance, in ways that are compatible with work' (World Bank 2018b, 126–7).

The Bank's own contribution to this proposed global revolution in work and social protection is its Human Capital Project and Human Capital Index, introduced in this report and up-dated in 2020. As initially introduced, it centred on an 'international metric'—an index 'designed to highlight how improvements in the current education and health outcomes shape the productivity of the next generation of workers' in which 'the components of the human capital index are aggregated by first transforming them into measures of their respective contributions to worker productivity relative to a benchmark corresponding to a complete education and full health' (World Bank 2018b, 56, 58). The essence of the project was captured in a table that estimated 'the productivity as a future worker of a child born in 2018' (World Bank 2018b, Table 3.1, 59) by combining measures of survival, schooling and health; and the chapter concluded by referring to related exercises (the Bank's Skills Towards Employability and Productivity surveys, and the OECD's Programme for the International Assessment of Adult Competencies surveys), and underlining the message that 'significant gaps in human capital persist across the world. These gaps—manifested in low education and health outcomes—hurt the future productivity of workers and future competitiveness of economies' (World Bank 2018b, 64). In short, protection from the cradle to the grave has long gone, and is replaced by the production on a global scale of young adults as willing and productive workers for capital. Social protection is not protection for human society, it turns out, but protection for capital.

In the meantime, the OECD had revised its 2006 *Jobs Strategy* in the light of subsequent developments. Published in 2018, the revised strategy placed the emphasis on the need 'to foster resilience and adaptability of the labour market to achieve good economic and labour market performance', with a triple focus on promoting an environment in which high-quality jobs could thrive, preventing labour market exclusion and protecting individuals against labour market risk, and preparing for future opportunities and challenges in a rapidly changing economy and labour market (OECD 2018, 3–4). In brief, it sought to provide guidance to policy makers on labour market and other policies that 'enable workers and firms to harness the opportunities provided by new technologies and markets, while helping them to cope with the required adjustments and ensuring that the fruits of growth are broadly shared' (OECD 2018, 14); and in so doing it incorporated the lessons taken from the successive editions of the *Skills Outlook* published in previous years.

The OECD's reflection on the future of work, published in the following year, built directly on this, opening with an evocation of transformational change that directly recalls the *Communist Manifesto* (1848):

The world is changing at lightning speed. Digitalisation, globalisation and demographic changes are having a profound impact on our lives, on our cultures, on our societies. These and other megatrends are constantly (and rapidly) transforming the way we interact with our friends and families; how and where businesses operate; what goods and services we consume; what dreams we dream. Our education and health, the distribution of income and wealth, the jobs we have and how we work are all particularly sensitive to these changes. It is a transformational era. Disruption is the new normal (OECD 2019a, 3).

Marx and Engels were more poetic: 'All that is solid melts into air'. Notably, the context was the same: the insight that the bourgeoisie 'cannot exist without constantly revolutionising the instruments of production, and thereby the relations of production, and with them the whole relations of society' (Marx and Engels 2010b, 487). So the OECD moves swiftly from the opportunities afforded by this revolution for higher productivity growth, better services and improved wellbeing to identify 'challenges, especially for labour'. The content is familiar: the vulnerability of many jobs to automation, the particularly poor prospects for unskilled workers, and the dangers of being left behind. It echoes the Bank's strategy and rhetoric of inclusion, urging that 'it is important that people feel that they will be supported if they lose out, and helped in their search for new and better opportunities' (OECD 2019a, 3). Their roles are complementary. Whereas the World Bank devoted most of its energy to a frontal attack on the informal economy, the OECD addresses 'non-standard' employment (defined as 'all temporary, part-time and self-employment arrangements, i.e. everything deviating from the "standard" of full-time, open-ended employment with a single employer': OECD 2019a, Box 2.3, 52), and sets out to establish it as the norm. This complements the work of the Bank by addressing the 'developed world' side of the process of convergence towards globally operative flexible conditions of employment geared to the needs of capital, covering the same terrain as the EU's *Pillar of Social Rights*. The Foreword from OECD Secretary-General Angel Gurría is followed by an editorial from the Director for Employment, Labour and Social Affairs Stefano Scarpetta, entitled 'A transition agenda for a *Future that Works* for all' (OECD 2019a, 14–16), with Bob Dylan's 'The Times They Are a-Changin'' (unattributed) as the lead-in. Scarpetta, at the OECD since 1991, save a couple of years at the World Bank (2004–6), is an organic intellectual of social protection and labour market reform *par excellence*, and a veteran of the OECD's *Jobs Strategy*, having directed its reworking in the late 1990s. These policies too, then, have been a long time in the making. And lest the central message should be missed, it is spelled out three more times in advance of the main text, in an infographic, an executive summary, and an Overview that includes a five-page listing of detailed policy directions (OECD 2019a, 17, 19–21, 23–36).

The underlying strategy in all of this is simple—to abolish the 'standard employment relationship', replacing the 'standard worker' with the 'non-standard worker' as the focal point of labour market and social protection policies, and putting a positive spin on 'non-standard' work. The starting point is that diversity in employment contracts can provide 'welcome flexibility for many firms and workers', so long as challenges surrounding the quality of non-standard work are met—the first being 'determined policy action . . . to ensure a more equal sharing of the costs of structural adjustment in the world of work' (OECD 2019a, 19). The costs are not to be shared equally between workers and firms, but equally between all workers. So the permanent worker employed by a single employer is declared obsolete, and the category of non-standard work serves to ratchet down levels of protection to a new lower floor: those in non-standard forms of work must have 'access to labour and social protection', but by definition it will fall short of a permanent, full-time contract with attendant benefits. Employers, in the meantime, are bound specifically and only by the doctrine of competitiveness—they must not abuse the market by collusion, agree 'non-compete' covenants, or fail to provide workers with full and clear information regarding the terms of their employment. Lifelong learning, including good quality training aligned to labour market needs, is essential, and social protection systems, which 'play a key stabilising role in the current context of heightened uncertainties about the pace and extent of labour market changes', require reform to make them 'sufficiently agile to respond to changes in people's need for support, ensuring that entitlements are portable across jobs, and adapting the scope of activation and employment support for evolving work patterns' (OECD 2019a, 20–1).

Collective bargaining rights, similarly, should be extended to non-standard workers and to workers in the 'grey zone'—'but the challenge is to ensure that labour market and competition policy remain aligned': 'An absence of collective bargaining rights can accentuate power imbalances that are inherent in the employment relationship, and could lead to a degree of monopsony [excessive power in the hands of the buyer] in the labour market'. This is bad for workers and for competitiveness, as stronger bargaining power in the hands of employers 'may imply that they can impose lower wages by inefficiently reducing labour demand' (OECD 2019a, 29–30):

> On the one hand, lack of competition in the labour market—for example because certain companies collude among themselves or resort to restrictive covenants to reduce workers' mobility and bargaining power—may mean

that innovative companies are prevented from exploiting new opportunities and recruiting the best people. On the other hand, insufficient enforcement of competition law disadvantages firms that abide by the rules.

(OECD 2019a, 30)

The OECD, in short, embraces a pure doctrine of competitiveness in all markets, centred on mobile and flexible 'non-standard' workers embedded in social protection regimes that oblige them to strive to maintain and renew a portfolio of market-relevant skills, and to compete on a global scale for work that is inherently precarious. When it devotes a chapter to the 'role of labour markets to adequately protect workers in a changing world of work', first ensuring their 'correct classification' in terms of employment status (OECD 2019a, 131), it jettisons the norm of full-time permanent work for a single employer. By setting its sights at the limit, on the grey zone between dependent and self-employed, it positions that status as the new norm to which labour market regulation and social protection should be calibrated. That this is the underlying logic is made clear when the OECD comments on the introduction of the statutory category of 'worker' in the UK Equality Act of 2010, to broaden the reach of employment regulations to those not deemed by the courts to enjoy 'employee' status. Here the 'worker' category 'is not precisely defined but is intended to cover any individual who works under a contract to provide a personal service, independently of whether he/she has a contract of employment'. The Act affords the worker protection against discrimination, and by implication a right to equal treatment with standard employees in basic working conditions. But although they are covered by selected labour regulations including those on working time, holiday pay and the minimum wage, and may be entitled to sick pay and parental pay, 'they do not benefit from minimum notice periods, health and safety provisions, protection against unfair dismissal and redundancy pay', and at the same time, 'they are responsible for their own social security contributions and tax (like the self-employed)'. In short, the 'worker' is entitled only to 'in-work' benefits, and is denied any that relate to continuity of employment or pension rights. The OECD is quick to point out the strategic shift that this implies:

While the original intention of the worker category was to broaden the reach of protective regulations to a greater number of workers, the creation of this separate category of workers may have shifted the objective of litigation down from obtaining employee status to merely obtaining worker status— as has been evidenced in recent course cases involving ride-sharing services (OECD 2019a, 143).

'Worker status', then, is the new norm the OECD favours. This efficiently does away with any rights arising from loss of work or termination of contract, making dismissal cost free. By the same token, it rejects the notion of a zero hours, zero rights status prevalent in some forms of 'platform' work where the platform operator resists designation as an employer. Rights *should* be extended to these workers, but they should *exclude* any notion of job security and hence ensure absolute flexibility: 'New regulations should be flexible and broad enough to encompass various types of employment, regardless of the means through which work is obtained' (OECD 2019a, 145). New forms of work are not to be resisted, then, but to be accommodated, and are presented as emerging 'in response to the real needs of both employers and workers': 'Diversity (and continuous innovation) in employment contracts gives both employers and workers the necessary flexibility to find arrangements that are in the best interests of both. The objective of policy should therefore be to accommodate these changes without abandoning the aim of protecting the weakest and ensuring fundamental rights for all' (OECD 2019a, 157).

In short, the OECD aims to encourage the adoption of *comprehensive* labour regulations that legislate job security out of existence for the formerly non-standard and now new standard worker. It does so by first identifying the 'interest of the worker' as identical to the needs of global capital, then advocating forms of collective bargaining and social dialogue that 'contribute to addressing the realities of global markets, increased competition and frag-mentation of production, and ensure that all workers and companies, includ-ing small and medium-sized enterprises, reap the benefits of technological innovation, organisational changes and globalisation' (OECD 2019a, 191–2). Spelling out the politics of this approach, the final chapter states the current form of the argument that effective social protection can both make labour markets work better, and blunt resistance to competitive labour *and* product markets. It 'provides a buffer against the individual and social costs of… adjustments and can ensure that those losing their jobs have the time to find good job matches or undertake training if needed. In doing so, it can also counter calls for policy responses that stifle economic dynamism, such as creating barriers to trade or innovation.' Social protection regimes should be restructured, and made portable across different forms of employment, while 'enforcing job-search responsibilities and other requirements for the part-time unemployed may be a necessary counter-weight to extending benefit rights to these groups' (OECD 2019a, 294–6). It then rejects the distinction between being *in* and *out* of work as a 'dichotomy [that] appears increasingly ana-chronistic', to focus attention on the 'under-employed':

In fact, in some countries, workers with intermittent employment and/or limited working hours already outnumber key categories of out-of-work individuals, such as those not working for family reasons, those unfit to work, or the longer-term unemployed. A strict focus on the jobless denies support from [sic, they mean 'to'] a large number of precarious workers who face barriers to higher-quality employment. It therefore becomes more and more unsatisfactory as basis for targeting activation and re-employment programmes.   (OECD 2019a, 318)

This leads inexorably, at the very end of the report, to the core of its strategic purpose, which is to question the narrow focus on weak work incentives as 'the only employment barrier for jobseekers', when 'a more fluid labour market with more options for when and how long to work creates more opportunities for acting on positive and negative incentives' (OECD 2019a, 320). First, it argues that 'incentives that favour specific employment forms can become more distortionary and economically damaging than they had been in the past'; second, 'tax-benefit provisions, which create sudden income drops or gains as people vary earnings or working hours, are more likely to affect working time and earnings when choices are no longer constrained to, say, 40, 30, or 20 hours per week'; and third, then, 'and perhaps most important, governments should review whether benefit reforms that are intended to tackle benefit coverage gaps create a need to rebalance the demanding and supporting elements of existing rights-and-responsibilities frameworks':

> An emergence of alternative working arrangements, with additional scope for arranging work or earnings patterns in a way that is compatible with benefit receipt, calls for additional efforts to formulate and enforce clear and reasonable responsibilities for benefit recipients. Likewise, extending the scope of job-search responsibilities and provisions for active participation in re-employment measures may be a necessary counter-weight to any extensions of benefit rights to new groups of jobseekers, such as part-time unemployed, those with intermittent employment, or those who entered unemployment after periods of self-employment.   (OECD 2019a, 320)

The logic is clear. The final piece in the puzzle of the reform of social protection to bring it into line with the new world of work, having established the formerly 'non-standard' worker as the new norm, is to extend to this new (part-time, intermittently employed or recently self-employed) worker the disciplines that they previously were able to avoid. With this shift, the worker as envisaged in social protection regimes is precisely the worker imagined in Marx's general law of social production.

The World Market

Following the focus on the worker in the 2019 *World Development Report*, its successor, *Trading for Development in the Age of Global Value Chains*, turns its attention to the world market, in a significant step towards the systematic construction of a model for a global economy based upon the universal subjection of the propertyless majority to the demands and disciplines of capital. Its focus is actually on *production* and the *labour market* as much as on *trade*: by exploring the spatial organisation of production and its domination by a minority of large firms involved in both importing and exporting, and focusing particularly on dynamic change in labour markets, it complements the 2019 Report. In doing so, it confirms that the Bank does not privilege 'Western' corporations or capital, but promotes the worldwide hegemony of capital under a regime of global competitiveness to which *all* states must conform. It promotes active state intervention to address imperfections in labour markets that hinder integration into global value chains: 'In low-income, labor surplus countries with large pools of unskilled labor transitioning from the agriculture sector,' it argues, 'externalities arising from the divergence between the market price and the opportunity cost of labor may call for additional targeted incentives for the private sector to invest in labor-intensive activities' (World Bank 2020b, 196). So the Bank explicitly encourages low-income countries to subsidise wage costs in order to increase their capacity to compete in global markets. This is not proposed as a means of integration into a traditional division of labour in the global economy. On the contrary, the imperative is to adopt policies that will avoid 'low-wage traps', and facilitate 'transitioning up the GVC typology' successively from special-isation in commodities to light manufacturing, then to advanced manufactur-ing and services, and finally to innovative GVC activities, with the Czech Republic repeatedly identified as a successful case (World Bank 2020b, 54–5, 74, 186–9). As always, the ambition of the Bank is to take advantage of the technological revolutions that have given rise to the fragmentation of produc-tion on a global scale to develop as extensive and competitive a world market and as productive a global proletariat as possible. It favours free trade because it imposes *competitiveness*: cheaper imports of finished goods subject domes-tic producers to competition, forcing them to become more competitive themselves or go out of business, while imports of intermediate goods (goods used in the production process) have the same effect on domestic suppliers of those goods, while reducing the production costs of the firms they supply, and raising *their* competitiveness. All this, of course, is consistent with the arguments made by the OECD from the 1970s onwards. The Bank values above all competitiveness in *labour markets*. The first response of firms facing increased competition is not to go out of business, but to replace labour with capital and/ or reduce wages, in order to restore profitability. In a flexible labour market (one in which wages can be reduced and workers laid off with relative ease) barriers to resource allocation are removed and competition in the domestic economy is encouraged. Only when free trade and labour market reform go together, and are pursued *in advanced and developing countries alike*, will workers be subjected to the full discipline of competition in the world market. All of this was set out in detail in an OECD paper (Andrews et al. 2018, 7–10) that the 2020 *World Development Report* draws on to argue that 'GVCs have contributed to lower inflation via *downward pressures on labor through heightened competition across countries to attract tasks*, in particular when low-wage countries are integrated in supply chains' (World Bank 2020b, 106, emphasis mine). This is the key mechanism on which the report depends, supported further by a body of recent work, originating in studies of FDI in global value chains, which argues that global trade 'integrates not only markets for products, services, finance and technology, but also, directly and indirectly, markets for labour' (Farole et al. 2018, 6). This paper is one of dozens of publications that have emerged since 2017 from the Bank's Jobs Group, all specifically intended to influence programmes and policies in client countries, and its three authors are all members of the core team that produced *Trading for Development*. They argue that 'the process of trade-induced growth entails the continual reallocation of resources away from less productive activities to more productive ones', in a process that inevitably creates winners and losers across countries, sectors, firms, and workers, as it changes the relative demand for certain skills:

> Specifically, the emergence of global value chains (GVCs) – whereby activities that used to be produced under one roof are now fragmented and distributed across networks spanning many countries ('offshored') – means *the trade and technology nexus is increasingly merged*. Producers play off trade, investment, and technology to maximize profits. This has fundamental impacts on where jobs go, who gets them, and what types of jobs they are. (Farole et al. 2018, 6, emphasis mine)

In short, the Bank and the OECD embrace global value chains because they bring about 'downward pressures on labour through heightened competition across countries to attract tasks'. This presupposes two relatively recent developments: the fragmentation of production down to the level of separate individual tasks, and advances in transport, logistics, and communications to a point where low-wage countries all around the world can participate. These together underpin a regime of genuine global competitiveness. So *Trading for Development* 'sets out a comprehensive domestic agenda for governments: investments in connectivity, improvements in business climate, and unilateral reductions in trade and investment barriers', combined with an international agenda of coordinated trade liberalisation, a universal regime for foreign investment, and the subjection of state-owned enterprises to rules of competition. Crucially, as always, this entails complementary programmes of reform in advanced and developing countries. First, 'reinvigorating the international trade system will require governments in certain advanced countries to first look inward to address the discontent and inequality associated with openness. More generally, advanced economies need to rethink the priorities of the welfare state to better help workers adjust to structural change'; second, developing countries 'need to expand social assistance and improve compliance with labor regulations in order to extend the jobs and earnings gains from participation in GVCs to more people across society. They also need to take steps to ensure that their domestic firms benefit from knowledge transfer from lead global firms' (World Bank 2020b, xiii). Set out right at the start by Chief Economist Pinelopi Koujianou Goldberg in the preface to the report, this is the basis of the World Bank prescription for a genuinely global capitalist economy.

The report takes for granted, then, that the fragmentation of production across global value chains is beneficial. GVCs 'are associated with structural transformation in developing countries, drawing people out of less productive activities and into more productive manufacturing and services activities' (World Bank 2020b, 3); they are more likely than non-GVC firms to employ women; and are associated with a reduction in poverty. But because they can also increase inequality within and between countries, and cause environmental damage, continued reform is necessary, to avoid or mitigate negative consequences. The key word here is 'adjustment'—adjustment to the logic of global competitiveness, that is, through policies that smooth the path of change in its favour, such as 'labor market policies to help workers who may be hurt by structural change; mechanisms to ensure compliance with labour regulations; and environmental protection measures': 'Adjustment assistance, which is especially important in middle- and high-income countries, will help workers adapt to the changing patterns of production and distribution that GVCs bring about. Adjustment policies can include facilitating labor mobility and equipping workers to find new jobs' (World Bank 2020b, 6). This in turn is the point of intersection with *The Changing Nature of Work*, and the global agenda of skills training and labour activation in response to changing demands for labour (a connection that is made directly, World Bank 2020b, 151–3).

Not all of this is new. The mapping out of the requisites for a comprehensive regime of global competitiveness and the means by which it can be brought to bear on the attitudes and behaviour of the world's poor had largely been accomplished over the period from the late 1980s on, while other forces brought about a genuinely global world market. What *is* new is that the regime that was already envisaged in the late 1980s can now be realised in practice, while more fine-grained sources of data make it possible to explore policy areas such female employment in more strategic detail than in the past. In the meantime, just as the material content of trade has changed as it has become dominated by goods that did not exist four decades ago, so has the world in which trade takes place.

At the same time, the Bank is concerned that renewed protectionism is threatening the relative freedom of trade, and thereby hindering the operation of the competitive pressures it brings about. Both the expansion of trade and the advancing global division of labour are slowing, and the distribution of GVC production across the developing world remains uneven. It responds first by looking for means to press the development of global value chains further, and second by addressing the factors that are slowing their expansion. It places great emphasis on the prospects for and means towards the increased employment of women in 'good jobs' in GVCs, observing first that the most successful developing world firms integrated into GVCs not only increase their productivity through greater capital intensity (more investment per worker), but also employ increasing numbers of workers, especially if they are involved in both exporting and importing. So 'GVCs are associated with structural transformation, with exports pulling people out of less productive activities and into more productive manufacturing jobs' (World Bank 2020b, 78). Noting that female workers tend to predominate (and specifically, that GVC firms are more likely than non-GVC firms to hire women), it illustrates the potential positive effects with the example of Bangladesh, where 'young women in villages exposed to the garment sector delay marriage and childbirth, and young girls gain an additional 1.5 years of schooling', and suggests similar trends in India, Kenya, and Senegal (World Bank 2020b, Box 3.5, 79–80). At the same time, it identifies a persistent gender gap in wages, as 'women are generally in lower-value-added segments of the value chain, mostly in labor-intensive production jobs and in occupations that require lower skills and pay less' (World Bank 2020b, 90, esp. Fig. 3.18). It attributes this, and the fact that very few women own or run GVC firms, to familiar causes: 'disadvantages in endowments, such as assets, education, skills, experience, networks, and social capital, as well as gender-biased regulations or discriminatory social norms', drawing particularly on a previous World Bank study (Staritz and Reis 2013) for support. The focus of the Staritz and Reis collection was on the extent to which barriers to the advance of women were also restraints on competitiveness in the global economy. The 2020 Report takes up the point: 'gender-intensified constraints can restrict a country's ability to remain competitive and upgrade to higher-value segments of the chain', and notes that this is 'a topic discussed in an as yet unpublished World Bank/World Trade Organization report on trade and gender, "How Can 21st Century Trade Help to Close the Gender Gap?"' (World Bank 2020b, 91). The two studies from this project available at the point of writing show just how keen the Bank is to find and promote global value chains in which women enjoy better career opportunities. The first, a case study of Chile, argues that even in the 'worst case' of the mining industry, technologically advanced large-scale mining offers more opportunities for women as jobs shift from manual labour on site to automated and remotely operated techniques of production. Its focus is directly on 'understanding the important role women should have as a strategic asset for competitiveness', in a context in which the Chilean Mining Skills Council estimates that projects in the pipeline will increase remote-operated and automated job profiles to 71 per cent of those in extraction, 90 per cent in processing, and 58 per cent in the currently lagging sector of maintenance (Fernandez-Stark et al. 2019, 2–3, 9). The second paper examines the rapidly expanding high value medical devices industry (anything from syringes and sutures to pacemakers) in Costa Rica and the Dominican Republic, and similarly addresses 'the relative opportunities for men and women in these higher value GVCs, and what, if any, gender sensitive policies are required to enhance a country's competitiveness in these sectors' (Bamber and Hamrick 2019, 2). Here women account for more than half the workforce, and 'this female participation holds steady as the sector grows, upgrades into new, higher value products and as wages rise; and... these predominantly female jobs are good quality jobs despite being primarily in production stages; that is, they are sustainable and characterised by permanent contracts and higher than average wages'. Upgrading is associated with stable or increasing female intensity of employment, and as the level of sophistication of production increases, women are favoured for technician and quality control roles. The authors attribute this relatively unusual situation to a number of factors: in the medical devices industry continuous up-grading is relatively easy, but considerable on the job training is required; the largely skilled/semi-skilled nature of the workforce and its acquired sector-specific expertise make retention desirable, and less than 1 per cent of workers are on temporary contracts (Bamber and Hamrick 2019, 12–17). This Costa Rican case is profiled in the 2020 Report (World Bank 2020b, Box 7.8, 188–9), and a subsequent joint report with the World Trade Organization developed the relationship between women and trade at length. 'In an integrated world', it argued, 'the competitive pressure generated by trade raises the cost of discrimination against women. Countries that do not allow women to fully participate in the economy are less competitive internationally—particularly those countries with export industries that globally have high female employment rates.' However, it warned, 'the positive effects of trade will materialize only if the barriers that hold women back are lifted and appropriate policies to deal with adjustment costs are put in place' (World Bank and World Trade Organization 2020, p. 3).

From this point, *Trading for Development* turns to the broader issue of the way a world market structured by GVCs should be managed. On the grounds that in a world of GVCs 'countries are increasingly related through rigid production linkages that bind them to a common fate', the Bank argues that they have an interest in cooperating to synchronise their economic activity, control inflation, maintain currency stability, and facilitate and extend opportunities for trade. 'In view of their rigid ties', the Bank goes on, 'GVCs would benefit from multilateral institutions helping to coordinate policy worldwide, including through the formulation of product standards, investment and intellectual property protections, or the timing of fiscal adjustments.' As noted above, the key driver here is downward pressure on wages arising from 'heightened competition to attract tasks' (World Bank 2020b, 103, 106). The Bank has in mind a comprehensive global regime, in which it would itself play a leading role with its international partners. Such a regime would necessarily involve risks for new entrants: the Bank recognises that 'as automation improves productivity, it also compresses labour's share of income in advanced economies', and 'certainly causes significant, and costly, labour market adjustments' (World Bank 2020b, 149, 151). But the labour market disruptions, rising skill premiums, and further declines in the share of income going to labour that accompany the intensification of competition point not to protectionism, or opting out of global value chains, but to 'the importance of sound social safety nets and redistributive and tax policies to ensure that gains are widely shared without distorting incentives to innovate' (World Bank 2020b, 154).

From this point on a clearly articulated global liberal developmental policy agenda unfolds, with the imperative to draw women, youth, and informal sector workers into the world market at its heart. Countries 'should exploit their comparative advantage by eliminating barriers to investment and ensuring that labor is competitively priced, by avoiding overvalued exchange rates and restrictive regulations'; they should follow the precepts of the Bank's *Doing Business* reports, and 'facilitate GVC-oriented FDI and support investors through the investment life cycle', adopting 'well-planned investment promotion strategies' of the kind introduced by Costa Rica, Malaysia, and Morocco; they should liberalise trade in goods and services to expand access to markets and inputs; they should 'overcome remoteness by improving their connectivity and lowering trade costs'; and they should 'strengthen enforcement of contracts, protection of property rights, and regulatory standards'. Beyond this, they should proactively 'promote linkages between domestic small and medium enterprises (SMEs) and GVC lead firms by coordinating local suppliers, providing access to information about supply opportunities, and supporting training and capacity building of SMEs'; 'help domestic suppliers gain access to finance and technology to support raising productivity and meeting global standards'; 'strengthen sector-specific human capital through targeted workforce development strategies, involving close coordination between the public and private sectors'; 'support firms in their efforts to upgrade management capabilities and strengthen the capacity for innovation'; and 'strengthen national innovation systems to support upgrading in GVCs' (World Bank 2020b, 161–2, and 186–9). And as this approach is not in itself guaranteed to be either inclusive or sustainable, it should be combined with policies that 'spread the jobs and earnings gains from GVC participation across society, thereby helping to lift the bottom 40 per cent': in agriculture value chains, the integration of smallholders is particularly important; policies should also 'support the inclusion of women and youth in GVCs, including by providing access to child care and training programmes and by addressing legal and social barriers to employment and earnings'; and compliance with labour standards should be improved, not least because this can lead to higher productivity and profits. In the advanced countries, where the welfare of workers left behind in communities where factories have closed is the primary threat to the sustainability of trade and GVCs, 'labour adjustment policies can be used to ensure that workers have the skills to move to new industries and places', and additionally a price should be set on environmental degradation, regulation should be introduced for specific pollutants and industries, trade agreements should be consistent with environmental goals, and standardised international data should be used to expose poor production practices and incentivise firms to improve (World Bank 2020b, 195). Again, the focus quickly turns to women and youth: 'the potential of GVCs to employ large numbers of young female workers means they may play a major role in supporting many countries' efforts to increase female labor force participation and reduce youth NEETs (not in employment, education, or training)' (World Bank 2020b, 197). The material here dovetails perfectly with that of *The Changing Nature of Work* (cited World Bank 2020b, 197–8, 202), reasserting the strategic value of GVCs, in the eyes of the Bank, for its agenda of competitiveness-enhancing inclusion. GVCs become the focal point of policy, and governments are urged to reform policies across the board—from skills development and employability to quality childcare and public-private pathways to GVC-specific employment.

Marx expected, as did Adam Smith, that under conditions of competition in the world market, wages would tend to settle at the level of subsistence, defined in relative social terms, and might well fall below it for periods of time. Viewed from this perspective, the Bank's agenda of 'inclusion' is an attempt to develop the global proletariat to a point where labour markets around the world operate on the basis of subsistence-level wages, with global value chains the key mechanism to structure global labour markets in this way. The Bank recognises this, but only up to a point. It acknowledges that wages in GVC factories may on occasion be less than 50 cents an hour, and comments that 'to readers in high-income countries where even the lowest-skilled factory jobs pay 20–30 times that level, this is a shockingly low wage'. 'However,' it continues, '*this does not necessarily mean that low wages are a problem in GVCs.*' 'What matters more,' it says, 'is whether the wages on offer are in line with productivity and whether they offer a reasonable "living wage" for workers' (World Bank 2020b, 198, emphasis mine). It is a problem for the Bank only if the process of constant investment and innovation to raise productivity is absent, as this in turn impairs both local and global dynamics of competitiveness: 'GVCs can be problematic if they contribute to the emergence of "low wage traps"—that is, where wage suppression is used to maintain international competitiveness.' Ideally, 'policies should protect workers' earnings while maintaining competitiveness to attract GVC investment.... Minimum wages should be set at a level that, at the very least, protects workers from poverty and vulnerability, while also keeping an eye on firm competitiveness' (World Bank 2020b, 198)—and raised at regular intervals, through a transparent process, linked to both productivity growth and the cost of living, while avoiding excessively sharp increases during significant economic downturns.

What, though, if productivity growth is insufficient, in a globally competitive labour market, to protect workers from poverty and vulnerability? The Bank has an instructive answer—one that both dissimulates, and reveals its uncompromising commitment to the politics of global competitiveness. 'In some countries', it suggests, *distortions in the domestic market may drive a significant wedge between a living wage for workers and the wage at which firms can remain competitive in international markets'* (emphasis mine). Short-term remedies include raising wages by means of a subsidy, or by investment to reduce the cost of public transport or provide more and cheaper housing. But in the medium term the government must remedy the 'market failure', by strategies such as education and skills policy and 'the immigration of skilled workers as a strategy for both competitiveness and inclusion' (World Bank 2020b, 200).

Here, then, the Bank pulls up short, preserving the liberal myth at the heart of the politics of global competitiveness by reliance on the proposition that a perfectly competitive global labour market without 'domestic distortions' would guarantee all workers freedom from poverty and vulnerability, when in truth there are no means of making this so. On the Bank's own account, spelled out in its doctrine of creative destruction and in Catherine Mann's insistence that structural reform is not a finite list of measures with an end-date, but a never-ending process, there can be no such guarantee. In the world the Bank imagines, poverty and vulnerability stem not from 'distortions in the domestic market' but from the *structure of the world market itself.* As Gimenez reminds us, the better markets work, the more they expel workers, continually creating and recreating a reserve army of labour, and a layer of workers in menial and unskilled jobs on rock-bottom wages. If global value chains do not abuse the human rights of precarious workers, there will always be some employer, driven by the demands of competitiveness, who will. True to form, the Bank acknowledges the problems that exist 'in global commodity chains such as agriculture and even in high-technology value chains, as confirmed by recent news reports documenting the casualization, discrimination, harassment, and retaliation encountered in some of the world's largest technology multinationals' (World Bank 2020b, 200), but it treats this as evidence of a need for regulation and enforcement, rather than as an intrinsic feature of global capitalist labour markets. Similarly, when it turns to adjustment in the advanced countries, it assumes that for the foreseeable future—if not indefinitely—it is possible for these countries to combine flexible labour markets with 'a generous, broad-based unemployment benefit system that cushions the negative income effects on displaced workers' (World Bank 2020b, 202). It can only do this by forgetting for the moment that its principal objective is to abolish the advantage that this implies.

Proletarianisation and Global Competitiveness

Four decades ago, the first *World Development Report* argued that progress in the developing countries would require a combination of three elements: 'maintaining high rates of growth in incomes; modifying the pattern of growth so as to raise the productivity and incomes of the poorer sections of the population; and improving the access of the poor to essential public services'; and it expressed the view that the employment problem in developing countries was not 'long-term joblessness as conventionally understood, but absence of productive earning opportunities, so that long hours of hard work yield only small incomes' (World Bank 1978, 26). It then proposed a formula for development to which it has stuck ever since:

> Because the poor tend to share less than proportionately in growth, since they have only limited access to productive assets, education, and employment, deliberate action is necessary in areas that affect the distribution of increases in income. These include the structure of economic incentives, the allocation of investments, and the creation of special institutions and programs to increase the productivity of the poor and their opportunities for employment.   (World Bank 1978, 65)

As the second decade of the twenty-first century drew to a close, the OECD and the World Bank shared precisely this focus, and had worked it up into a vision of a perfectly competitive world market, a universal framework of governance, and an accompanying social politics of global competitiveness aimed at extracting the maximum possible amount of labour from households around the world, in which a tendentially universal regime of social protection was the crowning element. On their own, though, efforts to boost the utilisation of labour on a global scale were of no avail if the target population lacked the qualities to be productive. The 2018 Human Capital Index sought, there-fore, to produce a population fit to work productively for capital. But the Bank was not entirely happy with its work. Updating the Human Capital Index in 2020, it admitted that the original index fell short of perfection:

> When today's child becomes a future worker [sic], in many countries she may not be able to find a job, and even if she can, it might not be a job where she can fully use her skills and cognitive abilities to increase her productivity. In these cases, her human capital can be considered *underutilized*.
>
> (World Bank 2020a, xvii–xviii)

To remedy this, the Bank now introduced 'two simple extensions...that adjust the HCI for labor market underutilization of human capital'. The first, the *basic UHCI* (Utilization-Adjusted Human Capital Index), measures the fraction of the working-age population that is employed, while the second, the *full UHCI*, measures 'better employment', defined as non-agricultural employees, plus employers, 'which are the types of jobs that are common in high-productivity countries'; and it proclaimed that the analysis of underutil-isation 'suggests that moving to a world with complete human capital and complete utilization of that human capital, long-run per capita incomes could triple' (World Bank 2020a, xviii).

The Human Capital Project envisages a world in which children 'reach school well-nourished and ready to learn, attain real learning in the classroom, and enter the job market as healthy, skilled and productive adults' (World Bank 2020a, 1). It perfectly captures the enduring perspective of the Bank, at a point where the world market is universal, and technological developments allow capital in principle to access labour on a global scale, but the majority of the working-age population of the world is stuck in low-intensity, low-productivity activity, the exploitability of potential workers is held back by deficiencies in endowments and skills, and the subsumption of labour to capital is still far from complete. Its perspective, as it always has been, is that the potential of capitalism on a global scale is enormous, and very far still from being realised. The development of the Human Capital Index, with its focus on the productivity of the individual, reinforces its classical liberal orientation, and underlines once again that its primary focus is not on competing states, or on dominant business interests, 'Western' or otherwise, but on 'the capital relation'—the relationship between labour and capital. It is explicitly tied here to wage labour or proletarianisation, the division of labour and productivity, in that 'better employment' 'involves work organized in a team consisting of at least an employer and an employee, where employees are paid for their work (rather than out of familial obligation). This allows a minimum degree of specialization and organization, which helps boost productivity and allows for people to use their skills' (World Bank 2020a, 92). These are goals that the Bank has been pursuing systematically over four decades, allying itself in doing so with the OECD, whose commitment to the politics of global competitiveness described here dates back to its founding in 1961. The process has been far from smooth, and remains far from complete. And in 2020 it was shaken to its core by the COVID-19 pandemic, coming hard on the heels of a 'global financial crisis' whose effects were still felt. Although the pandemic has not yet run its course, the final chapter addresses the response of the OECD and the World Bank, and asks what more it tells us regarding the politics of global competitiveness.

6

Capitalising on COVID-19?

On 11 January 2021 Ugo Gentilini, the World Bank's global lead for social assistance, posted an article on his 'Let's Talk Development' Bank blog page entitled 'A game changer for social protection? Six reflections on COVID-19 and the future of cash transfers' (Gentilini 2021). It addressed increased investment in social protection during the pandemic, predominantly through emergency cash transfers, and asked whether it could 'offer an opportunity to move the needle in scaling-up social protection more permanently'. Detailed World Bank analysis in the January 2019 issue of *Global Economic Prospects* had argued that on average 'economies with larger informal sectors tend to have lower productivity, slower physical and human capital accumulation, higher poverty and inequality, and smaller fiscal resources', and, importantly, that 'workers in the informal economy are largely excluded from the social security system and less protected against negative shocks than workers in the formal sector' (World Bank 2019, 129–30). As the pandemic spread, a World Bank-UNICEF global monitoring platform led by Gentilini monitored initiatives in social protection across emerging and developing economies in a 'living' (periodically updated) paper, documenting some 1,414 new planned or implemented social protection measures in 215 countries as of 11 December 2020, in the areas of social assistance, social insurance, and active labour market programmes (Gentilini et al. 2020, 2). In the blog post, he identified a number of factors that might either help or hinder a permanent shift, concluding that: 'Sometimes history presents an unexpected window of opportunity for change. When this occurred in the past, windows tended to close rapidly, and the path taken (or not taken) at those junctures could set the course for decades' (Gentilini 2021).

The COVID-19 pandemic that spread across the world from late 2019 onwards came hard on the heels of the 'global financial crisis', and unfolded against the background of an environmental crisis centred on global warming that was increasingly recognised as an existential threat. The immediate impulse behind the proposed extension of social protection in response to the pandemic was humanitarian, but there was more to it than that. Each of these overlapping crises posed a significant threat to the project of bringing into being an inclusive global capitalist system in a world market characterised

The Politics of Global Competitiveness. Paul Cammack, Oxford University Press. © Paul Cammack 2022.
DOI: 10.1093/oso/9780192847867.003.0007

by competitiveness at all levels, in which workers were reliable producers of surplus value for capital. In particular, the pandemic not only created a health emergency around the world and plunged the global economy into another sharp recession, but also directly threatened two of the key components of the OECD-World Bank model—the mobility of goods and workers within and across borders, and the education of the young generations who would be tomorrow's workers. At the same time, it created significant opportunities to push ahead with other aspects of the project—notably, the development of digital platforms and resources that could potentially transform the world of work, and the enrolment of informal sector workers and firms into reformed schemes of social protection. In the formal sector, world-wide, the pandemic disrupted the world of work, obliging firms to undertake radical re-organisation and at the same time throwing workers onto the defensive and side-lining the organisations through which they were represented. It thereby posed serious threats, but also created opportunities to press forward, under cover of COVID, with reforms that had proved hard to push through in the past. The manner in which the OECD and the World Bank responded offers rich insights into the character of their project, confirming both its inclusive global character, and its unswerving commitment to a growth-oriented polit-ics of global competitiveness. There is already ample evidence—not least in the 185 policy briefs produced by the OECD by the end of January 2021 in its 'Policy Responses to Coronavirus (COVID-19)' series and the dozens of assorted briefs and working papers produced by the World Bank—to identify its basic contours, and that is my purpose here. To provide relevant context, the first section below develops the theme of crisis as opportunity, and the second details the production by the OECD and the World Bank of a frame-work for addressing disaster management and climate change, and its appli-cation to the world of work. The third then examines their response to the pandemic, conducted under the slogan 'Building Back Better', first applied to reconstruction after the Asian tsunami of 2004 (Hallegatte et al. 2018), but now addressed to the world market and the global capitalist system.

Crisis as Opportunity

In advancing their project in the present century, both the OECD and the World Bank have identified crises as opportunities to push ahead with reforms, and both have drawn on notions of resilience and adaptability derived from parallel work in relation to the management of disasters and climate change. In 2007, IMF Chief Executive Dominique Strauss-Kahn insisted that the 'global financial crisis' was an opportunity to advance its standing and its goals (Mirowski 2013, 167). Similarly, the World Bank argued in *Doing Business 2007* that financial crises 'allow governments to address regulatory problems ignored in good times' (World Bank 2007b, 35), praising Thailand for having done so a decade earlier. It recalled Thailand's performance again in *Doing Business 2010*, in a section headed 'Times of Crisis – An Opportunity for Reform', remarking that historically, 'many reforms have been prompted by recession or financial crisis' (World Bank 2010, 5). And it went further, depicting 'consistent reformers' as following a longer-term agenda aimed at increasing the competitiveness of their firms and economy. 'Successful reformers', it concluded, 'stay focused thanks to a long-term vision supported by specific goals.... Setting long-term goals and keeping a steady course of reform might help economies recover from shocks, including the current global financial and economic crisis' (World Bank 2010, 8–9).

This passage ended by quoting Egyptian Minister of Investment Mahmoud Mohieldin as acknowledging that the global crisis 'is not just a crisis of the economy. It is a crisis of economic thinking. It is a crisis that is confusing many reformers', but concluding all the same that 'whatever crisis you are facing, you need to make life easier for those who are endeavouring and working hard to create opportunities for jobs, and this is the least that we can be doing' (World Bank 2010, 9). Through this device, the Bank rather cleverly conceded that the crisis called economic orthodoxy into question, while still insisting that the goal of 'creating opportunities for jobs' was as valid as ever. In doing so, it brought the approach to the crisis to focus precisely on the kind of regime it advocates—one in which labour markets are competitive, and individuals are responsible for equipping *themselves* to compete for available work. There was never the slightest chance that the crisis would lead it to question or abandon its project.

The OECD was if anything even more emphatic. The 2009 edition of *Going for Growth* addressed the issue directly, noting that the 'still unfolding global crisis and recession have inevitably raised questions about the extent to which markets can be trusted to deliver good outcomes and whether earlier reforms have contributed to make economies more vulnerable'; in response, it acknowledged that the crisis had 'uncovered major problems with the functioning of [financial] markets and demonstrated the failures of past regulatory and supervisory structures to ensure market stability', but found it 'important to emphasise that the debacle in financial markets does not call into question the beneficial effects of recommended reforms of product and labour markets', and concluded that 'the economic crisis facing OECD countries should not be allowed to slow down structural reforms, and opportunities for reforms should be exploited to strengthen economic dynamism and living standards' (OECD 2009, 4–5). It went on, in fact, to publish studies in 2010 and 2016 aimed to show not only that crises were inevitable, but also that they were on the whole beneficial. *Regulatory Reform for Recovery: Lessons from Implementation during Crises*, exploring responses to crisis in the 1990s, concluded that '[a]lthough greater competition and openness do not reduce the likelihood of future crises, they increase potential long-term growth and the ability to recover more quickly from crises' (OECD 2010e, 3). Crises were 'an opportunity to pass reforms that would not otherwise have enough support and that suddenly become possible given the heightened sense of urgency', and countries had 'generally fared best when they have used the crisis as an opportunity to accelerate reforms rather than slowing them' (OECD 2010e, 40, 57). The 2016 paper looked back over the whole post-1970 record of 'severe recessions and financial crises', concluding that overall a trajectory of periods of growth interspersed with sharp recessions and even occasional major crises could provide *optimal* conditions for advancing the liberalisation of labour and product markets: while pro-growth policies could make economies more vulnerable to such recessions, risk-mitigating (prudential) policies could still produce lower overall long-term growth (Caldera-Sánchez et al. 2016). Product and labour market policies conducive to higher productivity and employment generally had no adverse impact on crisis risks, while stronger active labour market programmes and lower barriers to trade resulted in higher average growth and fewer occurrences of severe recessions. So while excessive expansion of private credit and increased foreign indebtedness should be avoided, equity-based financial instruments, foreign direct investment, and the equity portion of portfolio investment all impacted positively on growth, with no significant impact on crisis risk (Caldera-Sánchez et al. 2016, 5–6). It followed that a model based upon competitive global labour and product markets and the free movement of investment capital was still the best guarantee of overall long-term growth: frequent severe recessions were inevitable, but were a price worth paying, not least, although this report did not say so, because they shook out 'inefficient' producers and freed resources to move into new forms of enterprise in the cycle of creative destruction.

A Unified Theory of Adaptability and Resilience

In the same period, *World Development Report 2010: Development and Climate Change* and *World Development Report 2011: Conflict, Security, and*

Development addressed the means by which other forms of crisis could be alleviated. The Bank, entirely accepting the need for urgent action on climate change, called for 'acting differently, because a climate smart world requires a transformation of our energy, food, production, and risk management systems' (World Bank 2009a, 10). New financial instruments could help to spread the costs of mitigation fairly, and the overall cost could be reduced by innovative carbon-pricing mechanisms, financial transfers, and targeted price signals. Beyond this, the Bank linked the issue of climate change to its broader framework for social protection: 'Social policies will become more important in helping people cope with more frequent and persistent threats to their livelihoods. Social policies reduce economic and social vulnerability and increase resilience to climate change. A healthy, well-educated population with access to social protection can better cope with climate shocks and climate change' (World Bank 2009a, 13). More broadly, access to markets for developing countries should be facilitated, subsidies on energy consumption removed, and regulatory standards made tougher, with industrial energy performance targets set to spur innovation and increase competitiveness, and financial incentives introduced to encourage energy companies to promote conservation, adopt renewable sources, and develop new and emerging technologies for carbon capture and storage, second-generation biofuels, and solar photovoltaics. The overall framework was premised on the idea that the financial crisis 'offer[ed] an opportunity for efficient and clean energy' (World Bank 2009a, Box 4.1, 190), and as is evident, it stayed true to the Bank's preference for growth- and market-oriented strategies. *Conflict, Security, and Development* heightened the focus on productive employment, repeatedly summarising its message in terms of investing in 'citizen security, justice and jobs'. From the Foreword, in which Bank President Robert Zoellick called for 'greater emphasis on early projects to create jobs, especially through the private sector' (World Bank 2011a, xii), and through the main text, the phrase occurred 114 times. The central motif of the report was a looping virtuous spiral, driven by 'restoring confidence' and 'transforming institutions', threatened by external stress, and buoyed up by 'external support and incentives', with violence and fragility as the starting point, and 'citizen security, justice, and jobs' its outcome: 'A repeated process enables space for collaborative norms and capacities to develop, and for success to build on successes in a virtuous cycle' (World Bank 2011a, Figure 2.1, p. 12 and Chapter 3). It is not surprising that in arguing for 'a need first to restore confidence and then to transform institutions that provide citizen security, justice, and jobs' (World Bank 2011a, 45) the World Bank should advocate solutions centred on private enterprise and the rule of law. But it is significant, all the same, that it did so without qualification at the height of the worst crisis of global capitalism in its history. As noted, this was not a consequence of oversight: it factored in such crises and sought to use them to move the agenda of global competitiveness forward.

The OECD similarly addressed global warming in the context of its commitment to private sector-led inclusive growth, in *Aligning Policies for a Low-carbon Economy* (OECD 2015a) and *Investing in Climate, Investing in Growth* (OECD 2017a). In the latter, Secretary-General Angel Gurría identified 'a unique opportunity to bring the climate and economic growth agendas together and to generate inclusive economic growth in the short term, while ensuring that we meet the climate challenge in the longer term' (OECD 2017a, 3). The 'unique opportunity' arose from the low cost of long-term finance, and the way to a 'resilient, inclusive and sustainable' growth path lay in investment in modern, smart and clean infrastructure, for which finance would be a key factor: 'capital must be mobilised from both public and private sources, supported by a variety of financial instruments supporting low-emission, climate resilient infrastructure' (OECD 2017a, 15): once finance was made available, industrial and business innovation would follow. So in the summary of 'main policy messages' that concluded the overview of the report, the OECD was able to stitch its response to climate change seamlessly into its broader agenda: 'Implement structural reform policies that boost both productivity and economic activity, as well as supporting the transition to low-emission, climate-resilient economies, through easier resource reallocation; faster technology development and diffusion; greater dynamism in labour markets; and measures to facilitate firm entry and exit' (OECD 2017a, 36). In the following year, its revised *Jobs Strategy* would highlight the need 'to foster resilience and adaptability of the labour market to achieve good economic and labour market performance' (OECD 2018, 3–4). Adaptability and resilience now covered everything, signifying 'the effectiveness with which individuals, institutions and societies absorb and adapt to economic shocks, and make the most out of the new opportunities arising from megatrends such as technological change (including automation and digitalisation), climate and demographic change and globalisation' (OECD 2018, 47). Climate change had become just another opportunity.

Over the same period the World Bank refined its own approach to crisis, bringing a broader set of ideas linking risk, resilience and opportunity together in the notion of 'adaptive social protection'. The starting point was its social protection and labour strategy, *Resilience, Equity, and Opportunity* (World

Bank 2012b), adopted for the period 2012–2022, which invoked a world 'increasingly becoming interconnected and risky, with economic shocks and epidemics flowing across national borders', and presented social protection and labour programmes as protecting against what might be called 'negative' risks, and *enabling* 'positive' risks (Cammack 2012): they 'directly improve resilience by helping people insure against drops in well-being from different types of shocks', and 'also promote opportunity by building human capital, assets, and access to jobs and by freeing families to make productive investments because of their greater sense of security' (World Bank 2012b, xi). It was followed a year later by *Building Resilience: Integrating Climate and Disaster Risk into Development. Lessons from World Bank Group Experience*, in which the Bank offered a framework for 'climate and disaster resilient development', bringing the strands of the 2010 and 2011 *World Development Reports* together. It built in doing so on the IPCC [Intergovernmental Panel on Climate Change] definition of resilience as the 'ability of a system and its component parts to anticipate, absorb, accommodate or recover from the effects of a hazardous event in a timely and efficient manner, including through ensuring the preservation, restoration or improvement of its essential basic structures and functions' (World Bank 2013b, 4). The core chapter, 'Towards Climate and Disaster Resilient Development', cemented the link to the broader Bank policy on managing risk by quoting directly from *World Development Report 2014: Risk and Opportunity: Managing Risk for Development*: 'Taking on risks is necessary to pursue opportunities for development. The risk of inaction may well be the worst option of all' (World Bank 2013a, Box 1, 4, cited World Bank 2013b, 15).

The notion of 'adaptive social protection' was set out at length in 2020, in a context in which the global landscape is 'fraught with interconnected and often devastating covariate shocks such as natural disasters, economic crises, pandemics, conflicts, and forced displacement': adaptive social protection is 'a response to widespread demand for the use of social protection as a tool to build the resilience of poor and vulnerable households to these kinds of covariate shocks' (Bowen et al. 2020, 1), and economic shocks, natural disasters, and climate change are formally brought into a single framework, with unemployment, asset loss, and food insecurity respectively seen as the routes by which shocks are transmitted. Crucially, adaptation in all three cases is conceived in terms of the accumulation of human capital and the potential for mobility:

With sufficient adaptive capacity, a more resilient household can make investments that reduce both its exposure and vulnerability to shocks over the longer term. This includes diversifying or adjusting livelihood portfolios away from sources of income that are especially vulnerable to the impacts of a shock; building a larger and more diversified asset base, including productive, financial, and human capital-related assets to enable these adjustments in livelihood portfolios; and/or leveraging such assets to relocate away from an area of spatially concentrated risk. *Indeed, the ultimate expression of adaptive capacity may be the household's ability to reduce its exposure to a shock altogether through relocation and planned migration when in situ adjustments to livelihood and assets portfolios fail and where remaining in place would lead to chronic vulnerability and even maladaptation.*

(Bowen et al. 2020, 4, emphasis mine)

Workers and households capable of versatility, flexibility, and mobility, that is to say, would be best equipped both to succeed in the labour market, and to escape the consequences of natural disasters. Physics may still lack a unified theory, but the World Bank does not.

Capitalising on COVID-19?

The upshot of all this was that the OECD and the World Bank were primed to address the COVID-19 pandemic in terms of the perspectives they had developed on resilient approaches to crisis, and to take advantage of it to drive their reform agenda forward. At the same time, some aspects of the crisis—such as the shock to global value chains and to the building of human capital—threatened to undermine it completely. As a result, as the full impact of the pandemic became apparent, the idea of crisis as opportunity began to shift to a more defensive posture, particularly on the part of the Bank, which came to see itself as struggling to avoid significant and long-lasting setbacks to its goals.

The COVID-related output of the two organisations has been voluminous, running into many hundreds of documents by the end of January 2021. It is approached here primarily through the OECD's *Economic Outlook* (June and December 2020) and the World Bank's *Global Economic Prospects* (June 2020 and January 2021). For specific issues related to employment, I draw also on the OECD's *Employment Outlook* (July 2020) and the World Bank's *Human Capital Index 2020 Update* (September 2020). All the points made can be illustrated many times over from other sources too, and I refer to some of the more significant. I address first the general framework within which the pandemic has been approached, and second some further specific aspects of the manner in which labour and the new world of work have been addressed.

From the start the two organisations responded strategically to the pandemic, in accordance with their established analytical frameworks and long-term goals. Each saw opportunities for advancing some aspects of their project, but quickly came to realise that it also presented very considerable threats, and tailored their response accordingly. Notably, each was emphatic that the way forward was to redouble efforts to drive the development of the world economy forward on liberal lines: from the start, in both cases, the goal of a global economy marked at all levels by competitiveness was kept to the fore, along with the insistence that it would have to include the world's poor as potentially productive workers, and incorporate policies aimed at addressing climate change and sustainability.

'Building Back Better' for a Resilient and Inclusive Recovery

In the early months of the pandemic, both organisations were primarily concerned with assessing the possible scale of the crisis, and estimating its economic impact. While their immediate focus was on the need for support for individuals, households, and firms, they cautioned that it was imperative to limit any adverse consequences for growth and competitiveness. As far as possible, relief should be consistent with long-term goals, and where short-term measures compromised these goals, they should be tightly controlled and curtailed as quickly as possible. The OECD's *Supporting People and Companies to Deal with the COVID-19 Virus: Options for an Immediate Employment and Social Policy Response* (March 2020) warned that containment measures would themselves have economic costs, and tied its advice to key aspects of its strategic agenda, recommending teleworking and flexible hours, the extension of paid sick leave and unemployment benefit to non-standard workers including the self-employed, and the provision of online training for workers temporarily laid off (OECD 2020d). While accepting the need to secure jobs and incomes, it warned that the challenge for policy makers was 'to strike the right balance between ensuring adequate take-up and maintaining cost-effectiveness, i.e. limit the extent to which jobs that would have been preserved anyway or are unviable even in the long-term are unduly subsidised': if restrictions on dismissals were not rapidly lifted once the epidemic was over, they might inhibit restructuring and slow the recovery, with some workers 'locked in unviable companies instead of being taken care of by public employment services that could offer re-training and other support' (OECD 2020d, 8, 9). Following up in April 2020, it warned that government support should be 'transparent, time-limited, proportionate, and non-discriminatory', and targeted at 'those companies and sectors that experience the most disruption as a direct result of the pandemic, with a view to avoiding windfall benefits or rescuing firms that would also have failed absent the pandemic'. This would 'help minimise the risk that stimulus spawns a new cohort of corporate zombies or national champions that could restrict competition, dampen domestic productivity growth, distort international markets, and impede the economic recovery and, in some cases, aggravate economic disparities' (OECD 2020c, 1). 'Competition policy will be crucial in building the recovery', OECD Secretary-General Angel Gurría reiterated at the OECD Competition Committee Round Table on Competition Policy in Times of COVID-19, held on 15 June 2020, pledging that the OECD would 'continue working with competition authorities and governments to build the post-COVID-19 world in a fairer, more inclusive and sustainable manner, so that together we can "build back better"' (OECD 2020e, 4).

The World Bank's *Protecting People and Economies* (May 2020) similarly recognised the immediate need to protect the vulnerable, noting that the relative paucity of government resources and the high level of informality across the economy in the developing world made this difficult. While a 'blanket' approach might at first be necessary, though, it could create perverse incentives. Measures to support jobs and firms should be 'time bound and transparent to avoid perverse incentives and longer-run market distortions', and in general 'policy choices should not only offset the immediate negative impact, but also create foundations for productivity-driven growth during the recovery period by seeking to minimize distortions and disincentives that can hamper recovery efforts' (World Bank 2020d, 42–3). In June, a substantial COVID-19 Crisis Response Approach Paper, *Saving Lives, Scaling-up Impact and Getting Back on Track*, identified three stages, relief, restructuring, and resilient recovery, the third of which entailed 'strengthening policies, institutions and investments for resilient, inclusive and sustainable recovery by Rebuilding Better'. This meant 'avoiding early policy mistakes, such as those that treat private business poorly (e.g. delaying payment to government suppliers, defaulting on independent power producers, debt moratoriums, continuation of subsidies and support to old technologies) which may permanently destroy viable enterprises, or limit potential competitiveness of new ones, and will deter future private investment' (World Bank 2020c, viii).

The OECD's Chief Economist, Laurence Boone, introduced the June 2020 *Economic Outlook* with the view that governments could provide safety nets to allow people and firms to adjust, 'but cannot uphold private sector activity, employment and wages for a prolonged period': 'Capital and workers from impaired sectors and businesses will have to move towards expanding ones', making the OECD's previous calls for a rise in public investment in digital and green technologies to promote long-term sustainable growth all the more urgent (OECD 2020g, 8). The main body of the report called for a 'renewed effort to implement reforms that strengthen productivity and employment growth in an inclusive way, and foster the reallocation of resources across sectors', warning that global efficiency and income would be harmed if businesses were led to diminish their supply chains and reduce inputs from efficient but distant suppliers (OECD 2020g, 14). A key challenge would be 'to find ways of identifying and supporting viable jobs and companies in the near term whilst allowing sufficient flexibility for necessary resource allocation to occur across sectors to minimise long-term scarring and restore productivity growth': 'Gradually raising the financial contributions from employers in [support] schemes could provide one way of identifying businesses who expect to remain viable for an extended period', while in the medium term 'reforms to spur business dynamism, addressing infrastructure shortages, and reducing policy uncertainty about the longer-term challenges from climate change, digitalisation and globalisation, would also strengthen incentives for businesses to invest and improve the prospects for sustainable gains in living standards' (OECD 2020g, 32–3). Efforts to support recovery should include effective incentives for firms to invest in energy-efficient technologies, and international supply chains that were under strain should be protected and improved:

> Their resilience should be stress tested on a regular basis to identify particular weaknesses and ensured by companies and governments through the development of strategic stocks and upstream agreements for the reconversion of assembly lines during critical times. Investment policies should foster the broader adoption of digital infrastructure and transport facilitation to help bridge distances and reduce trade costs along production chains, and resolve disruptions in face-to-face processes. Governments can support businesses in upgrading their industrial strategies through regulatory flexibility that helps promote innovation and supply diversification, and through extension of credit support programmes designed to improve the efficiency of logistics.   (OECD 2020g, 54)

The June 2020 *Economic Outlook* also noted that the effectiveness of fiscal stimulus and the need for specific measures would change over time, 'increasing trade-off between the need to support the economy, the need to foster the reallocation of resources to sectors with better long-term prospects, and fiscal costs' (OECD 2020g, 49). The December edition opened with a reference to brighter prospects as vaccines were beginning to come on line, and a clear message from Boone: the three priorities for policy makers were investing in essential goods and services such as education, health, physical, and digital infrastructure; decisive actions to reverse durably the rise in poverty and income inequality; and international cooperation. In particular, investment was urgent in digital infrastructure and skills, and in social support systems, to reach 'vulnerable groups outside the usual welfare system who have not been eligible for the additional help provided so far, for their own benefit and the benefit of society as a whole' (OECD 2020h, 8–9). The main report first noted the need for continued fiscal policy support 'as long as containment measures limit economic activity, and also subsequently to help restore sustainable economic growth', then encapsulated its core message with economy and precision:

> Exceptional crisis-related policies need to be increasingly focused on supporting viable companies, and accompanied by structural reforms that help to raise opportunities for displaced workers and vulnerable people, strengthen economic dynamism and mitigate climate change. Together, these can help foster the reallocation of labour and capital resources towards sectors and activities with sustainable growth potential, raising living standards for everyone. (OECD 2020h, 13)

In short, the crisis was an opportunity to allow less viable firms to go out of business. The subsequent section on policy requirements repeated the message, in a section whose heading is self-explanatory: 'Structural reform and better targeted support for companies and workers are needed to ensure a sustainable and inclusive recovery' (OECD 2020h, 49–55). Referencing the 2019 issues of *Employment Outlook* and *Going for Growth*, along with the comprehensive 2016 review of recessions since the 1970s (Caldera-Sánchez et al. 2016) and half a dozen papers from the *Responses to Coronavirus (COVID-19) Series* on topics ranging from skills and online learning to green recovery, it ran once again through the full range of its reform programme, focused as always on improving productivity through innovation and institutional reform.

Across the Atlantic, World Bank president David Malpass's foreword to the Bank's June 2020 issue of *Global Economic Prospects* placed the informal sector and low productivity front and centre, announcing at the start that for many emerging and developing countries 'effective financial support and mitigation measures are particularly hard to achieve because a substantial share of employment is in informal sectors', and highlighting the 'importance of allowing an orderly allocation of new capital towards sectors that are productive in the new post-pandemic structures that emerge': 'To succeed in this, countries will need reforms that allow capital and labour to adjust relatively fast—by speeding the resolution of disputes, reducing regulatory barriers, and reforming the costly subsidies, monopolies and protected state-owned enterprises that have slowed development' (World Bank 2020e, xiii–xiv). It then referenced 'systems that can build and retain more human and physical capital', 'the post-pandemic need for new types of jobs, businesses and governance systems', the need for faster advances in digital connectivity, to take advantage of the heightened value of 'teleworking capabilities, digital information, and broad connectivity', and the transformative role of digital financial services in 'allowing new entrants into the economy and making it easier for governments to provide rapidly expandable, needs-based cash transfers' (World Bank 2020e, xiv). Echoing the OECD's reference to 'scarring', the main body of the report addressed the 'lasting scars' of the COVID-19 pandemic and their potential to do long-term harm to growth and labour productivity, returning to the vulnerability that arose from high levels of informality in a six-page highlighted 'box', 'How does informality aggravate the impact of COVID-19?', prepared by Shu Yu, one of the many contributors to the 2019 analysis mentioned at the beginning of this chapter (World Bank 2019, 129–95). The answer given was familiar: 'Informality is associated with underdevelopment in a wide range of areas, such as widespread poverty, lack of access to financial systems, deficient public health and medical resources, and weak social safety nets' (World Bank 2020e, Box 1.4, 36). Governments were advised to consider untargeted and unconditional support in the first instance, and to expand existing safety nets to provide temporary relief, but also to utilise flexible platforms and technologies to reach informal workers, and to facilitate access to finance for informal firms. Later, the report addressed the danger that the deep recessions triggered by the pandemic would leave 'lasting scars through multiple channels, including lower investment; erosion of the human capital of the unemployed; and a retreat from global trade and supply linkages'. In other words, the pandemic threatened the central elements of the model that the Bank had pursued for the world economy since the 1970s. The expectation that the pandemic would 'exacerbate the multi-decade slowdown in potential output growth and productivity growth' highlighted 'the need to forcefully undertake comprehensive reform programs to improve the fundamental drivers of economic growth' (World Bank 2020e, 134).

Malpass again set the tone in the January 2021 edition of *Global Economic Prospects*:

> Governments, households, and firms all need to embrace a changed economic landscape. While protecting the most vulnerable, successful policies will be needed that allow capital, labor, skills, and innovation to shift to new purposes in order to build a greener, stronger post-COVID economic environment.... Investing in green infrastructure projects, phasing out fossil fuel subsidies, and offering incentives for environmentally sustainable technologies can buttress long-term growth, lower carbon output, create jobs, and help adapt to the effects of climate change. (World Bank 2021, xv)

His foreword ended on a positive note: 'We should seize the opportunity to lay the foundations for a durable, equitable, and sustainable global economy.' But the Executive Summary took a more sombre tone, suggesting that 'unless there are substantial and effective reforms, the global economy is heading for a decade of disappointing growth outcomes' (World Bank 2020e, xviii). This was the theme of a substantial chapter in the *Outlook*, and it signalled a shift, providing the clearest evidence so far of the level of threat the Bank perceived to the whole model of expansive global capitalism to which it was committed. What could be presented as exploiting a favourable opportunity might easily morph into struggling to stave off a catastrophe.

The global outlook in the first chapter suggested that the pandemic was 'expected to inflict lasting scars that push activity and income well below their pre-pandemic trend for a prolonged period' (World Bank 2020e, 3). It went on to identify a host of specific concerns that went beyond the issue of deep recession followed by slower growth to touch on fundamental components of the politics of global competitiveness. Not only was debt building up, but global value chains were disrupted by border closures and supply disruptions, and travel restrictions had thrown international tourism into virtual ruin. Aspirations to increase the acquisition of skills and engagement with the labour market were particularly at risk. Longer periods of unemployment might discourage workers from remaining in the labour force, 'which could appreciably erode skills given steep job losses'; school closures could reduce learning-adjusted years of education by as much as a full year, which 'combined with deskilling due to prolonged unemployment, will likely lower future earnings and dent human capital' (World Bank 2020e, 23); as many as 100 million people might be forced back into extreme poverty, while inequality would worsen as the most vulnerable had the least access to infrastructure and technology that might allow them to adapt; low interest rates following on from the global recession were in some ways problematic, as they might 'allow otherwise unviable firms to survive, crowding out the more dynamic firms that drive productivity growth'. At the same time they eroded bank profitability, undermined capital buffers, and set the stage for bank failures, while waves of bankruptcies could still not be ruled out; worse, the severity of the shock might cause behavioural changes as individuals and businesses became more risk-averse. This could lead to 'waning global integration', exacerbating trends already under way, fragmenting global links and lowering productivity. Civil and social unrest could rise, geopolitical risks would be heightened as cooperation faltered, and there remained an ever-present threat of further disruptions from natural disasters and weather-related events, threatening food security in low-income countries in particular in circumstances where it was estimated that the number of people facing food crises had more than doubled over 2020 (World Bank 2020e, 33–8, 44, 51–2).

This was the background to a chapter on the prospect of a 'decade of disappointments'—a novel attempt to model potential developments over a whole decade that was again the spur to a further insistence on the need for the 'comprehensive policy effort' already sufficiently set out above to obviate repetition. It estimated that without effective policy action or the emergence of unforeseen technological advances, anticipated annual average potential growth output, already expected to slow by 0.4 per cent globally and 1 per cent in emerging markets and developing economies before the pandemic, would fall by a further 0.3 and 0.6 per cent respectively (World Bank 2020e, 117). As a consequence, gains made over previous years would be lost. As regarded labour, for example: 'While job losses have been severe overall, COVID-19 has hit the services sector, which tend to have high female employment shares, particularly hard.... If steep employment losses in these sectors persist, they may eventually cause female workers to exit the labor force entirely, lowering potential output' (World Bank 2020e, 137). The comprehensive review of growth-enhancing policies it offers reproduces faithfully every aspect of the agenda on which the Bank doubled down in response to the global financial crisis, revealing that its confidence in the rightness of its agenda is undiminished. What is new, though, is the wavering of its confidence in the prospect of carrying the reform programme through. Even on its best estimates, the adoption of 'ambitious, but not unprecedented, reforms could stem, although not reverse, the potential growth slowdown projected over the 2020s'. But '[w]hile lasting economic damage is the most likely outcome of the pandemic, a scenario involving better growth outcomes cannot be ruled out' (World Bank 2020e, 148–9). On this account, the fortunes of the Bank's reform programme are hanging by a thread. Rather than an opportunity to be exploited, the Bank is looking at a disaster to be averted.

COVID-19 and the New World of Work

In their quest to create a productive global working class ready and willing to serve the needs of capital, the OECD has sought to reach the jobless and under-employed, and bring all workers under a uniform regulatory regime, while the World Bank has sought to transform the informal sector, and to endow workers with levels of health, education and skills that make them productive for capital. These long-running complementary projects were seriously threatened by the COVID-19 pandemic, as both institutions were acutely aware. In this area in particular the notion of seizing on the opportunity provided by the crisis threatens to flip over to striving to avoid disaster.

The OECD's June 2020 *Economic Outlook* noted that although unemployment had been at a fifty-year low in the OECD countries at the end of 2019, it was expected to rise to the highest level for 25 years. It identified an urgent need for 'renewed and well-targeted structural policy reforms in all economies': 'active labour market programmes and enhanced vocational education and training are needed to create opportunities for all, facilitate possible job reallocation after the removal of containment measures, and prevent the erosion of human capital' (OECD 2020g, 31–2). It included as an annex a paper on non-standard work from its *Policy Responses to COVID-19 Series* (OECD 2020a): this noted that non-standard or 'informal' workers accounted for around 40 per cent of the OECD-country workforce, ran through the disadvantages they faced in terms of social protection, and suggested that looking forward, countries should 'consider enhancing social protection schemes for non-standard workers', in order to 'reduce labour market segmentation and equalities' (OECD 2020h, 102). As some job losses were likely to occur over the medium term, as changes in the labour market might 'require workers to relocate from declining to expanding sectors and new jobs, potentially digitally-intensive jobs or jobs in the "gig economy"', it reiterated the need for effective active labour market policies and requalification schemes along with adequate income support to help job search for all workers, along with the development of new digitally delivered training programmes, and infrastructural investment to encourage remote work, more permanent social protection schemes, and 'the development of portable social benefits systems that move with workers' (OECD 2020h, 112). A companion paper on flattening the unemployment curve (OECD 2020b) was also incorporated, outlining approaches to preserving jobs that are viable in the medium term while allowing workers in distressed firms and industries to move to those with better growth prospects (OECD 2020h, 120–4).

These themes were much more prominent in the *Employment Outlook* published in July 2020 with the sub-title 'Worker Security and the COVID-19 Crisis', which was wholly focused on the reform of labour regulation to foster the transformation of employment through the re-building of a 'better, more robust, and inclusive labour market' (OECD 2020f, 12). Stefano Scarpetta's editorial ('From Recovery to Resilience after COVID-19') may stand in here for reasons of space for the document as a whole (which runs to 338 pages of detailed analysis). It homed straight in on workers in non-standard jobs, and went on to argue for better targeted support measures 'to ensure that those in need really get help, while fostering the incentives to go back to work for those who can'; 'stricter limits on the duration of subsidies and incentives to look for work, combine temporary secondary jobs and short-term subsidies, and take up training'; and a 'mutual benefits' approach in which firms in receipt of support in turn support efforts to help the unemployed return to work, boost employees' skills and ensure that nobody is left behind in a recovery, and individuals in receipt of support 'take active steps to search for work or improve their employability'. It then addressed the issue of gaps in social protection for non-standard workers, and argued that such workers 'need to be able to build up rights to the types of out-of-work support that are already available to standard employees' through sustainable and effectively targeted programmes: 'Making minimum-income protection more responsive, through timely reassessment of entitlements in the face of rapidly changing circumstances, remains an urgent policy priority'; companies 'should be encouraged to provide opportunities for work experience by hiring new graduates or offering apprenticeships, internship or work-related training'; 'A comprehensive recovery plan should include the expansion of cost-effective active labour market measures – such as counselling, job-search assistance, entrepreneurship programmes. Extending support to vocational education and training (VET) would also be crucial' (OECD 2020f, 13–16). As this suggests, the OECD was more than ever concerned about the possibility of losing touch with a generation of young workers, and more than ever committed to making the labour market homogenous on lines that made the non-standard worker the norm; and Scarpetta closed by referring policy makers to the OECD Jobs Strategy framework re-issued two years earlier, and declaring: 'It is not the time to rebuild the old. It is time to build better' (OECD 2020f, 17). The executive summary that followed echoed the same arguments, and analytical chapters discussed the trajectory that was taking the world 'from a health to a jobs crisis', the appropriate balance between income security and work incentives, with non-standard workers as the point of reference, trends in employment protection legislation, the challenges facing middle-skill workers, and the importance of vocational education and training.

The *Employment Outlook* was wholly focused on taking advantage of the pandemic to press for a thorough transformation of labour markets across the OECD, and the December issue of the *Economic Outlook* reinforced the same message, calling for crisis-related support measures to be 'flexible and state-contingent, evolving as the recovery progresses to support workers and ensure assistance is focused on viable companies': exceptional crisis-related policies should be 'accompanied by the structural reforms most likely to raise opportunities for displaced workers and improve economic dynamism, fostering the reallocation of labour and capital resources towards sectors and activities that strengthen growth, enhance resilience and contribute to environmental sustainability'; 'a lasting shift to remote working and the increasing digital delivery of services, including e-commerce, could... change the mix of jobs available and the location of many workplaces'; and in general, the policies put in place to foster the recovery were 'an opportunity to address... old and new challenges if economic stimulus measures and recovery plans combine an emphasis on restoring growth and creating jobs with the achievement of environmental goals'; support for employers should be fine-tuned to weed out jobs that are not viable, while investment in active labour market programmes and reforms to reduce barriers to labour mobility, along with enhanced vocational education and training 'to create new opportunities for displaced workers, lower-skilled workers, and those on reduced working hours' was a priority; and '[l]onger-lasting improvements in social safety nets may also be needed to prevent inequalities of income and opportunities from widening further' (OECD 2020h, 39, 49–50). Right on cue, the OECD returned to its principal policy objective—the need to reform social protection to enforce a single uniform regime:

At the same time, steps will have to be taken to move gradually from unconditional support to more targeted assistance that helps preserve incentives for work and job search. For instance, the gap between short-time work benefits and regular employment benefits may need to be better aligned in advanced economies with job retention schemes, especially in countries with particularly generous short-term work benefits.   (OECD 2020h, 51)

The OECD's suggestion that a 'renewed effort to implement reforms that strengthen productivity and employment growth in an inclusive way, and foster the reallocation of resources across sectors, is needed to counter... negative crisis-related shocks' (OECD 2020g, 14) was matched by the World Bank's position, set out in *Adaptive Social Protection* (September 2020) that in the wake of disaster, changes must be made so that individuals or communities are enabled to 'bounce back better', by which it means switch to 'higher-risk, higher-return' or 'more productive and resilient' livelihoods (Bowen et al. 2020, 5, 7, 16). However, the impact of the COVID-19 pandemic was judged to be particularly adverse to the Bank's project of transforming the informal economy in the developing world. This was the central message of the 2020 *Update* to the Human Capital Index launched in 2018, which began with the estimate that worldwide, on the eve of the COVID-19 crisis, 'the average newborn could only be expected to achieve 56 percent of her potential productivity as a future worker'. With so much still to be done, it warned that its initial simulations suggested that

school closures combined with family hardship are significantly affecting the accumulation of human capital for a generation of school-age children. The impacts appear comparable in magnitude to the gains many countries achieved during the previous decade, suggesting that the pandemic may roll back many years' worth of human-capital progress. In parallel, COVID-19's disruption of health services, losses in income, and worsened nutrition are expected to increase child mortality and stunting, with effects that will be felt for decades to come.   (World Bank 2020a, ix–x)

Although the Bank was quick to insist that ambitious, evidence-driven policy measures in health, education, and social protection could 'pave the way for today's children to surpass the human-capital achievements and quality of life of the generations that preceded them' (World Bank 2020a, xi), it was clear from its own analysis that the circumstances for such an initiative could not be less propitious. Every relevant indicator, from the components of the HCI itself to the newly introduced measures of basic and full utilisation of labour, was negatively affected, and governments around the developing world were faced with an adverse situation of falling revenues, rising costs, and mounting debt. The main body of the report documented this extensively, drawing out in particular the impact of the pandemic on *behaviour*. Especially in the poorest and most vulnerable households, where choices were forced when crisis struck, the impacts of the closure of schools and the sharp drop in economic activity were initially severe and intensified over the long term by the behavioural changes they induced: the poorest families were least able to support their children's education when schools closed, and were most likely to miss the contribution of school feeding programmes to nutritional status; and they would find it harder 'to justify sending older children back to school after a forced interruption, especially if households are under financial stress' (World Bank 2020a, 70). In the meantime, as the Bank recognised, the ideal of a versatile, flexible, and mobile workforce was still a long way off:

> Workers who have longer tenures in a company, if dismissed, are likely to face a considerable erosion of skills, as many skills they have accumulated may be particular to that employer. If these workers find employment in the future, and their new job requires different skills, they are likely to experience a considerable wage penalty. (World Bank 2020a, 73)

The COVID-19 pandemic represented a significant setback to the OECD/World Bank project overall, and as much a reality check as an opportunity to advance. It did afford, albeit fortuitously, an opportunity to assess the status of the project, sixty years on from the founding of the OECD.

Conclusion

Despite successive crises, despite the ravages of austerity, despite growing inequality, despite the apparently inexorable shift of the centre of gravity of the world market away from the 'West', despite the looming threat of global warming, and, it transpires, despite global pandemic, the OECD and the World Bank have never shifted their policy stance. Both organisations remain firm in their commitment to the continued development of capitalism on a global scale, embracing in doing so the verdict of the first Secretary-General of the OECD, Thorkil Kristensen, that there is no protection against the fundamental forces of history. The world economy on the eve of the global pandemic of COVID-19 was one of global competition, subject to rapid and disruptive multi-faceted technological and social change, in which protections from the market were few, and expectations of generalised prosperity had faded. But the orientation of the OECD and the World Bank towards developing the world market at every opportunity goes back to their roots, and defines them as institutions, and they have doubled down on it again in the face of the pandemic. They have always anticipated that periodic crises will occur, and that costs of adjustment will be high, in particular for unskilled workers in the advanced economies, so they urge governments to manage expectations downwards, and steer workers towards accepting periodic spells of unemployment, and constantly renewing and up-grading their marketable skills. As regards the emerging and developing areas of the world, their overwhelming preoccupation has been and remains with the huge distance at which they stand from the full incorporation of their labour force into the global economy as productive workers. It is indicative of the logic of their position that they express no concern at all about the growing dominance of Asia, and particularly of China, in the global economy, and the corresponding relative decline of the 'West', and particularly of Western Europe; and they are unmoved by practically universally declining fertility rates, and increasingly widespread trends towards the postponement or renunciation of motherhood. To cite the founding articles of the World Bank, they remain committed to the development of productive facilities and resources in less developed countries, while as regards present and future populations, they are still of the view that if anything there are too many people, and that, as the Human Capital Index signals, the imperative challenge is to maximise the health, education, and productive employment of such children as are born. So while neither the transformation of the world market over the last fifty years nor the related changes in demography, fertility, and family and household structure that have transformed the social landscape have been brought about directly by their actions, being the product of much deeper material forces, they continue to promote both without reservations.

All of this vindicates the ability of Marx's critique of political economy to illuminate the logic of their action. The drive of capital to 'subjugate every moment of production itself to exchange and to suspend the production of direct use values not entering into exchange' (Marx 1973, 408) dominates every aspect of life; the tendency for the 'varied, apparently unconnected and petrified forms of the social production process' everywhere to be 'dissolved into conscious and planned applications of natural science, divided up systematically in accordance with the particular useful effect aimed at in each case' (Marx 1976, 616–17) which is its concrete manifestation, is transforming even the production of life itself; and the increasing pressure on workers everywhere, under the compulsion of the 'general law of social production', to practise 'variation of labour, fluidity of functions, and mobility... in all directions', and to present themselves as 'totally developed' and 'absolutely available for the different kinds of labour required of them' (Marx 1976, 617–18) is brought to bear on everyone, regardless of gender, ethnicity, domestic circumstance or geographic location; 'the growth, accumulation and concentration of capital' still 'results in an uninterrupted division of labour, and in the application of new and the perfecting of old machinery precipitately and on an ever more gigantic scale'; and the OECD and the World Bank applaud all these developments. But the implications are still as they were for Marx. It is not individuals who are set free by free competition, but capital that is set free: 'The more productive capital grows, the more the division of labour and the application of machinery expands. The more the division of labour and the application of machinery expands, the more competition among the workers expands and the more their wages contract' (Marx 2010b, 225, 227). This is the politics of global competitiveness.

Bibliography

Ahuja, Anjana, Nicolle Liu, and Louise Lucas. 2018. 'Mastering Evolution: The World's First Gene-Edited Babies'. *Financial Times*, 30 November.

Andrews, Dan, Peter Gal, and William Witheridge. 2018. 'A Genie in a Bottle? Globalisation, Competition, and Inflation'. *OECD Economics Department Working Papers 1462*, ECO/WKP (2018)10 (20 March).

Arat-Koç, Sedef. 2018. 'Migrant and Domestic and Care Workers: Unfree Labour, Crises of Social Reproduction and the Unsustainability of Life under "Vagabond Capitalism"'. In *Handbook on the International Political Economy of Gender*, edited by Juanita Elias and Adrienne Roberts, pp. 411–26. Cheltenham: Edward Elgar.

Arias, Omar S., and Carolina Sánchez-Páramo (eds). 2014. *Back to Work: Growing with Jobs in Europe and Central Asia*. Washington DC: World Bank.

Armstrong, Pat, and Hugh Armstrong. 1983. 'Beyond Sexless Class and Classless Sex: Towards Feminist Marxism'. *Studies in Political Economy 10*, pp. 7–43.

Bailey, Alison. 2011. 'Reconceiving Surrogacy: Toward a Reproductive Justice Account of Indian Surrogacy'. *Hypatia 26*(4), pp. 715–41.

Baker, Philip, and Sharon Friel. 2016. 'Food Systems Transformations, Ultra-processed Food Markets and the Nutrition Transition in Asia', *Globalization and Health 12*(80), pp. 1–15.

Bakker, Isabella. 2020. 'Variegated Social Reproduction in Neoliberal Times: Mainstream Silences, Feminist Interventions. *NORA—Nordic Journal of Feminist and Gender Research 28*(2), pp. 167–72.

Bamber, Penny, and Danny Hamrick. 2019. *Gender Dynamics and Upgrading in Global Value Chains: The Case of Medical Devices*. Durham, North Carolina: Duke Global Value Chains Center.

Barbezat, Daniel. 1997. 'The Marshall Plan and the Origin of the OEEC'. In *Explorations in OEEC History*, edited by Richard T. Griffiths, pp. 33–48. Paris: OECD.

Barrett, Michèle. 2014 [1980]. *Women's Oppression Today: The Marxist/Feminist Encounter*. London: Verso.

Beechey, Veronica. 1979. 'On Patriarchy'. *Feminist Review 3*, pp. 66–82.

Benston, Margaret. 2019 [1969]. 'The Political Economy of Women's Liberation'. *Monthly Review 71*(4), 13–27.

Berg, Gunhild, and Bilal Zia. 2013. 'Harnessing Emotional Connections to Improve Financial Decisions: Evaluating the Impact of Financial Education in Mainstream Media'. *World Bank Policy Research Working Paper 6407*. Washington DC: World Bank.

Beroud, Samuel. 2017. '"Positive Adjustments": The Emergence of Supply-Side Economics in the OECD and G7, 1970–1984'. In *The OECD and the International Political Economy since 1948*, edited by Matthieu Leimgruber and Matthias Schmelzer, pp. 233–58. London: Palgrave Macmillan.

Bowen, Thomas, Carlo del Ninno, Colin Andrews, Sarah Coll-Black, Ugo Gentilini, Kelly Johnson, Yasuhiro Kawasoe, Adea Kryeziu, Barry Maher, and Asha Williams. 2020. *Adaptive Social Protection: Building Resilience to Shocks*. Washington DC: World Bank.

Breman, Jan, and Marcel van der Linden. 2014. 'Informalizing the Economy: The Return of the Social Question at a Global Level'. *Development and Change* 45(5), pp. 920–40.

Browne, James, Herwig Immervoll, Rodrigo Fernandez, Dirk Neumann, Daniele Pacifico, and Céline Thévenot. 2018a. 'Faces of Joblessness in Estonia: A People-Centred Perspective on Employment Barriers and Policies'. *OECD Social, Employment and Migration Working Papers 206*.

Browne, James, Herwig Immervoll, Rodrigo Fernandez, Dirk Neumann, Daniele Pacifico, and Céline Thévenot. 2018b. 'Faces of Joblessness in Ireland: A People-Centred Perspective on Employment Barriers and Policies'. *OECD Social, Employment and Migration Working Papers 209*.

Bulletti, Carlo, Antonio Palagiano, Caterina Pace, Angelica Cerni, Andrea Borini, and Dominique de Ziegler. 2011. 'The Artificial Womb'. *Annals of the New York Academy of Science 1221*, pp. 124–8.

Bürgi, Regula, and Daniel Tröhler. 2018. 'Producing the "Right Kind of People": The OECD Education Indicators in the 1960s'. In *Education by the Numbers and the Making of Society: The Expertise of International Assessments*, edited by Sverker Lindblad, Daniel Pettersson, and Thomas S. Popkevitz, pp. 75–91. Abingdon and New York: Routledge.

Caldera-Sánchez, Aida, Alain de Serres, Filippo Gori, Mikkel Hermansen, and Oliver Röhn. 2016. 'Strengthening Economic Resilience: Insights from the Post-1970 Record of Severe Recessions and Financial Crises'. *OECD Economic Policy Paper 20*, December. Paris: OECD.

Cammack, Paul. 1997. *Capitalism and Democracy in the Third World: The Doctrine for Political Development*. London and Washington: Cassell/Leicester University Press.

Cammack, Paul. 2001. 'Making the Poor Work for Globalisation?'. *New Political Economy* 6(3), pp. 97–408.

Cammack, Paul. 2002. 'Attacking the Poor'. *New Left Review 13* (Series 2), pp. 125–34.

Cammack, Paul. 2003. 'The Governance of Global Capitalism: A New Materialist Perspective'. *Historical Materialism 11*(2), pp. 37–59.

Cammack, Paul. 2004. 'What the World Bank Means by Poverty Reduction, and Why It Matters'. *New Political Economy 9*(2), pp. 189–211.

Cammack, Paul. 2006. 'The Politics of Global Competitiveness'. *Papers in the Politics of Global Competitiveness 1*. Manchester Metropolitan University.

Cammack, Paul. 2012. 'Risk, Social Protection and the World Market'. *Journal of Contemporary Asia 42*(3), pp. 359–77.

Camps, Miriam. 1975. *'First World' Relationships: the Role of the OECD*. Paris and New York: Atlantic Institute for International Affairs/Council on Foreign Relations.

Carroll, William K. 2010. *The Making of a Transnational Capitalist Class*. London: Zed Books.

Charnock, Greig, and Guido Starosta. 2016. 'Introduction: The New International Division of Labour and the Critique of Political Economy Today'. In *The New International Division of Labour: Global Transformation and Uneven Development*, edited by Greig Charnock and Guido Starosta, pp. 1–22. London: Palgrave Macmillan.

Chin, Jeannette, Vic Callaghan, and Somaya Ben Allouch. 2019. 'The Internet-of-Things: Reflections on the Past, Present and Future from a User-Centered and Smart Environment Perspective'. *Journal of Ambient Intelligence and Smart Environments 11*(1), pp. 45–69.

Clavin, Patricia. 2013. *Securing the World Economy: The Reinvention of the League of Nations, 1920–1946*. Oxford: Oxford University Press.

Clifton, Judith, and Daniel Díaz-Fuentes. 2011. 'The OECD and Phases in the International Political Economy, 1961–2011'. *Review of International Political Economy* 18(5), pp. 552–69.

Cox, Robert W. 1981. 'Social Forces, States and World Orders: Beyond International Relations Theory'. *Millennium* 10(2), pp. 126–55.

Cox, Robert W. 1983. 'Gramsci, Hegemony and International Relations: An Essay in Method'. *Millennium* 12(2), pp. 162–75.

Cox, Robert W. 1987. *Production, Power, and World Order: Social Forces in the Making of World History*. New York: Columbia University Press.

Cumings, Bruce. 1999. 'The Asian Crisis, Democracy, and the End of "Late" Development'. In *The Politics of the Asian Financial Crisis*, edited by T. J. Pempel, pp. 17–44. Ithaca: Cornell University Press.

DAC (OECD). 1996. *Shaping the Twenty First Century: The Contribution of Development Cooperation*. Paris: OECD.

Dalla Costa, Mariarosa. 2019 [1972]. 'Women and the Subversion of the Community'. In *Women and the Subversion of the Community: A Mariarosa Dalla Costa Reader*, edited by Camille Barbagallo, pp. 17–50. Oakland CA: PM Press.

Devlin, Hannah. 2017. 'Artificial Womb for Premature Babies Successful in Animal Trials'. *The Guardian*, 25 April.

Düll, Nicola, Céline Thévenot, Herwig Immervoll, James Browne, Rodrigo Fernandez, and Dirk Neumann. 2018. 'Faces of Joblessness in Portugal: A People-Centred Perspective on Employment Barriers and Policies'. *OECD Social, Employment and Migration Working Papers 210*.

Ellwood, David W. 1992. *Rebuilding Europe: Western Europe, America and Postwar Reconstruction*. London and New York: Longman.

Emmerij, Louis. 1989. *One World or Several?* Paris: OECD.

Engels, Friedrich. 2010 [1843]. 'Outlines of a Critique of Political Economy'. In *Marx and Engels, Collected Works*, Vol 3, pp. 418–43. London: Lawrence & Wishart.

Estevez-Abe, Margarita. 2015. 'The Outsourcing of House Cleaning and Low Skill Immigrant Workers'. *Social Politics* 22(2), pp. 147–69.

European Commission. 2010. *Europe 2020: A European Strategy for Smart, Sustainable and Inclusive Growth*. Brussels: European Commission.

European Commission. 2011. *Employment and Social Developments in Europe 2011*. Brussels: European Commission.

European Commission. 2012. *Employment and Social Developments in Europe 2012*. Brussels: European Commission.

European Commission. 2014. *Employment and Social Developments in Europe 2013*. Brussels: European Commission.

European Commission. 2017. *European Pillar of Social Rights*. Brussels: European Commission.

European Commission. 2018. *Employment and Social Developments in Europe 2018*. Brussels: European Commission.

Farole, Thomas, Claire Hollweg, and Deborah Winkler. 2018. 'Trade in Global Value Chains: An Assessment of Labor Market Implications'. *Jobs Working Papers 18*. Washington DC: World Bank.

Federici, Silvia. 2019. 'Social Reproduction Theory: History, Issues and Present Challenges'. *Radical Philosophy 2.04*, pp. 55–8.

Ferguson, Susan. 2020. *Women and Work: Feminism, Labour and Social Reproduction*. London: Pluto Press.

Fernandez, Rodrigo, Herwig Immervoll, Daniele Pacifico, and Céline Thévenot. 2016. 'Faces of Joblessness: Characterising Employment Barriers to Inform Policy'. *OECD Social, Employment and Migration Working Papers 192*.

Fernandez, Rodrigo, Herwig Immervoll, Daniele Pacifico, James Browne, Dirk Neumann, and Céline Thévenot. 2018. 'Faces of Joblessness in Spain: A People-Centred Perspective on Employment Barriers and Policies'. *OECD Social, Employment and Migration Working Papers 207*.

Fernandez-Stark, Karina, Vivian Couto, and Penny Bamber. 2019. *Industry 4.0 in Developing Countries: The Mine of the Future and the Role of Women*. Durham, North Carolina: Duke Global Value Chains Center.

Ferragina, Emanuele, and Martin Seeleib-Kaiser. 2015. 'Determinants of a Silent (R)evolution: Understanding the Expansion of Family Policy in Rich OECD Countries'. *Social Politics* 22(1), pp. 1–37.

Financial Times. 2016. 'Greencore to Acquire US Group Peacock Foods for $748m'. *Financial Times*, 14 November.

Firestone, Shulamith. 1970. *The Dialectics of Sex: The Case for Feminist Revolution*. New York: William Morrow and Co.

Fraser, Nancy. 2016. 'Contradictions of Capital and Care'. *New Left Review 100*, pp. 99–117.

Freedland, Mark. 2016. 'The Contract of Employment and the Paradoxes of Precarity'. *University of Oxford Legal Research Paper Series, 37*.

Gardiner, Jean. 1975. 'Women's Domestic Labour'. *New Left Review 89*, pp. 47–58.

Gentilini, Ugo. 2021. 'A Game Changer for Social Protection? Six Reflections on COVID-19 and the Future of Cash Transfers'. https://blogs.worldbank.org/developmenttalk/game-changer-social-protection-six-reflections-covid-19-and-future-cash-transfers (accessed 9 February 2021).

Gentilini, Ugo, Mohamed Almenfi, and Pamela Dale. 2020. *Social Protection and Jobs Responses to COVID-19: A Real-Time Review of Country Measures*. Washington DC: World Bank.

Gill, Stephen. 1990. *American Hegemony and the Trilateral Commission*. New York: Cambridge University Press.

Gill, Stephen. 1995. 'Globalisation, Market Civilisation, and Disciplinary Neoliberalism'. *Millennium 24*(3), pp. 399–423.

Gill, Stephen. 1998. 'New Constitutionalism, Democratisation and Global Political Economy'. *Pacifica Review 10*(1), pp. 23–38.

Gimenez, Martha E. 2019. *Marx, Women, and Capitalist Social Reproduction: Marxist Feminist Essays*. Leiden and Boston: Brill.

Gowan, Peter. 1999. *The Global Gamble: Washington's Faustian Bid for World Dominance*. London: Verso.

Griffiths, Richard T. (ed.). 1997. *Explorations in OEEC History*. Paris: OECD.

Hallegatte, Stephane, Jun Rentschler, and Brian Walsh. 2018. *Building Back Better: Achieving Resilience through Stronger, Faster, and More Inclusive Post-Disaster Reconstruction*. Washington DC: World Bank.

Hartmann, Heidi L. 1979. 'The Unhappy Marriage of Marxism and Feminism: Towards a More Progressive Union'. *Capital & Class 8*(1), pp. 1–33.

Harvey, David. 2003. *The New Imperialism*. Oxford: Oxford University Press.

Harvey, David. 2005. *A Brief History of Neoliberalism*. Oxford: Oxford University Press.

Henderson, Michael. 1981. 'The OECD as an Instrument of National Policy'. *International Journal 36*(4), pp. 793–814.

Hewitson, Gillian. 2014. 'The Commodified Womb and Neoliberal Families'. *Review of Radical Political Economics* 46(4), pp. 489–95.

Hill, Amelia. 2017. 'A World without Retirement'. *The Guardian*, 29 March.

Holman, Otto. 2001. 'The Enlargement of the European Union towards Central and Eastern Europe: The Role of Supranational and Transnational Actors'. In *Social Forces in the Making of the New Europe: The Restructuring of European Social Relations in the Global Political Economy*, edited by Adam David Morton and Andreas Bieler, pp. 161–84. Basingstoke: Palgrave.

Holzmann, Robert, and Stern Jorgensen. 2000. 'Social Risk Management: A New Conceptual Framework for Social Protection, and Beyond'. *Social Protection Discussion Paper, 0006*. Washington DC: World Bank.

Howarth, David, and Tal Sadeh. 2011. 'In the Vanguard of Globalization: The OECD and International Capital Liberalization'. *Review of International Political Economy* 18(5), pp. 622–45.

ILO. 2019. *World Employment Social Outlook: Trends 2019*. Geneva: ILO.

IMF. 2019. *World Economic Outlook: Global Manufacturing Downturn, Rising Trade Barriers*. Washington DC: IMF.

Immervoll, Herwig, and Mark Pearson. 2009. 'A Good Time for Making Work Pay? Taking Stock of In-Work Benefits and Related Measures across the OECD'. *OECD Social, Employment and Migration Working Papers 81*.

Inman, Mary. 1940. *In Woman's Defence*. Los Angeles: Committee to Organize the Advancement of Women.

Jackson, Peter, Helene Brembeck, Jonathan Everts, Maria Fuentes, Bente Halkier, Frej Daniel Hertz, Angela Meah, Valerie Viehoff, and Christine Wenzl. 2018. *Reframing Convenience Food*. London: Palgrave.

Jakiela, Pamela, and Owen Ozier. 2016. 'Does Africa Need a Rotten Kin Theorem? Experimental Evidence from Village Economies'. *Review of Economic Studies* 83(1), pp. 231–68.

Kalleberg, Arne L., and Kevin Hewison. 2013. 'Precarious Work and the Challenge for Asia'. *American Behavioral Scientist* 57(3), pp. 271–88.

Kristensen, Thorkil. 1963. 'Economic Relations between Europe and the Other Continents'. *OECD Observer 3*, pp. 14–18.

Kristensen, Thorkil. 1966. 'Problems Facing the Western World: Money, Trade and Food'. *OECD Observer 22*, pp. 3–7.

Lange, Elena Louisa. 2021. 'Gendercraft: Marxism-Feminism, Reproduction, and the Blind Spot of Money'. *Science & Society 85*(1), pp. 38–65.

Leerkes, Arjen. 2016. 'Back to the Poorhouse? Social Protection and Social Control of Unauthorised Immigrants in the Shadow of the Welfare State'. *Journal of European Social Policy* 26(2), pp. 140–54.

Leimgruber, Matthieu. 2012. 'The Embattled Standard-Bearer of Social Insurance and Its Challenger: The ILO, the OECD, and the "Crisis of the Welfare State", 1975-1985'. In *Globalizing Social Rights*, edited by Sandrine Kott and Joëlle Droux, pp. 293–309. Geneva: ILO.

Leimgruber, Matthieu, and Matthias Schmelzer. 2017a. 'Introduction: Writing Histories of the OECD'. In *The OECD and the International Political Economy Since 1948*, edited by Matthieu Leimgruber and Matthias Schmelzer, pp. 1–22. London: Palgrave Macmillan.

Leimgruber, Matthieu, and Matthias Schmelzer. 2017b. 'From the Marshall Plan to Global Governance: Historical Transformations of the OEEC/OECD, 1948 to Present'. In *The OECD and the International Political Economy since 1948*, edited by Matthieu Leimgruber and Matthias Schmelzer, pp. 23–61. London: Palgrave Macmillan.

Luxton, Meg. 2018. 'The Production of Life Itself: Gender, Social Reproduction, and IPE'. In *Handbook on the International Political Economy of Gender*, edited by Juanita Elias and Adrienne Roberts, pp. 37–49, Cheltenham: Edward Elgar.

Mahon, Rianne. 2011. 'The Jobs Strategy: From Neo- to Inclusive Liberalism?' *Review of International Political Economy 18*(5), pp. 570–91.

Mann, Catherine. 2014. 'Raising Global Growth: Why the G20 Is "Going Structural"'. *OECD Observer 300*, pp. 12–13.

Marcussen, Martin, and Jarle Trondal. 2011. 'The OECD Civil Servant: Caught between Scylla and Charybdis'. *Review of International Political Economy 18*(5), pp. 592–621.

Marx, Karl. 1973 [1857–8]. *Grundrisse: Introduction to the Critique of Political Economy*. London: Penguin/New Left Review.

Marx, Karl. 1976 [1867]. *Capital*, Volume 1. London: Pelican.

Marx, Karl. 2010a [1844]. 'Economic and Philosophic Manuscripts'. In *Marx and Engels, Collected Works*, Vol. 3, pp. 229–346. London: Lawrence & Wishart.

Marx, Karl. 2010b [1849]. 'Wage Labour and Capital'. In *Marx and Engels, Collected Works*, Vol. 9, pp. 197–228. London: Lawrence & Wishart.

Marx, Karl. 2010c [1861–3]. 'Economic Manuscript of 1861–63 (Continuation)'. In *Marx and Engels, Collected Works*, Vol. 32, pp. 7–543. London: Lawrence & Wishart.

Marx, Karl, and Friedrich Engels. 2010a [1845–6]. 'Critique of the German Ideology'. In *Marx and Engels, Collected Works*, Vol. 5, pp. 19–608. London: Lawrence & Wishart.

Marx, Karl, and Friedrich Engels. 2010b. 'Manifesto of the Communist Party'. In *Marx and Engels, Collected Works*, Vol. 6, pp. 477–519. London: Lawrence & Wishart.

Mazzucato, Mariana. 2020. 'Capitalism's Triple Crisis'. *Social Europe*. http://acdc2007.free.fr/mazzucato420.pdf.

McCarthy, Helen. 2020. *Double Lives: A History of Working Motherhood in Modern Britain*. London: Bloomsbury.

Mezzadri, Alessandra. 2019. 'On the Value of Social Reproduction'. *Radical Philosophy 2.04*, pp. 33–41.

Mezzadri, Alessandra. 2021. 'A Value Theory of Inclusion: Informal Labour, the Homeworker, and the Social Reproduction of Value. *Antipode 53*(4), pp. 1186–205.

Mies, Maria. 2014 [1986]. *Patriarchy and Accumulation on a World Scale: Women in the International Division of Labour* (2nd ed.). London: Zed Press.

Mirowski, Philip. 2013. *Never Let a Serious Crisis Go to Waste*. London: Verso.

Molyneux, Maxine. 1979. 'Beyond the Domestic Labour Debate'. *New Left Review 116*, pp. 3–27.

Monteiro, C. A., J. C. Moubarac, J. G. Cannon, S. W. Ng, and B. Popkin. 2013. 'Ultra-Processed Products Are Becoming Dominant in the Global Food System'. *Obesity Review 14 Supplement 2*, pp. 21–8.

Montgomerie, Johnna, and Daniela Tepe-Belfrage. 2017. 'Caring for Debts: How the Household Economy Exposes the Limits of Financialisation'. *Critical Sociology 43*(4–5), pp. 653–68.

Murphy, Craig N. 1994. *International Organization and Industrial Change: Global Governance since 1850*. Cambridge: Polity Press.

Newman, Susan, and Michal Nahman. 2020. 'Nurture Commodified? An Investigation into Commercial Human Milk Supply Chains'. *Review of International Political Economy*, DOI: 10.1080/09692290.2020.1864757, pp. 1–36.

Nunn, Alex, and Paul Beeckmans. 2015. 'The Political Economy of Competitiveness and Continuous Adjustment in EU Meta-Governance'. *International Journal of Public Administration 38*(12), pp. 926–39.

Nunn, Alex, and Daniela Tepe-Belfrage. 2017. 'Disciplinary Social Policy and the Failing Promise of the New Middle Classes: The Troubled Families Programme'. *Social Policy and Society* 16(1), pp. 119–29.

OECD. 1963. 'Twenty Nations Exchange Their Policy Ideas for Mutual Economic Benefit'. *OECD Observer 3*, pp. 3–7.

OECD. 1979. *The Impact of the Newly Industrialised Countries on Industry and Trade in Manufactures*. Paris: OECD.

OECD. 1994. *The OECD Jobs Study: Facts, Analysis, Strategies*. Paris: OECD.

OECD. 1995. *Linkages: OECD and Major Developing Economies*. Paris: OECD.

OECD. 1997a. 'Globalisation and Linkages: Macro-Structural Challenges and Opportunities'. *OECD Economic Studies, 28*.

OECD. 1997b. *The World in 2020: Towards a New Global Age*. Paris: OECD.

OECD. 2005. *Economic Policy Reforms: Going for Growth*. Paris: OECD.

OECD. 2006a. *Boosting Jobs and Incomes: Policy Lessons from Reassessing the OECD's Jobs Strategy*. Paris: OECD.

OECD. 2006b. *OECD Employment Outlook 2006*. Paris: OECD.

OECD. 2007a. *Annual Report 2007*. Paris: OECD.

OECD. 2007b. *Economic Policy Reforms: Going for Growth 2007*. Paris: OECD.

OECD. 2009. *Economic Policy Reforms: Going for Growth 2009*. Paris: OECD.

OECD. 2010a. *Economic Policy Reforms: Going for Growth 2010*. Paris: OECD.

OECD. 2010b. *OECD Economic Surveys: China*.

OECD. 2010c. *Perspectives on Global Development 2010: Shifting Wealth*. Paris: OECD.

OECD. 2010d. *Tackling Inequalities in Brazil, China, India and South Africa: The Role of Labour Market and Social Policies*. Paris: OECD.

OECD. 2010e. *Regulatory Reform for Recovery: Lessons from Implementation during Crises*. Paris: OECD.

OECD. 2012a. *Going for Growth 2012*. Paris: OECD.

OECD. 2012b. *Perspectives on Global Development 2012: Social Cohesion in a Shifting World*. Paris: OECD.

OECD. 2013. *Skills Outlook 2013: First Results from the Survey of Adult Skills*. Paris: OECD.

OECD. 2015a. *Aligning Policies for a Low-Carbon Economy*. Paris: OECD.

OECD. 2015b. *Skills Outlook 2015: Youth, Skills and Employability*. Paris: OECD.

OECD. 2017a. *Investing in Climate, Investing in Growth*. Paris: OECD.

OECD. 2017b. *The Next Production Revolution: Implications for Governments and Business*. Paris: OECD.

OECD. 2017c. *Skills Outlook 2017: Skills and Global Value Chains*. Paris: OECD.

OECD. 2018. *Good Jobs for All in a Changing World of Work: The OECD Jobs Strategy*. Paris: OECD.

OECD. 2019a. *OECD Employment Outlook 2019: The Future of Work*. Paris: OECD.

OECD. 2019b. *Economic Policy Reforms 2019: Going for Growth*. Paris: OECD.

OECD. 2020a. 'Distributional Risks Associated with Non-Standard Work: Stylised Facts and Policy Considerations'. *OECD Policy Responses to Coronavirus (COVID-19)*. Paris: OECD.

OECD. 2020b. 'Flattening the Unemployment Curve? Policies to Support Workers' Income and Promote a Speedy Labour Market Recovery'. *OECD Policy Responses to Coronavirus (COVID-19)*. Paris: OECD.

OECD. 2020c. 'Government Support and the COVID-19 Pandemic'. *OECD Policy Responses to Coronavirus (COVID-19)*. Paris: OECD.

OECD. 2020d. 'Supporting People and Companies to Deal with the COVID-19 Virus: Options for an Immediate Employment and Social-Policy Response'. *OECD Policy Responses to Coronavirus (COVID-19)*. Paris: OECD.

OECD. 2020e. *Competition Policy in Times of Crisis: Supplement to Competition Policy in Eastern Europe and Central Asia*. Paris: OECD.

OECD. 2020f. *Employment Outlook 2020: Worker Security and the COVID-19 Crisis*. Paris: OECD.

OECD. 2020g. *OECD Economic Outlook, 2020 Issue 1* (107). Paris: OECD.

OECD. 2020h. *OECD Economic Outlook 2020 Issue 2* (108). Paris: OECD.

ONS (Office for National Statistics). 2012. *Measuring National Well-being—Households and Families, 2012*. London: Office for National Statistics.

ONS. 2019. *Families and Households in the UK: 2019*. Newport: Office for National Statistics.

ONS. 2020a. *Labour Market Overview, UK: February 2020*. Newport: Office for National Statistics.

ONS. 2020b. *Births in England and Wales: Summary Tables* (Dataset, 22 July). Newport: Office for National Statistics.

ONS. 2020c. *Childbearing for Women Born in Different Years, England and Wales: 2019*. Newport: Office for National Statistics.

ONS. 2021a. *EMP17: People in Employment in Zero Hours Contracts* (Database, 23 February). Newport: Office for National Statistics.

ONS. 2021b. *Families and Households* (Database, 2 March). Newport: Office for National Statistics.

Pacifico, Daniele, James Browne, Rodrigo Fernandez, Herwig Immervoll, Dirk Neumann, and Céline Thévenot. 2018a. 'Faces of Joblessness in Italy: A People-Centred Perspective on Employment Barriers and Policies.' *OECD Social, Employment and Migration Working Papers 208*.

Pacifico, Daniele, Herwig Immervoll, James Browne, Rodrigo Fernandez, Dirk Neumann, and Céline Thévenot. 2018b. 'Faces of Joblessness in Lithuania: A People-Centred Perspective on Employment Barriers and Policies'. *OECD Social, Employment and Migration Working Papers 205*.

Pande, Amrita. 2014. *Wombs in Labor: Transnational Commercial Surrogacy in India*. New York: Columbia University Press.

Panitch, Leo, and Sam Gindin. 2012. *The Making of Global Capitalism: The Political Economy of American Empire*. London: Verso.

Pearson, Mark, and Stefano Scarpetta. 2000. 'An Overview: What Do We Know about Policies to Make Work Pay?' *OECD Economic Studies 31*, pp. 11–24.

Pelzman, Joseph. 2013. '"Womb for Rent": International Service Trade Employing Assisted Reproduction Technologies (ARTs)'. *Review of International Economics 21*(3), pp. 387–400.

Polanyi, Karl. 1944. *The Great Transformation*. New York: Farrar & Rinehart.

Pradella, Lucia. 2015. *Globalisation and the Critique of Political Economy: New Insights from Marx's Writings*. London and New York: Routledge.

Rai, Shirin M., Catherine Hoskyns, and Dania Thomas. 2014. 'Depletion'. *International Feminist Journal of Politics 16*(1), pp. 86–105.

Rainhorn, Daniel, and Samira El Boudamoussi (eds). 2015. *New Cannibal Markets: Globalization and Commodification of the Human Body*. Paris: Fondation Brocher.

Robinson, William I. 2004. *A Theory of Global Capitalism: Production, Class and State in a Transnational World*. Baltimore: Johns Hopkins University Press.

Rosenberg, Nathan. 1974. 'Karl Marx on the Economic Role of Science'. *Journal of Political Economy*, *82*(4), pp. 713–28.

Rupert, Mark. 1995. *Producing Hegemony: The Politics of Mass Production and American Global Power*. Cambridge: Cambridge University Press.

Saraceno, Chiara. 2015. 'A Critical Look to the Social Investment Approach from a Gender Perspective'. *Social Politics 22*(2), pp. 257–69.

Schmelzer, Matthias. 2014. 'A Club of the Rich to Help the Poor? The OECD, "Development", and the Hegemony of Donor Countries'. In *International Organizations and Development, 1945–1990*, edited by Marc Frey, Sönke Kunkel, and Corinna R. Unger, pp. 171–95. London: Palgrave Macmillan.

Schmelzer, Matthias. 2017. '"Born in the Corridors of the OECD": The Forgotten Origins of the Club of Rome, Transnational Networks, and the 1970s in Global History'. *Journal of Global History 12*(1), pp. 26–48.

Schroeder, Fred E. H. 1986. 'More "Small Things Forgotten": Domestic Plugs and Receptacles, 1881–1931'. *Technology and Culture 27*(3), pp. 525–43.

Schumpeter, Joseph A. 1954. *Capitalism, Socialism and Democracy*. 4th edition. London: Allen & Unwin.

Shields, Stuart. 2003. 'The "Charge of the Right Brigade": Transnational Social Forces and the Neoliberal Configuration of Poland's Transition'. *New Political Economy 8*(2), pp. 225–44.

Smith, Adam. 1999. *The Wealth of Nations, Books 1–3*. London: Penguin.

Staritz, Cornelia, and José Guilherme Reis (eds). 2013. *Global Value Chains, Economic Upgrading, and Gender: Case Studies of the Horticulture, Tourism, and Call Center Industries*. Washington DC: World Bank.

Sundaram, Ramya, Ulrich Hoerning, Natasha de Andrade Falcao, Natalie Millan, Carla Tokman, and Michelle Zini. 2014. *Portraits of Labor Market Exclusion*. Washington DC: World Bank.

Sunder Rajan, Kaushik. 2017. *Pharmocracy: Value, Politics and Knowledge in Global Biomedicine*. Durham and London: Duke University Press.

Tepe-Belfrage, Daniela, and Jill Steans. 2016. 'The New Materialism: Re-claiming a Debate from a Feminist Perspective'. *Capital & Class 40*(2), pp. 303–24.

Thaler, Richard N., and Cass R. Sunstein. 2008. *Nudge: Improving Decisions about Health, Wealth and Happiness*. London: Penguin Books.

van Apeldoorn, Bastiaan. 2002. *Transnational Capitalism and the Struggle over European Integration*. London and New York: Routledge.

van Apeldoorn, Bastiaan. 2013. 'The European Capitalist Class and the Crisis of Its Hegemonic Project'. In *Socialist Register 2014: Registering Class*, edited by Leo Panitch, Greg Albo, and Vivek Chibber, pp. 189–206. London: Merlin Press.

van der Pijl, Kees. 1984. *The Making of an Atlantic Ruling Class*. London: Verso.

van der Pijl, Kees. 1998. *Transnational Classes and International Relations*. London and New York: Routledge.

Vogel, Lise. 2013 [1983]. *Marxism and the Oppression of Women: Toward a Unitary Theory*. Chicago: Haymarket Books.

Wade, Robert H. 2001. 'Making the World Development Report 2000: Attacking Poverty'. *World Development 29*(8), pp. 1435–41.

Walby, Sylvia. 2015. *Crisis*. Cambridge: Polity Press.

World Bank. 1944. *IBRD Articles of Agreement*. http://siteresources.worldbank.org/EXTABOUTUS/Resources/ibrd-articlesofagreement.pdf.

World Bank. 1978. *World Development Report, 1978*. Washington DC: World Bank.

World Bank. 1979. *World Development Report, 1979.* Washington DC: World Bank.
World Bank. 1980. *World Development Report, 1980.* Washington DC: World Bank.
World Bank. 1981. *World Development Report 1981.* Washington DC: World Bank.
World Bank. 1982. *World Development Report 1982.* Washington DC: World Bank.
World Bank. 1983. *World Development Report 1983.* Washington DC: World Bank.
World Bank. 1984. *World Development Report 1984.* Washington DC: World Bank.
World Bank. 1985. *World Development Report 1985.* Washington DC: World Bank.
World Bank. 1986. *World Development Report 1986.* Washington DC: World Bank.
World Bank. 1987. *World Development Report 1987.* Washington DC: World Bank.
World Bank. 1988. *World Development Report 1988.* Washington DC: World Bank.
World Bank. 1989. *World Development Report 1989.* Washington DC: World Bank.
World Bank. 1990. *World Development Report 1990: Poverty.* Washington DC: World Bank.
World Bank. 1991. *World Development Report 1991: The Challenge of Development.* Washington DC: World Bank.
World Bank. 1992. *World Development Report 1992: Development and the Environment.* Washington DC: World Bank.
World Bank. 1993. *World Development Report 1993: Investing in Health.* Washington DC: World Bank.
World Bank. 1994. *World Development Report 1994: Infrastructure for Development.* Washington DC: World Bank.
World Bank. 1995. *World Development Report 1995: Workers in an Integrating World.* Washington DC: World Bank.
World Bank. 1996. *World Development Report 1996: From Plan to Market.* Washington DC: World Bank.
World Bank. 1997. *World Development Report 1997: The State in a Changing World.* Washington DC: World Bank.
World Bank. 1999a. *World Development Report 1998/99: Knowledge for Development.* Washington DC: World Bank.
World Bank. 1999b. *World Development Report 1999/2000: Entering the 21st Century.* Washington DC: World Bank.
World Bank. 2001a. *Social Protection Sector Strategy: From Safety Net to Springboard.* Washington DC: World Bank.
World Bank. 2001b. *World Development Report 2000/2001: Attacking Poverty.* Washington DC: World Bank.
World Bank. 2002a. *World Development Report 2002: Building Institutions for Markets.* Washington DC: World Bank.
World Bank. 2002b. *Private Sector Development Strategy—Directions for the World Bank Group.* Washington DC: World Bank.
World Bank. 2003a. *World Development Report 2003: Sustainable Development in a Dynamic World.* Washington DC: World Bank.
World Bank. 2003b. *World Development Report 2004: Making Services Work for Poor People.* Washington DC: World Bank.
World Bank. 2004a. *World Development Report 2005: A Better Investment Climate for Everyone.* Washington DC: World Bank.
World Bank. 2004b. *Doing Business in 2004: Understanding Regulation.* Washington DC: World Bank.
World Bank. 2005. *World Development Report 2006: Equity and Development.* Washington DC: World Bank.
World Bank. 2006a. *World Development Report 2007: Development and the Next Generation.* Washington DC: World Bank.

World Bank. 2006b. *Gender Equality as Smart Economics: A World Bank Group Gender Action Plan (Fiscal Years 2007–2010)*. Washington DC: World Bank.

World Bank. 2007a. *World Development Report 2008: Agriculture for Development*. Washington DC: World Bank.

World Bank. 2007b. *Doing Business 2007: How to Reform*. Washington DC: World Bank.

World Bank. 2009a. *World Development Report 2010: Development and Climate Change*. Washington DC: World Bank.

World Bank. 2009b. *Doing Business 2009*. Washington DC: World Bank.

World Bank. 2010. *Doing Business 2010: Reforming Through Difficult Times*. Washington DC: World Bank.

World Bank. 2011a. *World Development Report 2011: Conflict, Security and Development*. Washington DC: World Bank.

World Bank. 2011b. *World Development Report 2012: Gender Equality and Development*. Washington DC: World Bank.

World Bank. 2012a. *World Development Report 2013: Jobs*. Washington DC: World Bank.

World Bank. 2012b. *Resilience, Equity, and Opportunity: The World Bank's Social Protection and Labor Strategy 2012–2022*. Washington DC: World Bank.

World Bank. 2013a. *World Development Report 2014: Risk and Opportunity—Managing Risk for Development*. Washington DC: World Bank.

World Bank. 2013b. *Building Resilience: Integrating Climate and Disaster Risk into Development. Lessons from World Bank Group Experience*. Washington DC: World Bank.

World Bank. 2014. *World Development Report 2015: Mind, Society, and Behavior*. Washington DC: World Bank.

World Bank. 2016. *World Development Report 2016: Digital Dividends*. Washington DC: World Bank.

World Bank. 2017. *World Development Report 2017: Governance and the Law*. Washington DC: World Bank.

World Bank. 2018a. *World Development Report 2018: Learning to Realize Education's Promise*. Washington DC: World Bank.

World Bank. 2018b. *World Development Report 2019: The Changing Nature of Work*. Washington DC: World Bank.

World Bank. 2019. *Global Economic Prospects, January 2019: Darkening Skies*. Washington DC: World Bank.

World Bank. 2020a. *The Human Capital Index 2020 Update: Human Capital in the Time of COVID-19*. Washington DC: World Bank.

World Bank. 2020b. *World Development Report 2020: Trading for Development in the Age of Global Value Chains*. Washington DC: World Bank.

World Bank. 2020c. *Saving Lives, Scaling-up Impact and Getting Back on Track: World Bank Group COVID-19 Crisis Response Approach Paper*. Washington DC: World Bank.

World Bank. 2020d. *Protecting People and Economies: Integrated Policy Responses to COVID-19*. Washington DC: World Bank.

World Bank. 2020e. *Global Economic Prospects, June 2020*. Washington DC: World Bank.

World Bank. 2021. *Global Economic Prospects, January 2021*. Washington DC: World Bank.

World Bank and World Trade Organization. 2020. *Women and Trade: The Role of Trade in Promoting Gender Equality*. Washington DC: World Bank.

Yates, Luke, and Alan Warde. 2017. 'Eating Together and Eating Alone: Meal Arrangements in British Households'. *British Journal of Sociology* 68(1), pp. 97–118.

Index

For the benefit of digital users, indexed terms that span two pages (e.g., 52–53) may, on occasion, appear on only one of those pages.

Africa 80–2, 141–2
ageing 94–5
    active ageing 67, 108, 137–8
    European Commission 108
    OECD 67–8, 137–8
    see also pensions; retirement
Arias, Omar S. 110
Asia 10–11, 38–9, 63–4, 183–4
    1997 Asian financial crisis 10–11
    South Asia 81–2, 141–2
automation 109–10, 118–19, 126, 140–1, 147–8, 157–8, 169

Ball, George 7–8
Bangladesh 155–7
Bank of International Settlements 6
Barrett, Michèle 29–32
Bennholdt-Thomsen, Veronika 28–9
Benston, Margaret 28–30
Beroud, Samuel 57
Boone, Laurence 138, 173–5
Bourguignon, François 90–1
Bowen, Thomas 170–1, 182
Brazil 11–12, 136, 138–9
Bretton Woods system 3–8, 10–11
    politics of global competitiveness 12–14
'BRIICS' countries (Brazil, Russia, India, Indonesia, China, South Africa) 69–71
Buret, Eugène 32–3

Camdessus, Michel 10–11
Camps, Miriam 50–1, 72–3
Canada 10–11
capital
    freedom of capital 12–14, 17–18
    hegemony of capital on global scale 14–15, 82–3, 152–3

household as overtaken by capital 34–5
social protection as protection for capital 145–6
as social relation 73–4
transnational capital 3–5, 8–10, 38–9
universalisation of 19, 21–2, 25–6
capital accumulation 105, 184–5
    OECD 139
    proletariat and 24–5
    World Bank 82–3, 91–2, 139
capitalism
    industrial capitalism 17–18, 22–3, 34, 45–6
    League of Nations 49
    manufacturing capitalism 2–3
    reproduction of 15–16, 28–32
    as social phenomenon 1
    social production under capitalism 22–5
    see also global capitalism
capitalist development 15–16, 27–8, 30–2, 36–7, 41–2
    OECD 42–4, 139
    World Bank 42–4, 75–6, 84, 103, 123
capitalist production
    class struggle and 19
    exploitation 24–5, 82–3
    laws of 23–4
    Marx, Karl 18–25, 27–8, 60, 123–4
    OECD 60
    as process of reproduction 24–5
    workers' life and 22–3
    World Bank 82–3, 123–4
    see also production
capital/labour relationship 1, 162–3
    hegemony of capital over labour 14–15, 72–3, 96–7, 139
    Marx, Karl 17, 19, 141

Charnock, Greig 21–2
children
    child labour 32–3
    European Commission 133–4
    exploitation of workers' children 22–3
Chile 155–7
China 11–12, 75, 145, 183–4
    OECD and 64–5, 69–72, 136, 138–9
civil society 87
class conflict 3–5, 14–15
Clavin, Patricia 45–9
Clifton, Judith 6–7, 10–11
climate change 164–6, 170, 172
    OECD 138–9, 169, 173–5
    World Bank 123, 167–70, 177
    see also environmental issues
commodification
    of domestic production 38–40
    of the human body 40–1
competition/competitiveness
    ERT 3–5
    EU 107–8
    managing the disruption created by 68,
        73–4
    Marx, Karl: free competition 18, 28,
        42–4, 85–6, 118–19, 184–5
    neo-liberal competitiveness discourse 3–5
    OECD 45, 55–6, 66–8, 72–4, 103,
        118, 149
    World Bank 83–5, 87, 91–2, 101–4,
        126–7, 152–3
    see also global competitiveness; politics of
        global competitiveness
constitutionalism 3–5
contracts 149
    atypical contracts 132
    OECD 150
    open-ended contracts 36–7
    part-time contracts 36–7
    short-term contracts 36–7
    termination of contract 150
    World Bank 127
    'zero hours' contracts 35–6, 38–9, 150
    see also employment
Costa Rica 155–9
Cotis, Jean-Philippe 68–9
COVID-19 pandemic 162–5, 183–5
    adaptability and resilience, unified theory
        of 167–71

'Building Back Better' 164–5, 172–81
capitalising on COVID-19? 171–83
climate change and sustainability
    172–4, 177
crisis as opportunity 164–7
crisis as threat to global capitalist
    project 164–5, 177–9
digital technology 169, 173–7, 179–80
education and training 164–5, 172–3,
    177–83
employment 172–3, 175–83
global competitiveness 172, 183–4
GVCs 171, 177–8
human capital 171, 175–7, 179–80,
    182–3
informal sector 164–5, 173–7,
    179–80, 182
liberalism 172
'non-standard' employment 172–3,
    179–81
OECD 16, 164–5, 171–5, 179–84
politics of global competitiveness 16,
    164–5, 177–8
poverty 177–8
reforms 164–7, 173–81
social protection 164–5, 174–5,
    179–82
state support 172–7, 183–4
taxation 173–5
teleworking 172–3, 175–7, 179–80
unemployment 36–7, 172–3,
    177–80
women 178–9
World Bank 16, 164–5, 171–3, 175–9,
    182–4
Cox, Robert 2–3
CSCE (Conference on Security and
    Cooperation in Europe) 5–6
Cumings, Bruce 7–8
Czech Republic 11–12, 136, 152–3

Dalla Costa, Mariarosa 28–32, 41–2
deregulation 60–1, 72–3, 96–7
developing countries
    GVCs 154–7
    OECD 51–5, 63–4
    World Bank 75–82, 141, 154–7, 161,
        183–4
Díaz-Fuentes, Daniel 6–7, 10–11

digital technology
   COVID-19 pandemic 169, 173–7,
      179–80
   digital economy 126–7
   digital revolution 35, 119–20, 125–7,
      131, 139–40
   OECD 118–20, 169, 173–4
   World Bank 2016 *Report*, *Digital*
      Dividends 105–6, 122, 125–7
   see also technology
division of labour 1, 15–16, 184–5
   'domestic sphere'/household 15–16
   gender division of labour 32, 34
   general law of social production 131
   Marx, Karl 20, 32, 34
   OECD 105–6
   technology 35
   World Bank 91–2, 99–100
   see also labour
Dominican Republic 155–7
Dylan, Bob 147–8

EBRD (European Bank for Reconstruction
      and Development) 7–8
education and training
   COVID-19 pandemic 164–5, 172–3,
      177–83
   European Commission 109–10, 112,
      132–4
   for girls 79, 93–4
   OECD 57, 116
   reform in 57, 125–6
   rural education 93
   vocational education and training 179–81
   for women 93–5, 112
   World Bank 79, 92–5, 122, 125–6,
      129–30
   see also skills
Ellwood, David W. 49–50
emerging and developing economies
      10–11, 141–2, 164
   OECD 45, 55–6, 62–3, 68–70
Emmerij, Louis 57–8
employment
   'better employment' 162–3
   COVID-19 pandemic 172–3, 175–83
   disabled people 108–12, 133–4
   European Commission 105–13, 115–16,
      132–3

female labour 32–4, 36–40, 91–6, 102,
      111–13, 155–7, 178–9
   freelancing 35, 127
   full time work 36–7, 109–10, 114–15,
      133–4, 147–9
   job security 36–7, 150
   'non-standard' employment 112–13,
      147–9, 151–2, 172–3, 179–81
   OECD 62–3, 66–7, 69–71, 113–14,
      146–52, 172–3, 179–81
   OECD: employability skills for the
      twenty-first century 116–22
   part-time work 36–7, 109–10, 112–15,
      147–8, 150–2
   self-employment 39–40, 132–4, 147–9,
      151–2
   under-employment 39–40, 105–6,
      108–9, 139–40, 150–1,
      172–3, 179
   World Bank 78, 90–1, 95–7, 101–4,
      110, 142–4, 162–3, 167–9
   youth 90–1, 96, 102, 107–8, 116–17
   see also contracts; labour flexibility;
      labour mobility; labour versatility;
      social politics of global
      competitiveness; workers; workers'
      rights
Engels, Friedrich 32
   Communist Manifesto 20, 146–8
   German Ideology 17, 20
   Outlines of a Critique of Political
      Economy 17–18
   science and technology 26
   world market 20
environmental issues 64–5, 138–9, 154–5,
      158–9, 164–5, 181
   see also climate change
ERT (European Round Table of
      Industrialists) 3–5, 12–14
EU (European Union)
   competitiveness 107–8
   female labour 36–7
   labour market reform 12–14
   labour mobility 138–9
   neo-liberalism 8–10
   politics of global economy 5–10
   single market and single currency 8–11,
      49–50
   unemployment 61

European Commission 3–5
  2000–2010 *Lisbon Strategy* 107–8
  children 133–4
  education and training 109–10, 112,
    132–4
  employment 105–13, 115–16, 132–3
  Employment and Social Developments in
    Europe series 105–9
  Europe 2020 105–9
  European Pillar of Social Rights 139–40,
    147–8
  European Pillar of Social Rights as
    constitution for the general law 130–4
  gender equality 108
  general law of social production 105–7,
    130–4
  household 108–13
  joblessness project 105–13, 115–16
  OECD and 45, 113–16
  politics of global competitiveness 12–14,
    105–8
  Portraits of Labour Market
    Exclusion 110–13
  poverty 107–10
  reform 112–13
  social protection 111–13
  unemployment 110–12, 132–4
  women 108–13, 133
  World Bank and 110–11, 113–16
  youth 107–8, 132
exploitation
  capitalist production 24–5, 82–3
  Marx, Karl 22–3
  World Bank 84

family 32–41, 183–4
  procreation 30–2, 34–5, 40–1
  see also fertility; household
Farole, Thomas 152–3
Federici, Silvia 41–2
feminism, *see* Marxist feminism
Ferguson, Susan 28–9
Fernandez, Rodrigo 113–15
fertility 32, 183–4
  fertility reduction 78–9, 81–2, 94–6,
    183–4
  human development and 78–9
  World Bank 78–9, 81–2, 94–6
Firestone, Shulamith 40–1

Ford, Henry 3–5
Fordism 3–5, 12–14
Fraser, Nancy 41–2

G7 (Group of Seven) 5–8, 10–14
Gass, James 57
GATT (General Agreement on Tariffs and
  Trade) 6
gender issues
  European Commission 108
  gender division of labour 32, 34
  gender gap in wages 155–7
  World Bank 93–5, 97–100, 155–7
  WTO 155–7
general law of social production 15–16,
  25–6, 105–6
  constitutionalisation of 131, 138
  core project: combatting
    joblessness 105–16
  division of labour 131
  European Commission 105–7
  European Pillar of Social Rights as a
    constitution for the general law 130–4
  'making work pay' 105–8
  Marx, Karl 15–17, 24–7, 89–90, 105,
    125–6, 130–1, 133–4, 139–40, 151–2,
    184–5
  OECD 16, 42–4, 67, 130–1
  OECD: employability skills for the
    twenty-first century 116–22
  politics of global competitiveness 105–6
  social protection reform 105–6
  social reproduction 27–8
  World Bank 16, 89, 93
  World Bank: governance of the general
    law 105–6, 122–31
General Motors 7–8
Gentilini, Ugo 164
Germany: Hartz reforms 145
Ghana 124–5
Gill, Stephen 3–5, 11–14
Gimenez, Martha 24–5, 30–2, 160–1
Gindin, Sam 6–11
global capitalism
  COVID-19 pandemic as threat to global
    capitalist project 164–5, 177–9
  governance of 14–15
  international organisations and 14–15,
    45–7, 49

OECD 1, 10–11, 15–16, 46, 54–6, 66–7,
    71–3, 183–4
    US 6–7, 10–11
    World Bank 1, 15–16, 46, 82–4, 95,
        105–6, 183–4
    see also capitalism
global competitiveness 3–5
    COVID-19 pandemic 172, 183–4
    EU 8–10
    GVCs 154–5, 160–1
    regime of 152–5, 157–8
    see also competition/competitiveness;
        politics of global competitiveness
global financial crisis 105–6, 130–1, 164–7,
    178–9
    OECD 56, 68–9, 71–2, 106–7, 116, 166–7
    World Bank 95, 97–8, 102–4, 166–9
globalisation 139–40
    economic globalisation 5–6
    ERT 12–14
    OECD 65–6, 118–19
    transformation of social practices 3–5,
        12–14
    World Bank 86–7
Goldberg, Pinelopi Koujianou 154
government, see state
Gowan, Peter 6–8, 10–11
Gramsci, Antonio F. 2–3
Greenspan, Alan 7–8
Gurría, Angel 56, 147–8, 169, 172–3
GVCs (Global Value Chains) 154
    COVID-19 pandemic 171, 177–8
    developing countries 154–7
    global competitiveness 154–5, 160–1
    OECD: Skills and Global Value
        Chains 105–6, 118–21
    poverty 154–5, 159–61
    proliferation of 118–19
    reform/structural adjustment 154–9
    wages 159–60
    women 154–9
    World Bank: Trading for Development in
        the Age of Global Value Chains
        139–40, 152–61

Hartmann, Heidi 36–7
Harvey, David 6
hegemony 2–3, 10–11
    Europe 3–5

hegemonic world order 2–3, 10–11
hegemony of capital on global scale
    14–15, 82–3, 152–3
hegemony of capital over labour 14–15,
    72–3, 96–7, 139
    US 2–3, 5–6, 8–11, 49–50
Henderson, Michael 51–2
historical materialism 17–18, 20
Hoffman, Paul 49–50
Holman, Otto 8–10
Holzmann, Robert 88–9
household (domestic sphere) 183–4
    commodification of domestic
        production 38–40
    composition of 37–9
    division of labour 15–16
    drawing 'inactive' household members
        into the labour market 42–4
    European Commission 108–13
    impact of industrial capitalism on 34–5
    as limit for capital 28
    male breadwinner 36–9
    OECD 113–15
    as overtaken by capital 34–5
    replacement of domestic production by
        market or state provision 30–2, 38–9
    rural household 91–3
    science and technology 34–5, 38
    women's unpaid labour and
        reproduction of capitalism 15–16,
        28–32
    World Bank 75–6, 79, 81–2, 91–100,
        123–4
    see also family
human capital
    COVID-19 pandemic 171, 175–7,
        179–80, 182–3
    human capital accumulation 96,
        170–1, 182
    World Bank 90–1, 94–6, 98–9, 122,
        140–3, 170–1, 182–3
Human Capital Index (World Bank)
    145–6, 162–3, 183–4
    2018 Human Capital Index 161–2
    2020 Human Capital Index 161–2
    Human Capital Index 2020 Update 171,
        182–3
    UHCI (Utilization-Adjusted Human
        Capital Index) 162

Human Capital Project (World Bank)
145–6, 162–3
human development 78–9

IBRD (International Bank for
Reconstruction and Development) 1
see also World Bank
IFIs (international financial
institutions) 8–11
ILO (International Labour
Organisation) 39–40, 47, 57
IMF (International Monetary Fund) 2–3,
5–8, 14–15, 85–6
1944 United Nations Monetary and
Financial Conference 2–3
1997 *World Economic Outlook* 3–5
2019 *World Economic Outlook* 136
US and 10–11
see also Trilateral Commission
Immervoll, Herwig 106–7, 113–14
India 11–12, 124–5, 141–2, 155–7
OECD and 64–5, 69–72, 136, 138–9
Indonesia 11–12, 64–5, 136, 138–9
industrial revolution 26, 45–6
inequality 1, 42–4, 154–5, 183–4
industrial capitalism 45–6
OECD on 66, 71–2, 174–5
World Bank on 164, 177–8
informal sector 28, 39–42
COVID-19 pandemic 164–5, 173–7,
179–80, 182
from informal into formal
economy 125–6, 139–40
OECD 42–4
social protection 164–5, 174–5
World Bank 42–4, 125–6, 141–2, 158–9,
164, 175–7, 179, 182
Inman, Mary 28–9
International Bureau of Weights and
Measures 45–6
International Finance Corporation 100
international organisations
global capitalism and 14–15, 45–7, 49
governance of global economy 105–6
industrial capitalism and 45–6
liberalism 46
International Telegraph Union 45–6
IPCC (Intergovernmental Panel on Climate
Change) 169–70

Japan 8–10
jobs, *see* employment
Johnson, Donald 135
Jorgensen, Stern 88–9

Kanbur, Ravi 87
Kennedy, John F. 7–8, 50–1
Kenya 123–5, 155–7
Kim, Jim Yong 97–8, 122, 129–30
Kim Dae Jung 7–8
King, Alexander 51–2
Korea 7–8, 10–11
Kristensen, Thorkil 51–5, 183–4

labour
labour regulation 106–7, 127, 150,
180–1
social labour 21–2
see also capital/labour relationship;
division of labour; employment
labour flexibility 35–6, 42–4, 105–6,
184–5
casual work 127
European Commission 133–4
'flexicurity' 62–3, 145
OECD 102, 135–7, 149–50
World Bank 102, 127, 129–30, 152–3
see also employment
labour market
competitiveness in 152–3
EU, labour market reform 12–14
global labour market 118–20, 160–1
hiring and firing 100–1, 133, 145, 152–3
OECD: labour reform 11–14, 55, 58,
68–9, 136–7, 180–1
online labour markets 127
rural labour market 92
World Bank: labour reform 141, 145,
152–3
see also employment
labour mobility 42–4, 105–6, 127, 129–30,
133–4, 139–40, 149, 184–5
COVID-19 pandemic and 164–5
EU 138–9
see also employment
labour versatility 105–6, 129–30
see also employment
Lange, Elena Louisa 42
Latin America 63–4, 141–2

League of Nations 45–6
  capitalism 49
  EFO (Economic and Financial
    Organisation) 47–9
  liberalism 49
  protectionism 48–9
  taxation 49
Leimgruber, Matthieu 51–2, 57
liberalism
  international organisations 46
  League of Nations 49
  liberal universalism 7–8
  OECD 54–5, 65, 116
Loveday, Alexander 48–9
Luxemburg, Rosa 28–9
Luxton, Meg 41–2

macroeconomic policies
  OECD 57, 62–5, 71, 135–7
  World Bank 85–6, 88–9, 100–1, 103–4
Malaysia 158–9
Malpass, David 175–7
Malthus, Thomas Robert 22–3
Mann, Catherine 60, 138, 160–1
Marshall Plan 3–5, 7–8, 12–14, 49–50
Marx, Karl 15–17
  capital accumulation 24–5
  capitalism and forms of production
    15–16
  capitalist production 18–25, 27–8, 60,
    123–4
  capital/labour relationship 17, 19, 141
  critique of political economy 17, 19,
    184–5
  division of labour 20, 32, 34
  exploitation 22–3
  family and production 32–5
  female labour 32–4
  free competition 18, 28, 42–4, 85–6,
    118–19, 184–5
  freedom of capital 17–18
  gender issues 32
  general law of social production 15–17,
    24–7, 89–90, 105, 125–6, 130–1,
    133–4, 139–40, 151–2, 184–5
  machinery 26–7, 32–5, 184–5
  science and technology 26, 34–5
  socialization of labour 22
  wages 22–5, 159–60

world market 20–1, 27
world money 21
Marx, Karl: works and lectures
  Capital 1, 17–19, 22–3, 25, 30–3,
    105, 141
  Communist Manifesto 20, 146–8
  'Economic Manuscripts of 1861–63' 21
  Economic and Philosophic
    Manuscripts 17–18, 22–3, 32–3
  German Ideology 17, 20
  'Wage Labour and Capital' 20
Marxist feminism 15–17, 28–30
Mexico 10–11
Mies, Maria 28–30
migration 29–30, 65, 91–2
  care and domestic labour 38–9, 42
  European Commission 108
  immigration of skilled workers 160
  OECD on 65, 119–20
  as workforce 42–4, 108
Mill, John Stuart 22–3
Millan, Natalia 113–14
Mitterrand, François 8–10
Mohieldin, Mahmoud 166
Molyneux, Maxine 29–30
Monteiro, C. A. 38–9
Morocco 158–9
multinationals, see transnationals
Murphy, Craig 45–6, 72–3

NAFTA (North American Free Trade
  Association) 3–5, 10–11
neo-liberalism 3–8
  disciplinary neo-liberalism 3–5, 8–11
  EU 8–10
  neo-liberal competitiveness discourse
    3–5
  OECD, neoliberal reform 60
NICs (Newly Industrialised Countries)
  50–1, 54–6, 64–5

OECD (Organisation for Economic
  Cooperation and Development)
  1948–1990 45, 49–58
  1990–2013 45, 58–72
  antecedents 45–9
  benchmarking 68–9
  capitalist development 42–4, 139
  capitalist production 60

OECD (Organisation for Economic
  Cooperation and Development)
  (*cont.*)
  competition/competitiveness 45, 55–6,
    66–8, 72–4, 103, 118, 149
  confrontation of economic policies 52–3
  core principles of 52–8
  COVID-19 pandemic 16, 164–5, 171–5,
    179–84
  division of labour 105–6
  economic integration 66–7, 135–6
  education and training 57, 116
  employment 62–3, 66–7, 69–71, 113–14,
    146–52, 172–3, 179–81
  employability skills for the twenty-first
    century 116–22
  European Commission and 45, 113–16
  founding of 2–3, 7–8, 45, 50–1
  general law of social production 16,
    42–4, 67, 116–22, 130–1
  global capitalism 1, 10–11, 15–16, 46,
    54–6, 66–7, 71–3, 183–4
  global financial crisis 56, 68–9, 71–2,
    106–7, 116, 166–7
  globalisation 65–6, 118–19
  household 113–15
  joblessness project 113–16
  Jobs Strategy 66–7, 69–71, 146, 180–1
  liberalism 54–5, 65, 116
  macroeconomic policies 57, 62–5, 71,
    135–7
  membership 11–12, 50–1
  migration 65, 119–20
  non-Members 11–12, 50–1, 64–6, 135–9
  OECD/World Bank considered
    together 2, 12–14, 45, 71–2, 77–8,
    88–9, 103, 106–7, 129–30, 136, 139,
    152–3, 161–3, 183–5
  as political organisation 54–5, 139
  politics of 72–4
  politics of global competitiveness 2,
    11–15, 42–4, 57–8, 62–3, 72–3,
    113–14, 162–5
  politics of global economy 5–8, 10–11
  protectionism 12–14, 45, 53–4, 56, 61,
    66, 72–3
  Secretariat 10–11, 51–2
  shifting wealth and social cohesion
    68–72

skills 106–7, 116–22, 129–30, 135–6
social politics of global
  competitiveness 135–8, 146–52
social protection 12–14, 66–8, 72, 106–7,
  148–50
socio-economic rights 71–2
soft governance 10–11
state 119–20, 135
surveillance at 52, 68–9
taxation 106–7, 117, 136–7
technology 62–3, 117, 138, 169, 173–4
towards a new global age 63–8
unemployment 58–61, 69, 115–16,
  135–6, 179–80
women 42–4, 115
world market 16, 45, 50–1, 56–8, 62–3,
  71–3, 118–19
youth 116–17
see also Trilateral Commission
OECD: Development Advisory
  Committee 50–1
OECD: Development Centre 7–8, 50–1,
  54–5, 57–8
OECD: documents and publications
  *Aligning Policies for a Low-carbon
    Economy* 169
  *Development Partnerships in the New
    Global Context* 63–4
  Economic Outlook 171, 173–5, 179–80
  Economic Studies 106–7
  Employment Outlook 2006 62–3
  *Employment Outlook 2019: The Future of
    Work* 139–40, 147–52, 175
  Employment Outlook 2020 171, 180–1
  Going for Growth series 68–70, 103,
    166–7, 175
  *Impact of the Newly Industrialising
    Countries on Production and Trade in
    Manufactures* 55–6, 64–5
  Inflation: The Present Problem 57
  *Investing in Climate, Investing in
    Growth* 169
  Jobs Strategy 146–8, 169
  Jobs Study 11–14, 58–63, 106–7
  *Linkages: OECD and Major Developing
    Economies* 63–5
  The Next Production Revolution 117,
    130–1
  One World or Several? 57–8

Perspectives on Global Development series 68
Perspectives on Global Development, Shifting Wealth 68–70
Policy Responses to COVID-19 series 164–5, 175, 179–80
Regulatory Reform for Recovery: Lessons from Implementation during Crises 166–7
Shaping the 21st Century... 63–4
Social, Employment and Migration Working Papers 113–14
Supporting People and Companies to Deal with the COVID-19 Virus... 172–3
The World in 2020: Towards a New Global Age 11–12, 63, 65–7, 135–7
see also OECD Skills Outlook series
OECD: functions/roles 47
  coordinating economic policy 5–8
  developmental assistance to less developed countries 51–5, 63–4
  development of the world economy 50–1, 54–5, 57–8, 60
  policy coordination, mutual surveillance, and peer review 52, 72–3
  world trade 50–1
OECD Observer 51–2
OECD: reform/structural adjustment 56–8, 64–7, 69, 72–3, 116, 119–20, 135, 137–8, 148
  COVID-19 pandemic 166–7, 173–5, 179–80
  educational reform 57
  governance reform 136–7
  labour reform 11–14, 55, 58, 68–9, 136–7, 180–1
  neoliberal reform 60
  social protection 181–2
  welfare reform 45, 55, 57, 61–2, 68
OECD Skills Outlook series 106–7, 116, 121–2, 130–1, 146
  2015: Youth, Skills and Employability 116–17
  2017: Skills and Global Value Chains 105–6, 118–21
OEEC (Organisation for European Economic Cooperation) 2–3, 45, 49–50, 57
out-sourcing 34–5, 38–9, 65

Padoan, Pier Carlo 69
Panitch, Leo 6–11
Paye, Jean-Claud 57–9
Pearson, Mark 106–7
pensions 69, 88, 142–3, *see also* ageing; retirement
Poland 10–11
  Balcerowicz Plan 7–8, 145
Polanyi, Karl 3–5
politics of global competitiveness 3–5, 12–15, 184–5
  COVID-19 pandemic 16, 164–5, 177–8
  European Commission 12–14, 105–8
  G7 12–14
  general law of social production 105–6
  OECD 2, 11–15, 42–4, 57–8, 62–3, 72–3, 113–14, 162–5
  social reproduction and 27–32
  World Bank 2, 12–15, 42–4, 75–6, 84–5, 97–8, 101–3, 140–2, 152–5, 160–1, 164–5, 167–9
  see also competition/competitiveness; social politics of global competitiveness
politics of global economy
  critical approaches to 2–12
  EU 5–10
  OECD 5–8, 10–11
  US 2–3, 5–11
poverty 42–4
  COVID-19 pandemic 177–8
  European Commission 107–10
  GVCs 154–5, 159–61
  World Bank 12–14, 78–9, 82–3, 87, 123, 154–5, 159–61
Pradella, Lucia 21–2
production
  bourgeois mode of production 1, 34, 40–1, 130–1
  fragmentation of 35, 56, 118–20, 152–4
  internationalisation of 3–5
  World Bank: productivity of the poor 75–6, 78–9, 123–5
  see also capitalist production
the proletariat
  capital accumulation and 24–5
  World Bank: global proletariat 16, 75–6, 83–4, 89–90, 103–4, 127, 152–3, 159–60

proletarianisation 14–15
　　global competitiveness and 161–3
　　of the household 16
　　of informal sector 16
　　by the OECD 42–4
　　transformation of workers into
　　　proletarians 22
　　by the World Bank 42–4, 82–9, 103–4,
　　　162–3
protectionism
　　agricultural protection 48–9, 53–4
　　EFO (League of Nations) 48–9
　　OECD 12–14, 45, 53–4, 56, 61, 66, 72–3
　　World Bank 12–14, 76–8, 155

racism 12–14
Reagan, Ronald 8–10
reform/structural adjustment 8–10, 12–15,
　　49–50, 160–1
　　behavioural reform 89–90, 97–8, 103–4,
　　　122–3, 177–8, 182–3
　　COVID-19 pandemic 164–7, 173–81
　　educational reform 57, 125–6
　　EU 12–14, 112–13
　　GVCs 154–9
　　marketising reform 12–14
　　regulatory reform 68–9, 103, 112–13,
　　　141, 145
　　social protection 150–2, 181–2
　　Western Europe 49–50
　　see also OECD: reform/structural
　　　adjustment; welfare reform; World
　　　Bank: reform/structural adjustment
Reis, José Guilherme 155–7
retirement
　　age of retirement 67, 137–8
　　European Commission 133–4
　　OECD 67, 137–8
　　World Bank 143–4
　　see also ageing; pensions
Robinson, William 5–6
Rosenberg, Nathan 26–7
Rupert, Mark 3–5, 7–8, 12–14
Russia 11–12, 136, 138–9

Sánchez-Páramo, Carolina 110
Scarpetta, Stefano 147–8, 180–1
Schmelzer, Matthias 6–7, 51–2
Schulz, Wilhelm 32–3

Schumpeter, Joseph A. 72–3, 78–9
science 26
　　family/household and 34–5, 38
　　procreation and 30–2, 40–1
Senegal 155–7
Shu Yu 175–7
Simon, William 8–10
skills
　　cognitive, social and emotional
　　　skills 119–21, 129–30
　　employment and 116
　　labour market and 116
　　low-skilled workers 62–3, 109–10, 115,
　　　117, 135–6
　　OECD 106–7, 116, 129–30, 135–6
　　OECD: employability skills for the
　　　twenty-first century 116–22
　　skilled workers 125–6
　　unskilled workers 92, 115, 125–6, 136–7,
　　　147–8, 183–4
　　World Bank 122, 127, 129–30
　　see also education and training
SMEs (small and medium
　　enterprises) 107–8, 119–20, 158–9
Smith, Adam 69, 78–9, 116, 159–60
social politics of global competitiveness 16,
　　135–40
　　OECD 135–8, 146–52
　　politics of global competitiveness
　　　139–40, 160–1
　　proletarianisation and global
　　　competitiveness 161–3
　　social protection 139–46, 148–52
　　women 139–40
　　work 140–52
　　World Bank 136, 138–46, 152–61
　　world market 152–61
　　see also employment
social production
　　capitalism and 22–5
　　science and technology 26
　　World Bank 75–6, 89–100
　　see also general law of social production
social protection
　　adaptive social protection 169–70, 182
　　COVID-19 pandemic 164–5, 174–5,
　　　179–82
　　ERT 12–14
　　Europe 3–5

European Commission 111–13
general law of social production 105–6
informal sector 164–5, 174–5
non-standard workers 179–81
OECD 12–14, 66–8, 72, 106–7, 148–50,
  181–2
as protection for capital 145–6
reform of 150–2, 181–2
World Bank 12–14, 75–6, 88–9, 106–7,
  125–6, 140–6, 167–70, 182
see also social politics of global
  competitiveness
social reproduction 15–17
crisis of 41–4
general law of social production 27–8
politics of global competitiveness
  and 27–32
World Bank 75–6
social reproduction theorists 15–17, 28–30
South Africa 69–71, 123–4
Soviet Union 10–11, 51–2, 75
Staritz, Cornelia 155–7
Starosta, Guido 21–2
state
COVID-19 pandemic 172–7, 183–4
OECD on 119–20, 135
transnational state 5–6
World Bank on 83, 85–6, 101–3, 127–8,
  142–4, 152–3
Stern, Nicholas 90–1
Strauss-Kahn, Dominique 165–6
structural adjustment, see reform/structural
  adjustment
Sundaram, Ramya 110–13

taxation
COVID-19 pandemic 173–5
League of Nations 49
OECD 106–7, 117, 136–7
payroll taxes 106–7, 142–5
World Bank 125–7, 141–5, 157–8
technology
division of labour 35
family/household and 34–5, 38
general law of social production 26
growth and 60
household/wage labour relationship
  30–2
OECD 62–3, 117, 138, 169, 173–4

trade and 153
World Bank 87–8, 91–2, 94, 96, 125–7,
  141–2, 152–3
see also digital technology
Thailand 165–6
Thatcher, Margaret 8–10
trade
free trade 10–11, 48–9, 152–3, 155
OECD 50–1
technology and 153
world trade 50–1
trade unions 49–50, 59, 84
unionisation 72, 84
transnationals 14–15, 38–9, 56, 160–1
transnational capital 3–5, 8–10, 38–9
transnational capitalist class 2–6, 14–15
transnational state 5–6
'Treaty of Detroit' 7–8
Trilateral Commission 2–5
see also IMF; OECD; World Bank

UAW (Union of Auto Workers) 7–8
UK (United Kingdom)
2010 Equality Act 149
austerity politics 36–7
female labour 36–7
manufacturing capitalism 2–3
Pax Britannica 2–3
welfare reform 36–7
'zero hours' contracts 35–6
UN (United Nations) 5–6, 45–6
UNCTAD (UN Conference on Trade and
  Development) 53–5
unemployment 39–40
COVID-19 pandemic 36–7, 172–3,
  177–80
EU 61
European Commission 110–12, 132–4
OECD 58–61, 69, 115–16, 135–6,
  179–80
unemployment benefits 62–3, 69, 133–4,
  151, 160–1, 172–3
US 61
World Bank 102–3, 145, 161
youth 115
Universal Postal Union 45–6
US (United States) 8–10
Bretton Woods system and 10–11
Dollar-Wall Street regime 10–11

US (United States) (*cont.*)
  global capitalism 6–7, 10–11
  hegemony 2–3, 5–6, 8–11, 49–50
  IFIs and 8–11
  IMF and 10–11
  Pax Americana 2–3
  politics of global economy 2–3, 5–11
  unemployment 61
  World Bank and 8–11

Van Apeldoorn, Bastiaan 3–5, 8–10, 12–14
Van Lennep, Emile 54–5, 57
Van der Pijl, Kees 5–8, 12–15
Vogel, Lise 29–30
'Volcker Shock' 8–10

wages
  dependence on waged labour 106–7
  European Commission 133
  family wage 36–7
  gender gap 155–7
  GVCs 159–60
  household/wage labour relationship
    30–2
  living wage 109–10, 159–60
  low-wage 54, 60–5, 127, 152–4
  low-wage traps 152–3, 159–60
  Marx, Karl 22–5, 159–60
  minimum wages 72, 133, 159–60
  subsidy for 152–3, 160
  subsistence-level wages 159–60
Warde, Alan 38–9
welfare 35–6
welfare reform 36–7, 39–40, 42–4
  OECD 45, 55, 57, 61–2, 68
  World Bank 88–9, 106–7, 154
Werlhof, Claudia 28–9
women 28–9, 139–40
  COVID-19 pandemic 178–9
  domestic work 41–2
  education for girls and women 79,
    93–5, 112
  empowerment 87–8, 99–100
  European Commission 108–13, 133
  female labour 32–4, 36–40, 91–6, 102,
    111–13, 155–7, 178–9
  GVCs 154–9
  OECD 42–4, 115
  procreation 30–2, 37–8

reproduction of labour-power 34, 41–2
unpaid labour in domestic sphere and
  reproduction of capitalism 15–16,
  28–30
World Bank 42–4, 87–8, 91–6, 98–100,
  102, 142–3, 158–9, 178–9
'zero hours' contracts 35–6
work, *see* employment
workers
  capitalist production and workers' health
    and life 22–3
  general law of social production 15–16,
    25–6
  precarity of 25–6
  'worker' category 149
  worker status 149–50
  working day 22–3
  working time 62–3, 149, 151
  in the world market 17–22
  see also skills
workers' rights 36–7
  collective bargaining rights 148
  competitive capital vs rights of
    workers 49, 71–2
  European Pillar of Social Rights 130–4,
    139–40, 147–8
  OECD 150
World Bank 5–8
  1944 United Nations Monetary and
    Financial Conference 2–3
  1979–1989 76–82
  1982 recession 80–1
  1990–2001 82–9
  2001–2013 89–100
  benchmarking 100–1
  capitalist development 42–4, 75–6, 84,
    103, 123
  capitalist production 82–3, 123–4
  cash transfer programmes 93–5, 99–100,
    164, 175–7
  civil society 87
  competitiveness 83–5, 87, 91–2, 101–4,
    126–7, 152–3
  COVID-19 pandemic 16, 164–5, 171–3,
    175–9, 182–4
  democracy 128–9
  developing countries 75–82, 141, 154–7,
    161, 183–4
  development 161

division of labour 91–2, 99–100
economic growth 79
education and training 79, 92–5, 122, 125–6, 129–30
employment 78, 90–1, 95–7, 101–4, 110, 142–4, 162–3, 167–9
empowerment 85–8, 99–100
European Commission and 110–11, 113–16
fertility 78–9, 81–2, 94–6
free trade 152–3, 155
functions/roles 14–15, 75, 86, 103, 128–9
gender issues 93–5, 97–100, 155–7
general law of social production 16, 89, 93
general law of social production, governance of 105–6, 122–31
global capitalism 1, 15–16, 46, 82–4, 95, 105–6, 183–4
global financial crisis 95, 97–8, 102–4, 166–9
globalisation 86–7
household 75–6, 79, 81–2, 91–100, 123–4
human capital 90–1, 94–6, 98–9, 122, 140–3, 170–1, 182–3
human development 78–9
informal sector 42–4, 125–6, 141–3, 145, 164, 175–7, 179, 182
International Bank for Reconstruction and Development 75
joblessness project 110–11, 113–16
localisation 86–7
macroeconomic policies 85–6, 88–9, 100–1, 103–4
OECD/World Bank considered together 2, 12–14, 45, 71–2, 77–8, 88–9, 103, 106–7, 129–30, 136, 139, 152–3, 161–3, 183–5
as political organisation 139
politics of global competitiveness 2, 12–15, 42–4, 75–6, 84–5, 97–8, 101–3, 140–2, 152–5, 160–1, 164–5, 167–9
poverty 12–14, 78–9, 82–3, 87, 123, 154–5, 159–61
productivity of the poor 75–6, 78–9, 123–5

proletariat/global proletariat 16, 42–4, 75–6, 82–90, 103–4, 127, 152–3, 159–60, 162–3
protectionism 12–14, 76–8, 155
skills 122, 127, 129–30
social intervention 75–6, 78
social politics of global competitiveness 136, 138–46, 152–61
social production 75–6, 89–100
social protection 12–14, 75–6, 88–9, 106–7, 125–6, 140–6, 167–70, 182
social reproduction 75–6
social risk management 88–9
state 83, 85–6, 101–3, 127–8, 142–4, 152–3
taxation 125–7, 141–5, 157–8
technology 87–8, 91–2, 94, 96, 125–7, 141–2, 152–3
unemployment 102–3, 145, 161
US and 8–11
women 42–4, 87–8, 91–6, 98–100, 102, 142–3, 158–9, 178–9
world market 75–8, 80–3, 86, 88–9, 139–40, 152–3
youth 90–1, 96, 102, 158–9
see also Human Capital Index; Human Capital Project; Trilateral Commission
World Bank: Doing Business series 75, 89–90, 100–4, 158–9
Doing Business 2004: Understanding Regulation 100–2
Doing Business 2005: Removing Obstacles to Growth 102
Doing Business 2006: Creating Jobs 102
Doing Business 2007: How to Reform 102, 165–6
Doing Business 2009 102
Doing Business 2010: Reforming through Difficult Times 102–3, 165–6
Doing Business 2011 101–2
World Bank: reform/structural adjustment 89–91, 97–8, 100–1, 110, 125–6, 128–9, 144–5
behavioural reform 89–90, 97–8, 103–4, 122–3
COVID-19 pandemic 165–6, 175–9
labour reform 141, 145, 152–3
political economy of reform 75–6, 89, 102

World Bank: reform/structural adjustment
    (*cont.*)
  regulatory reform 103
  welfare reform 88–9, 106–7, 154
World Bank: *World Development Reports*
    and publications 75–6, 89–90, 100,
    103–4
  1978 *Report* 12–14, 16, 76–8, 83, 103, 161
  1978–89 *Reports* 75–82
  1979 *Report* 78–9
  1980 *Report* 77–9
  1981 *Report* 79
  1982 *Report* 80–1
  1983 *Report* 81–2
  1984 *Report* 79, 81–2
  1985 *Report* 77–8, 81–2
  1986 *Report* 81–2
  1987 *Report* 77
  1988 *Report* 81–2
  1989 *Report* 81–2, 123–4
  1990 *Report, Poverty* 75–6, 83, 89, 142–3
  1990–2001 *Reports* 83
  1991 *Report, The Challenge of
    Development* 83
  1992 *Report, Development and the
    Environment* 84
  1993 *Report, Investing in Health* 84
  1994 *Report, Infrastructure for
    Development* 84
  1995 *Report, Workers in an Integrating
    World* 12–14, 84
  1996 *Report, From Plan to Market* 84–5
  1997 *Report, The State in a Changing
    World* 3–5, 11–12, 85–6
  1998/99 *Report, Knowledge for
    Development* 86
  1999/2000 *Report, Entering the 21st
    Century* 86–7
  2001 *Report, Attacking Poverty* 86–8,
    90–1
  2001 strategy document, *From Safety Net
    to Springboard* 88–9
  2002 *Report, Building Institutions for
    Markets* 90–1
  2002 *Private Sector Development
    Strategy—Directions for the World
    Bank Group* 100
  2003 *Report, Sustainable Development in
    a Dynamic World* 90–1

2004 *Report, Making Services Work for
    Poor People* 75–6, 90–1
2005 *Report, A Better Investment Climate
    for Everyone* 75–6, 90–1, 100
2005 *Report, Equity and
    Development* 90–1
2006 *Report, Development and the Next
    Generation* 90–1
2008 *Report, Agriculture for
    Development* 91–3
2008 *Reshaping Economic
    Geography* 93–4
2009 *Report, Development and Climate
    Change* 93–4
2010 *Report, Development and Climate
    Change* 167–70
2011 *Gender Equality and
    Development* 93–5
2011 *Report, Conflict Security and
    Development* 93–4, 167–70
2013 *Report, Jobs* 95–7, 101–4, 110,
    142–3
2014 *Back to Work: Growing with Jobs
    in Europe and Central Asia* 110,
    112–13
2014 *Report, Risk and Opportunity—
    Managing Risk for Development*
    97–100, 103–4, 169–70
2015 *Report, Mind, Society and
    Behavior* 105–6, 122–4
2016 *Report, Digital Dividends* 105–6,
    122, 125–7
2017 *Report, Governance and the
    Law* 105–6, 122, 127–31
2018 *Report, Learning to Realize
    Education's Promise* 105–6, 122,
    125–6, 129–31
2019 *Report, The Changing Nature of
    Work* 125–6, 139–46, 154–5,
    158–9
2020 *Report, Trading for Development in
    the Age of Global Value Chains*
    139–40, 152–61
Adaptive Social Protection 182
*Building Resilience: Integrating Climate
    and Disaster Risk into Development . . .*
    169–70
Global Economic Prospects 164, 171,
    175–8

Protecting People and Economies 173
Resilience, Equity, and Opportunity
    169–70
Saving Lives, Scaling-up Impact and
    Getting Back on Track 173
'trilogy' of reports 105–6, 122, 125–8,
    130–1
World Bank-UNICEF global monitoring
    platform 164
world market 17, 152–61
    Engels, Friedrich 20
    Marx, Karl 20–1, 27
    OECD 16, 45, 50–1, 56–8, 62–3, 71–3,
        118–19
    production for accumulation
        purpose 21–2
    universalisation of capital 21–2
    workers in 17–22
    World Bank 75–8, 80–3, 86, 88–9, 139–
        40, 152–3

world order 2–3
    hegemonic world order 2–3, 10–11
    new world order 3–5, 10–12, 55
World War II 2–3, 7–10
WTO (World Trade Organisation) 3–6,
    14–15, 85–6, 155–7

xenophobia 12–14

Yates, Luke 38–9
youth
    employment 90–1, 96, 102, 107–8,
        116–17
    European Commission 107–8, 132
    OECD 116–17
    unemployment 115
    World Bank 90–1, 96, 102, 158–9

Zini, Michele 113–14
Zoellick, Robert 167–9